MEMPHIS TENNESSEE GARRISON

Ohio University Press Series in
Ethnicity and Gender in Appalachia

SERIES EDITOR: LYNDA ANN EWEN

MEMPHIS TENNESSEE GARRISON

*The Remarkable Story of a
Black Appalachian Woman*

Edited by Ancella R. Bickley
and Lynda Ann Ewen

Historical Afterword by Joe W. Trotter

OHIO UNIVERSITY PRESS

ATHENS

Ohio University Press, Athens, Ohio 45701
© 2001 by Ohio University Press
Printed in the United States of America
All rights reserved

09 08 07 06 05 04 03 02 01   5 4 3 2 1

This book is published by Ohio University Press with financial assistance
from The West Virginia Humanities Council, a state program of
the National Endowment for the Humanities.

 West Virginia Humanities Council

Joe W. Trotter wishes to thank the Macmillan and Carlson Publishing Companies,
respectively, for permission to reprint portions of his essay "West Virginia" and, with
H. LaRue Trotter, "Memphis Tennessee Garrison" in "Memphis Tennessee Garrison
and West Virginia's African American Experience: Historical Afterword."

Frontispiece photograph courtesy of Mrs. Ruth Carruthers.

Library of Congress Cataloging-in-Publication Data
Garrison, Memphis Tennessee, 1890–1988.
    Memphis Tennessee Garrison: the remarkable story of a Black Appalachian
woman / edited by Ancella R. Bickley and Lynda Ann Ewen ; historical afterword
by Joe W. Trotter.
        p. cm. — (Ohio University Press series in ethnicity and gender in Appalachia)
    Includes bibliographical references (p.) and index.
    ISBN 0-8214-1373-2 (cloth : alk. paper) — ISBN 0-8214-1374-0 (pbk. : alk. paper)
    1. Garrison, Memphis Tennessee, 1890–1988—Interviews. 2. African American
women —West Virginia—McDowell County—Biography. 3. African Americans—
West Virginia—McDowell County—Biography. 4. African Americans—Civil rights—
West Virginia—History—20th century. 5. African Americans—West Virginia—Social
conditions —20th century. 6. West Virginia—Race relations. 7. McDowell County
(W. Va.)—Biography. I. Bickley, Ancella R. II. Ewen, Lynda Ann, 1943– III. Title.
IV. Series.

F247.M2 G375 2001
975.4'4900496073'0092—dc21
[B]

00-067755

contents

✻

illustrations

✴

Photographs

Maps

preface

✶

When Lynda Ann Ewen found the transcript of Memphis Tennessee Garrison's oral history, she felt as though she had gone to a yard sale and discovered a painting by Grandma Moses or an unknown manuscript by Frederick Douglass tucked in behind an old sewing machine or bicycle. Except, of course, most everyone knows who Grandma Moses and Frederick Douglass were. Those who know anything about the struggle for civil rights in West Virginia know of Memphis Tennessee Garrison. The problem is that no one else does.

Certainly, all of us in Appalachian studies are acutely aware of how Appalachians have been left out or, if included, distorted to fit preexisting stereotypes. It is almost passé now to talk about how women and African Americans have been written out of history—and especially African American women. We are, therefore, exceptionally lucky that someone had the foresight to record an interview with Memphis Tennessee Garrison and that, although the manuscript of the interview had languished for nearly thirty years, it was there.

Oral history is an avenue by which "unheard voices" can be recorded and archived for following generations. Ewen, as new director of the Oral History of Appalachia Program (OHAP) at Marshall University in the fall of 1995, eagerly set out to reclaim the neglected voices of those who had shaped who Appalachians were and what they had become in the tri-state area (Kentucky, Ohio, and West Virginia). She also vowed to bring to light those voices archived in relative obscurity in the Special Collections of Morrow Library at Marshall University in Huntington, West Virginia.

Ewen had heard of Memphis Tennessee Garrison in connection with the annual West Virginia NAACP dinner named in her honor. But she was just a name. Only when OHAP began a civil rights project with the support of Alan Gould and the Drinko Academy did Ewen begin to hear mention of Garrison's role in past civil rights struggles. Realizing the importance of the archived interview, she read the Garrison transcript and recognized what a treasure it was. The transcript was based on an oral history recorded at Marshall University by Bernard Cleveland of the Social Studies Department in about 1968. It is thanks to Dr. Cleveland's personal interest in undertaking the interview and Marshall University's support of his work that Memphis Tennessee Garrison's story was preserved.

The "voice" of the story is that of Memphis Tennessee Garrison as edited by Ancella R. Bickley. Bickley has carried on a crusade to find and retain the rapidly disappearing historical records—both written and oral—of African Americans in West Virginia. She knew of Garrison's important role and enthusiastically joined this project.

As a sociologist, Ewen sees Memphis Tennessee Garrison as a "player" in the great social civil rights movement that has helped define democracy in America. The introduction places Garrison in this drama and underlines the significance of her role at that time. It is important to remember that hindsight allows us to recognize relationships that individuals, caught in the moment, may have understood intuitively but would not have been able to conceptualize clearly. Ewen also has the twin advantages of knowing how the later scenes played out and of having read scholarly analyses by others who have studied the period. Thus, her introduction—which places Garrison on that stage—suggests perspectives Garrison herself may not have fully understood or conceptualized.

The editors are deeply grateful to the Department of Sociology, particularly to Kenneth Ambrose for his support of OHAP. The Drinko Academy and Alan Gould have also played an important role in the support of the Garrison project as well as of other projects related to Appalachian African American history. The encouragement given by Gillian Berchowitz, Senior Editor of the Ohio University Press, not only for this book but also for an entire series dedicated to Appalachian ethnicity and gender, is much appreciated as well.

A special debt is owed to Mary Thomas of the Center for the Study of Ethnicity and Gender in Appalachia at Marshall University and Gina

Kates, secretary for OHAP, who helped rescue the Garrison material from the obscurity of its shelving.

Among others who have given freely to this project are Joe W. Trotter of Carnegie Mellon University and Rita Wicks-Nelson. Dr. Trotter, a historian with in-depth knowledge of black Appalachian life, has long had a special interest in Memphis Tennessee Garrison; he willingly took time from an extremely busy schedule to develop an accompanying essay that provides a historical review setting the context within which some of the events of Garrison's life played themselves out. Renée Hill and Dr. Wicks-Nelson offered encouragement and aid by reading the manuscript and suggesting points where further clarification would be helpful.

Elizabeth Scobell, Ancella Livers, and Paul Casdorph offered historical information and suggested background resources. Cora Teel and Lisle G. Brown of Special Collections at Marshall University's Morrow Library and Stuart McGehee and Eva McGuire from the Eastern Regional Coal Archives provided information and photographs. Len LaCara from the *Huntington Herald Dispatch* permitted the use of a photograph, and Mack Gillenwater and Neil Cadle of the Marshall University Geography Department provided maps of McDowell County. Alma Carter, Allen Garrison, and Barbara Rhea, relatives of Memphis Tennessee Garrison, shared family information and reminiscences; and her niece, Ruth Carruthers, shared pictures, obituary, and other background material.

The editors also wish to thank Carolyne Brown, Herbert Henderson, Charles Holley, Dolores Johnson, John Settle, and Evelyn Payne Starling, some of Garrison's friends and former students, who offered remarks used in the document, particularly in its concluding pages.

Our husbands, Nelson R. Bickley and H. John Taylor, have continued to support and encourage us in our work. Thank you.

introduction

✳

In 1909 the United States was in the grip of a wave of race riots and lynchings. It was clear that an organized response was required. After a race riot in Springfield, Illinois, that year, black leaders and white reformers formed the National Association for the Advancement of Colored People (NAACP). In the following two decades racial hysteria mounted. Crosses were burned, and books and pamphlets extolling the virtues of the white Aryan race were distributed everywhere—including schools, public libraries, and churches. Nativist groups fanned a frenzy directed against immigrants of color.[1] This tide of racism rolled over America, and by the mid-1930s there was strong sentiment in support of the emerging Nazi party in Germany.

In 1916 the NAACP had 68 branches in the North and West but only 3 in the South. By 1919 the number of branches had exploded to 310, of which 131 were in the South. The organization continued to grow and provided the main leadership in the civil rights movement up until the emergence of the Southern Christian Leadership Conference.

The explosion of membership in the early days of the NAACP was the result of the tireless work of the grassroots organizers. Traveling remote, muddy roads at night to meet, often clandestinely, with community people who needed organizational protection, these grassroots organizers were overwhelmingly black women.[2] Poorly paid or not paid at all, threatened, and often exhausted, these foot soldiers of the NAACP built a base for the organization. In its early years the NAACP fought for, and won, antilynching legislation and nullification of restrictive covenants— clauses in real estate deeds that pledged white buyers never to sell the property to blacks. In 1923, the court ruled in favor of an NAACP suit, declaring that exclusion of blacks from juries was inconsistent with the right to a fair trial. Thus, in just a few years, formidable obstacles to black voting, integrated communities, and integrated juries had been removed through concerted legal action.

Historians have compiled the names of some of these women of the NAACP, along with membership figures, dates, and public and legislative activity. But such research fails to answer more important questions. What kind of consciousness led to such selfless determination? What wellsprings did these unsung women draw on for their continued resistance?

The answers to those kinds of questions require a different kind of data. This book provides answers and insights into some of these questions, for it is the extraordinary memoir of one of the most important of those unknown women. Memphis Tennessee Garrison, born in 1890, was the daughter and granddaughter of slaves. She lived most of her life in Gary, West Virginia, center of one of the most important coal mining areas in America's industrial history.

Memphis Tennessee Garrison was a political leader at a time when women's leadership was rarely acknowledged. She extolled racial pride at a time when "black is beautiful" had not become a slogan. She was an Appalachian at a time when folks from the mountains were considered backward hillbillies. She was an intellectual and educator when those traits were considered incompatible with being an Appalachian black woman.

This memoir documents the soul of a woman who, at the end of her eighth decade, reflects on her own development and the lessons of a remarkable life. It cannot be read as traditional history, for her story is told through her personal lenses. But it is history, nonetheless, for it reveals to us the inner workings of the soul of a woman changing her world, and the world of others.

Resistance

During its time, American slavery was the most brutal and degrading form of slavery known to history. Not surprisingly, it produced an "oppositional culture."[3] Oppressed and exploited, enslaved men and women created responses that allowed them not only to have some control over their daily lives, but to resist and fight back. This culture of resistance, then, is not just the action of individuals but is collectively owned through community music, art, storytelling, and group activity.[4]

Memphis Tennessee Garrison's family roots lay in this oppositional culture. She tells the story of her grandmother with great pride. *My mother would tell me about old Granny Roddy. . . . They'd bring the new overseers in, new white men, and they'd say, "You can whip any of these slaves but Roddy. Don't touch her. If you do, she'll kill you." So we used to like to talk about her because she was big and brave, you know—bad. So that's why I remember her. When we were little we would argue about history. I would say something about her. I always could defend my side by referring to Granny Roddy; she wouldn't let them whip her. She would kill them.*

Memphis Tennessee Garrison's childhood was clearly shaped by the stories of resistance her grandfather and mother told. When someone asks her if she was bitter about slavery in her family, she avoids answering the question directly. Rather, she tells the story of a slave woman who had tried to run away. Later this woman had a child. *She wasn't a real bright child, but she was loved by this woman with a love that was terrific. That was all she had, it seemed. I think it was my grandfather who told me, because it happened at the place where he got a whipping. . . . The overseer got mad with this woman and wanted to punish her, so when the traders came by . . . he sold this little girl and he knew that would hurt the woman worse than anything he could do. The woman'd come from the field, working the field all day, and she came in looking for the little girl. The overseer was making fun of her. He let her look and then finally he told her that he'd sold the child to the nigger trader, and the woman killed him. . . . My grandfather said she made one step toward the overseer, then grabbed him and choked him to death. . . . In her anger and in her sadness, she had the strength of two men.*

She acknowledges that she doesn't know who the woman is or if the story is factually true, but that is not the point. For Garrison, the story is a truth about the ability of slave women to fight back. She goes on to say, *I was glad that she choked him.* For her, the question is not one of violence. Rather, the lesson is that people have limits beyond which they cannot be pushed. The story affirms that her people drew those lines.

Our current perceptions of social justice and social change are viewed through lenses created by the struggles of the civil rights movement and the women's movement. Our "cultural vocabulary," so to speak, has given us concepts of militancy, feminism, Black Nationalism, and integration. Modern perceptions might see some of Garrison's activities as accommodationism. But it is important that the contemporary reader remember the perceptions held by those who struggled prior to those movements.

Garrison's lenses were created in a different time. She acted in a different context. Her views of her race and gender restrictions were formed in the context of the restrictions placed upon the lives of slaves. She saw, and seized, opportunities and potentials that were simply nonexistent for her ancestors in slavery. What we see in Garrison's story is the remarkable ability to grasp any small opening for resistance, any little opportunity for change—and maximize it. She was like so many other black women who, as Kim Marie Vaz notes, "drew on institutions in the Black community to stretch the tight spaces they are assigned."[5] She represents the generations of women who acted decisively and with great courage within the possibilities of their times—what they were able to do under the historical conditions.

By working "within the cracks," so to speak, Memphis Tennessee Garrison helped widen those cracks until they became the breaches through which the social movements of the 1960s could flow. Without the patient, lifelong efforts of persons like her, those mobilizations and marches could not have occurred.

Prior to joining the NAACP, Garrison worked within her community as an individual. The coalfields of McDowell County, West Virginia, were among the richest coal seams in the nation, and Gary, home of U.S. Steel, had one of the largest mines in the country. As Garrison makes clear, the backbone of that workforce—those who laid the railroad tracks, manned the coke ovens, and dug the coal—were black workers.[6] Memphis Tennessee Garrison mediated labor issues, community issues, and race issues on behalf of both the owners and the community. There was no organizational base from which she could have adopted a more independent or vocal role. *I don't care who you were, if you buck the company and they* consider it not in their best interest, and that's true everywhere, they get rid of you. The company did control the housing and the company store. I guess that's true overall, of all the coal companies. They had a certain amount of power. Even in that, they ruled the political world.

Garrison's role changed markedly in 1918 when she became aware of the NAACP, which provided her with an organizational base. By 1921 she had organized a branch in Gary, the third such branch in West Virginia (after Charleston and Wheeling). It is not clear whether she perceived the connection between her developing militancy and a supportive organizational base. She saw herself, again, as a person who did what was possible under the conditions. *The NAACP was for helping those people that weren't having anything. . . . And this lynching—you see that year they lynched 347 Negroes in these United States. They were lynching a Negro a day, nearly! And this organization was organizing wherever people knew so that they could do something about that, find a way to help. That was the searching, to get the lynching of our people stopped.*

But she was keenly aware of even the limits of her new base. *The local branch of the NAACP didn't touch the discrimination in the coal mines. They would talk about it at the meeting, but there was nobody who was able to move in on it. We hadn't come to that time.*

As the NAACP grew stronger, Garrison's role broadened. Her extraordinary talents as an organizer were recognized first within West Virginia, and then nationally. In her typically understated voice, she described her role in West Virginia. *The NAACP was also established in Raleigh County and Logan County. I was in Raleigh; I was in Beckley when they had their first mass meeting; I was there to set up and to see where their offices were. I spoke to them and they were ready to set up. In Logan—Laredo—I set up. And there was one in Mercer County that I set up. . . . Maybe over in the other district, over in Warren they'd say, "We'd like to have one at our place." I'd tell them, "I'll come to you. Get your fifty people and call me, and I'll come." In that period between 1921 and 1931 when they began to cut into it with the Depression, I'd set up many branches. They'd go down, and they'd tell me and I'd go get them back together again. . . . I've crawled around those mud roads and got stuck and somebody'd come pull me out.*

The national NAACP identified Garrison as a troubleshooter. She never claimed to have special talents or skills, but clearly possessed them. She described trips to Indiana, Denver, Richmond, and Cincinnati. In regard to the latter she said: *I stayed fourteen weeks there as a field secretary on special assignment. I brought that branch from 65 members to around 7,000, somewhere in that neighborhood. You've worked when you've done that, no hours —night and day.*

The NAACP was Garrison's lifelong passion—it was her way to "choke" the system and demand justice. It was in this organizational arena that she was able to carry on the oppositional culture of her people. But it was not the only organizational arena in which she provided leadership. She always understood that her effectiveness required more than race militancy. Power and politics underlay everything in the coalfields, and she had to move in that arena as well.

Politics and Leadership

Her roots in a slave history also shaped Garrison's politics. Her loyalty lay with the Republicans until the Kennedy era. To Garrison, changing parties for personal advancement was a disloyal act—Republicans were the party of Lincoln.

In explaining the changing political climate in West Virginia, she discussed the switch by black voters to the Democratic Party, and her stubborn affiliation with the Republicans. *It was normal for me to say Republican, because they were the party of Lincoln and it was normal for me to think Lincoln was the greatest leader because history had told me so, and my mother was a slave. . . . The start of it was in the Depression, but they have remained the majority because of what they have done. The Democrats have turned to be the liberal party, and Negroes have come in because they were. They began to give better jobs, and they began to give you everything the Republicans gave you. . . . I remained a Republican because I wanted to. If I had changed, I would have felt like I was being disloyal to what I had always believed in, and if other people had remained through a lot of things and stayed what they were, I could do the same. When I would think about changing, my grandfather would come up in my mind. When my mother would rub his back—the old man was old then and of course he ached—my mother was there and she'd rub his back for him and those welts, those on his back, those striped welts every which way, ridges just like . . . a washboard only they weren't even. But they were those kinds of ridges. I'd say, "Granddaddy, what's wrong with your back?" He said, "That's the bullwhip, Honey, but you ain't going to never feel it, 'cause you's free." I could not think of that and put down anything else but Republican. Anything that had saved me from that, any man who had spoken out against that, who had put his life on the line and died for us, I couldn't forget. Greater love has no man than this, that he'd give up his life for his fellow man. That's all Christ did; that's why when they shot Lincoln, the man who did it said, "Now the South has been avenged." And it was the South who put those marks on my grandfather's back. That's history, that's Booth, that's what he said. And I just say that I have to be a Republican.*

Garrison's loyalty, however, was not blind. To get the resources she needed for her students and to get support for community activities required casting her lot with those who had the power. She described the company influence on the school board and school district: *The person who owned the most in that district or the company who owned the most, who worked the most men in that district would be the persons who would be influential. They were the people who had the votes to get what they wanted. At one time when we had school districts, the company ruled that district. For instance, Adkins District was ruled by United States Steel. . . . All of those boards of education, all of the district boards of education were under the supervision of the United States Steel. The boards were elected on the county ticket, but the persons elected had been picked by company people. In the primary they picked them and they were elected, and they functioned according to company wishes, and the big boss of the company was usually the president of the board. When they were elected, they elected him the president.*

Although the NAACP provided her with an outlet for political organizing, what drove Memphis Tennessee Garrison's organizing was her devotion to her students and to black youth in general. Feminist scholars have noted the difference between white women activists of this period and black women activists. Middle-class white women reformers focused on "charity" and usually had very delimited goals. But black women focused on "their people," seeing the goal of "uplifting the race" as both noble and attainable.[7] Garrison articulated this commitment in terms of a deep spiritual duty—one which she shouldered joyfully. But she could not have been effective without playing the political game.

So she played it to win. Even when she lost an election, as she did when she ran for school board, she saw it as a victory. *I won the nomination in the primary over four other persons. I got the highest number of voting in my own party. I always think I have a chance to win. And I don't take all the votes. If nobody voted for me, I don't count it that I've lost the votes. I said that to somebody and they said, "Why?" "Because," I said, "somebody sitting right there knows they should have voted for me. Just certain pressures kept them from it. I haven't lost. I have those people right there who know they should have voted for me. And the time will come when they will vote. I haven't lost for one reason or the other. They were pressured into wiping me off. I never lose." I was the only woman and the only Negro running, and I ran a pretty close race in the general election.*

It is this concern with issues—a focus on the problems rather than on the people—that distinguishes Garrison's political analysis. Although she fought for more opportunities and resources for black people, her analysis was not in terms of black people *versus* white people. Nor does it seem that she saw herself as a "black" candidate. Her story is not linked to those of other successful black politicians from McDowell County elected in that same time period. It is doubtful that the other politicians shared Garrison's agenda, and thus they are not part of her story.

Garrison's goals appear to have arisen out of her strong religious background, which was based more on her spiritual life than within an organized religion. Indeed, she took a pragmatic view of the black church, arguing that her money did more good when donated directly to the people in need, rather than going into the hands of preachers. *When somebody would say something about giving to the church, I would say that I tithe, but I would say, "I wouldn't give a preacher all of that money. I don't give the preacher all that." Whatever is good to be done, I use that money for that. When it's out [spent], it's out. That tenth goes to whatever somebody needs—to some child, to helping somebody through school, to sending fifty dollars or something when somebody is in a hard place. That to me is what it's all about, not going there giving that preacher that money. You see, I'm the rebel.*

Garrison was raised in the church, and her memories of Sunday school and her mother's devout faith profoundly influenced her. As an adult, however, she moved beyond the boundaries of the time—refusing to be limited by the agendas, and rivalries, of the local black churches. By not affiliating, she was better able to work with, and speak for, the community as a whole. And besides, the church did not at this time represent a political base. Not until the rise of the Southern Christian Leadership Conference (SCLC) in the 1950s did the black churches become the local heart of the civil rights movement. Memphis Tennessee Garrison resembled the earlier leaders of the NAACP who were educated professionals and came out of the reform movements or labor and suffrage struggles.

Garrison's memoir makes it clear that she built and utilized networks. Although she never used the word (and may never have thought about it in this way) she was a skilled networker, wending her way through white men and women, black men, and other black women with consummate skill. The black community was tightly organized through clubs, churches, schools, and kinship. In a segregated society, the networks acted both to protect black people from a hostile environment and, at the same time, to provide the social resources needed for growth and development.[8]

Because she believed in the righteousness of her cause, Garrison was not afraid to use her influence and resources to make people respond to her agenda. This is, perhaps, the real hallmark of leadership—creating an agenda that motivates others. The ability to lead and mobilize people is clearly Garrison's most important source of power, for she had neither independent wealth nor a large and influential family. Her mother was widowed early in life and made a living doing domestic service and laundry; only later in life did Garrison's mother learn to read. But Garrison's mother encouraged and supported Garrison's insatiable thirst for knowledge. Garrison was thus able to pursue as much of a formal education as was available to black women at that time.

As a black schoolteacher, Memphis Tennessee Garrison automatically became part of one of the most influential and powerful networks in the black community. In West Virginia, black teachers were organized into the West Virginia State Teachers' Association. Not surprisingly, Garrison became the first woman to be elected president of the organization. In her matter-of-fact way, she describes her election: *In time, about 1929–30, there was estimated to be about 1,100 or 1,200 Negro teachers in the entire state. The meeting at which I was selected president of the WVSTA was at Bluefield. I didn't come for the night meeting—the first night—but I was there the next morning for the meeting. Posted out in the hall was who was running for president—it just struck me about the election, something that I had passed in the hall. Then I began to announce that I was going to run for president. I was unanimously elected. Three or four other persons said that after it was announced who was running, they just pulled off.*

Later in life Garrison's networks included better-known people—including famous politicians and civil rights leaders. But in her reminiscences, these persons have no more special place than do her outstanding students, or members of her family. This was a woman who clearly had no elitist pretensions. She used connections to famous people in the same way she used connections to anybody else—to further her causes.

A political agenda that meets the needs of a community is certainly a criterion for leadership. But leaders must also be intimately familiar with, and trusted by, the community they are leading. Garrison's skills with people, as well as her knowledge of people, were honed in her multifaceted relationship to community.

Community

As a young child, Memphis Tennessee came with her family to Gary, West Virginia, just as the community was being built. Throughout her life, Gary was *her* hometown—her homeplace, as we say in Appalachia. As a girl she watched the town build up—largely through the efforts of black labor. She returned as a schoolteacher and married soon thereafter. In following the acceptable avenues open to women of the time—marriage and a teaching career—Memphis Tennessee Garrison embraced the path given to her, and followed it to the limits of its possibility.

Over and over again Garrison's memoir reveals that her true love was teaching, something she did full-time or part-time for fifty years. She understood that training the next generation for leadership was in itself

1. West Virginia and surrounding states, showing McDowell and Mercer Counties

a remarkable contribution. But she did more than that. Her commitment to working with what we today would call remedial, or "special education," students reflects a commitment to developing human potential in every child, regardless of the child's chance to succeed in the eyes of the larger world. She reflects on what it meant to her: *With some of them it's like coming out of the shell. Something touches them somewhere and opens up the whole thing to them. But suppose they hadn't had somebody trained to help them reach that point.*

Teaching was not only a vocation for Garrison—it was her passion. She took responsibility for the bodies and souls of her students. She tells the story of feeding the children during the Depression: *There was a restaurant right next to the school; an old lady ran it, and I contracted with her to have a big dish of cereal and some hot bread and butter ready for those children at recess time in the morning. She had cows and milk, and for almost two whole years, at least for a whole year, I fed those children. I never made any to-do about it because I was afraid the parents would be too proud or something so we*

just called it our recess party. And those little children, it was those little ones—
I had the little ones, those first two grades. I paid for the food myself; the lady
wouldn't charge me anything for fixing it.

In her telling she is not asking for praise—she is stating her analysis of
the situation. She understood, long before the War on Poverty instituted
school breakfasts, that children cannot learn when they are hungry. The
rest of her teaching experiences were also subjected to her analysis.
She experimented with teaching methods and obtained successes where
others had failed. She mentions, almost in passing, that in the 1930s she
sought out help from, and then shared her successes with, the Horace
Mann School of Education at Columbia University.

Memphis Tennessee Garrison's teaching was not restricted by the walls
of the schoolhouse. The entire community was her classroom. Her activity in bringing the arts, politics, and education to the coalfields was
also a response to people's hunger for learning and culture. The story of
the opera singer performing on rugs from the furniture company is almost funny. Yet it was not humorous to Memphis Tennessee Garrison.
She told it to support her strong belief that "culture" was a necessary
and welcomed part of the community's life. She brought a variety of
prominent speakers to Gary, including Matt Henson, the black explorer
who co-discovered the North Pole. She brought in plays and nationally
prominent musicians. Indeed, one could argue that teachers such as she
laid the groundwork in black communities for the generation of young
black leaders who stepped forward in the late 1950s and 1960s.

West Virginia attorney Herbert Henderson, a civil rights leader and
NAACP activist, was one of those deeply influenced by Memphis Tennessee Garrison. He wrote about her cultural activities in the community: "I knew of Mrs. Garrison ever since I was in high school, too many
years ago for me to think of. Every black person in McDowell County
knew about Memphis Tennessee Garrison. You couldn't grow up there
if you didn't know about her. We knew about Gary; we knew about the
things that she brought to Gary. We knew how she had U.S. Steel to
bring in the Count Basies, bring in the black entertainers, the black intellectuals, the Marian Andersons. She was just it."

This deep involvement in the community—from writing columns in the local newspaper to raising money for youth recreation—created a reservoir of trust and respect that Garrison drew on as she fought her battles. There were those who opposed her and obstructed what she saw as necessary progress. But she loved her community, most of its members loved her, and she knew it.

Appalachia and Coal

Appalachians are among the most viciously stereotyped of all American ethnic groups today. The media have struggled to correct racist and distorted images of African Americans, Hispanics and Latinos, Jews, and Asian Americans. But caricatures of dumb hillbillies—poor white folks from the hollow, chewing tobacco and committing incest—still abound in television, literature, and even education. The issue is more than representation in the media. American culture itself has embraced the notion of isolated hillbillies.[9]

The reality of Appalachia is strikingly in opposition to the stereotype. Instead of a homogenous "isolated people," Appalachians are in fact a diverse group—originating in early mixtures of Native American peoples (including the Cherokee, Shawnee, and Iroquois Nations), African Americans, and Celtic Europeans.[10] Major immigrations of Southern blacks, Italians, Hungarians, Germans, and Belgians (to name a few) came later, and were "Appalachianized." Sprinkled throughout the region are Lebanese and Eastern European Jewish immigrants.

By treating Appalachians as somehow peculiar and separate from the rest of the country, American history has been able to overlook the story of those who supplied the timber and coal for the development of the United States. Workers in timbering and mining died by the hundreds of thousands to fuel American expansion. Women were often the glue that held families together after the death of the breadwinner. These sacrifices were made in hundreds of relatively small communities scattered throughout the mountains. There has never been an assessment of the loss of life and and the crippling injuries that occurred as a result of early timbering.[11] And while historians have totaled the numbers lost in major coal disasters, no one has researched the total number of miners killed in accidents involving only one, two, or three miners. When President of the United Mine Workers John L. Lewis launched the UMWA campaign for federal mine inspectors, he was quoted by the UMWA *Journal* on April 15, 1940: "In the last thirty years the coal industry has killed 50 thousand mine workers, and injured three and one-half million, a record approached by no civilized country in the world."[12]

Unions came to the coalfields as a result of the low wages and dangerous and debilitating working conditions in the mines. The struggle for unionization was a violent one: the danger in the workplace was violent; the operators' resistance to miners' organization was violent; and the miners' response was violent.[13] And it was the coalminers from southern West Virginia who were the guts of this union movement. At the height of the union movement, nearly one-third of the miners were African American, and another large percentage was foreign-born.[14]

Later, UMWA-supported organizers took industrial unionism to the giant cities of American industry—Detroit, Chicago, Toledo, and Cleveland. Indeed, one might say that the standard of living of America's industrial working class is largely due to the courage and stubbornness of coalfield unionists. Memphis Tennessee Garrison moved to Gary, West Virginia, in the 1890s, before the age of eight, and lived there until she was sixty-two, when she moved to Huntington. Gary miners and their families created communities that became centers of struggle to build unions, better education, and expanded civil rights. At the end of her interview, Garrison makes it clear that her story is also the story of her people's role in this industry.

Garrison's narrative reveals the multidimensional richness of life for the people of this coal camp—a hard life but one well lived in many ways. Her depiction flies in the face of images of poor, downtrodden black folk. These are people who send their children to school, and then to college. These are people who support a wide variety of cultural activities.

In her telling, Garrison reflects the ways in which class and race have intersected in the American working class. Perhaps the most complex aspect of Garrison's life is her early role as welfare worker and mediator on behalf of the coal company. Purists would be disappointed that she was not pro-union, or at least anti-company. But Garrison's acute sense of power, and the manipulation of that power, led her to accept a position with the company in which she felt she could be effective.

Garrison's own grandfather had played a similar role on the plantation. He was the preacher and the slave owner's mouthpiece for the church service. But after the sermon was delivered, he would "sing" the *real* meaning of the Biblical text as the slaves worked in the fields. *And he said that there's a certain way that you could turn—now he didn't know anything about crosscurrents and air and all—but that sound would carry. He wanted to send a message. . . . And he said he'd just clear his throat and let out a long groan like he's going to say something and they'd come alive in that field to listen. And then he'd sing. In order to let him know that they heard him, they would answer with a moan or something they put in. . . . He was communicating to them the correct reading of that text he'd preached on Sunday. He said his folks knew.*

Again, the lessons from slavery have been learned. It is not surprising that one of the most popular of the slave folktales is that of Brer Rabbit —who begs the fox *not* to throw him into the briar patch, knowing that the fox will then throw him into the best place for him to hide. To accuse Garrison of accommodating to the coal operator, or selling out, would be to ignore the realities she faced.

Race relations in other coalfield communities were often strained and sometimes violent. Blacks who stood up or talked back ran the risk of being lynched. But not in Gary. Garrison best explained the role she played in her story of how she had a racist white miner removed to prevent a violent confrontation in the community: *This man stood on the porch and made the remark to one of the other white fellows, "What are you doing living among these niggers? We lynch 'em where I come from." One of the Negro men went in his house and got his gun and came out . . . I was rounding the corner. . . . And I said, "Where are you going? He told me what had happened next door. . . . I said, "Well, now, you put your gun up because I promise you that if you put your gun up and go on to Welch and shop and do something,*

*I promise you he'll have moving orders before you get back. I give you my word."
. . . I went right to that office and I said, "You're going to have a riot if you don't
do something right now." . . . They told him to pack up and I guess they moved
that night. The next morning the house was empty.*

Garrison looked back upon this period of her life as rewarding and
fulfilling. *And those were the things that kept me down in this coalfield. I didn't
have anything to leave for. If I wanted entertainment, there was entertainment
of a kind. If I wanted to work and get money, there was money and work. There
was teaching, and if I wanted a vacation there was a husband who had a good
job with the company and he got two weeks' vacation. My life was filled with
activity. . . . People'd say, "What're you doing down there in those mountains?"
Well, they'd say that to me as if you were coming out of the jungle or something, and I had so much to do, my life was so full.*

Garrison worked for the company from 1931 to 1946. Then the union
came in. U.S. Steel had been able to forestall organization by the UMWA
by sponsoring its own union—a "company union." As one of the richest and most powerful corporations in America at that time, U.S. Steel
had the resources to provide certain benefits to its workers—the price it
paid to keep outside organizers away. Because Garrison did not perceive
the UMWA as acting particularly in the interests of black people, she felt
no obligation to support it.

Once the UMWA organized the miners at U.S. Steel, Garrison's role
changed. *The political picture changed due to the fact that unions were coming
in. That made a difference in the whole setup—everything. I didn't work for
them any under the union. The union came in and they were organized and I
wasn't any more a part of it after that. They had new people and a new setup
of rules for the laborer and the whole picture changed. Any role that I might
have had was either obsolete or it was taken over otherwise. I knew that it was
time to quit and when that year was up, that was it.*

Although Garrison does not articulate all the reasons, the change in
her relationship to the coal industry was certainly affected by her growing commitment to the NAACP and activities outside Gary, West Virginia. And as one listens to her telling of her life journey, family clearly
played a central role.

Family

Garrison's family were freed slaves who worked hard after the Civil War and were able to buy land and support themselves. This was "family land," and although Garrison called Gary "home," she recognized her roots in the land owned by her maternal grandfather and great-uncles in Virginia. She told the story of how a large portion of that land was lost through terror and how she ultimately was forced to sell the remainder for much less than its worth. This story, of course, is one that is echoed in the life histories of thousands of American black families.

Garrison had only one sibling, an older brother. Her father, Wesley Carter, died when she was young and her mother never remarried. Her mother, Cassie Thomas Carter, became a central figure in her life—supporting her and challenging her to grow and expand her horizons. Garrison described her mother as *unlettered but highly intelligent.* She used as an example a story about the bones in pigs' feet—how her mother outsmarted a young schoolteacher headed for medical school. When Garrison began teaching and married, her mother kept house for her, staying with her until she died in 1941.

A friend of the family told us that Garrison's mother also had a scarred back from whippings during slavery. While there can be no doubt of the accuracy of this report based on personal observation, Garrison made no mention of this in her interview—a surprising omission in light of the importance in her life of seeing her grandfather's scarred back. We can speculate that the omission may have been due to her wish to protect her mother's privacy. Unfortunately we will never know why she neglected to add this to her story. Yet we must assume that the brutal treatment of her revered mother would have deeply affected her.

Garrison's understanding of the profound influence her mother had on her life is revealed when she speaks of her grieving: *In the memoirs of the little book that they gave me at her funeral I wrote,*

> *I had a wonderful mother.*
> *Her memory will never grow old.*
> *God gave her the smile of sunshine;*

He made her a heart of pure gold.
She was a good friend and neighbor
To everyone she knew.
Although he saw fit to take her,
He knew just what to do.
But to me she will live forever,
That wonderful mother I knew.

And that was it. I stopped grieving for her. After I got something—I have to get
something to hang onto and then I don't grieve. I just stopped grieving for her. I
knew she'd been and she'd passed, and I didn't grieve any more.

Memphis Tennessee Carter married William Garrison, a mine electrician and mine contractor, in 1918. She related the story of their courtship but little else about their relationship. It seems that her husband supported her activities, or at least she gave no sense that it was otherwise. She mentioned that she would have liked to have had children, but they did not. She did not explain. But she did see her support of other people's children as her way of making up for the lack of her own.

A mother who kept her house, a husband who supported her activities, and the absence of children were all conditions that enabled Memphis Tennessee Garrison to make her contributions more visibly than many other women. She freely acknowledged these factors. Without this kind of support system in the early part of the twentieth century, it was difficult for a woman to engage actively in a public life.

As she grew older, the children she had mentored and supported through school became her family network. When she moved to Huntington later in her life, former students became part of her support. But she hardly "retired." For example, there were no black Girl Scout troops in the city. When the women of the city heard Garrison had moved there, as she said, they *descended on me. . . . That was in the fall of '52. I was just moving to town, hadn't even straightened up. I said, "Give me until spring and I'll see what I can do."* She set up troops for a hundred girls. She also organized a book drive for Africa, and continued to work with the NAACP.

Garrison influenced a whole new generation of young black people in Huntington. NAACP leader and attorney Herbert Henderson tells of how he came to know her: "She had no close relatives here, but she had relationships. Rev. Smith and I and others would go there and sit and listen. We'd talk and listen. She was a very wise person. . . . She's the one who taught me. . . . We spent hours poring over the various conventions, leaders, people in the NAACP from all over the country. That's how I fell in love with the NAACP. So did a lot of other people, I think."

Henderson notes especially Garrison's influence on young black women: "Many of the female students from McDowell County at Bluefield State College were there because Mrs. Garrison sent them. She'd say, 'Take your two dresses and go on. You can make it.'"

In Appalachia the line between biological kin and community kinship has always been blurred. Cultural anthropologists call the latter "fictive kin." But no matter the terminology, it is clear that Memphis Tennessee Garrison was surrounded throughout her life, even in her very last years, by people who loved, respected, and cared for her.

Conclusion

Memphis Tennessee Garrison contradicts all the images and stereotypes of Appalachia. She is Appalachian to the core, declaring her connection to the mountains and her community as an intrinsic part of her being. There were times in her life when she might easily have left the region, and she always refused. She defended her roots not only in terms of the love of the land, but love of the people. She never saw them as backward or ignorant.

A culture in which fame is determined by structures that are racist, sexist, and materialistic will not anoint as "famous" such persons as Memphis Tennessee Garrison. What was her contribution compared to that of presidents, the executives of multimillion-dollar companies, or movie stars? She was never rich, nor was her name ever on a marquee. Yet the lives of thousands of Appalachian people, of African Americans, and of all Americans were immensely enriched because of her efforts. This book, then, is not only the story of Memphis Tennessee Garrison but also a challenge to the very way in which we think of fame or leadership. It is acknowledgment of the heroic role of "ordinary" people who become extraordinary. It is also an invitation to recognize those who are bypassed by official history because they don't fit preconceived notions of fame.

In the end, you, the reader, will evaluate the life of Memphis Tennessee Garrison. We believe that most of you will feel as we do—that she deserves her place in the lists of important women, important black Americans, and important Appalachians.

Lynda Ann Ewen

note on the editing

✼

As editor of the original interview, I have preserved Memphis Tennessee Garrison's voice while helping the flow of the "story." For Garrison, one event triggers recollections of another. Stories about one person lead to more stories about that person and about others. The result is not a neat chronology or clear analysis and, to a reader, may often seem rambling. My dilemma, in preparing this book for publication, was to minimize the meandering effect without distorting Garrison's own vision of her life. The careful reader will notice several places where stories are repeated or events retold. I have retained these redundancies because they were essential to a point Garrison was making. I made an effort to arrange related parts of the interview in sections that help the reader see connections. As an aid to readers unfamiliar with certain aspects of this historical period or place, I have added names, dates, and brief identifying phrases as bracketed insertions. I have included some essential explanations as footnotes, and occasionally I have supplied more detailed information in numbered notes at the end of the book. Lynda Ann Ewen has provided brief introductions to each section, highlighting key points and supplying a context for the reader. In all our work with this document, we have attempted in every way possible to preserve the integrity of this amazing voice.

As an oral history, this is a reconstruction of nearly eighty years as seen through the eyes of a remarkable woman. Memphis Tennessee Garrison is not always entirely accurate in her recollection of facts, but there is no doubt that she has remembered those things that were important—not only in her own life, but for the community, state, and nation that she served. What is amazing is the way she speaks. Her voice is simultaneously one of analysis, reflection, and storytelling.

Following the interview itself, several people who knew Memphis Tennessee Garrison share their recollections and feelings about her in an epilogue. The final commentary points out the significance of Garrison's story for black history in Appalachia. The concluding section by Joe W. Trotter presents a more detailed background of the history of African Americans in West Virginia.

We are keenly aware that Garrison's story raises historical, political, and sociological questions that require research beyond the scope of this book. We hope that some readers will carry this work forward.

Ancella Bickley

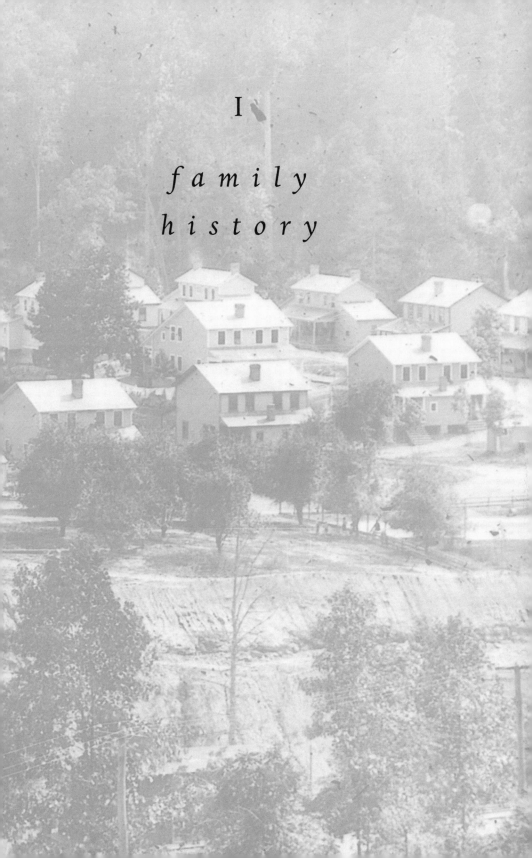

I

family

history

I F there is a theme in the first two chapters, it is one of suffering. Memphis Tennessee Garrison's standpoint on life was
framed by the suffering of people—particularly "her people."
These chapters establish her perspective. Life was hard, and
there was suffering. Slaves were beaten and scarred. People
like her father had their lives cut short by accidents or violence. But life was also rich, and there were rewards, both
material and spiritual, for those who could fight the good
fight.

What is remarkable in her telling of her family's slave experiences is her ability to separate the social institution of
slavery—which was evil—from the people caught up in it.
She identified those slave owners who "had hearts" and tried
to protect their mixed children. Garrison's ability to separate
social institutions from individuals is a theme echoed throughout her story. She made a distinction between the coal company operators as part of an oppressive system and decent
people within the company, such as "the Colonel." She recognized the contradictions between the political parties that
stood for certain ideals and the people who misused their political power within them. Even the NAACP is scrutinized in
this light, for although her loyalty to that organization never
wavered, she was able to see the failures and problems of individuals within the organization.

Sociologists talk about "generational consciousness." Those
of us born in the baby boom of the 1940s were the children
of parents on whose consciousness the Depression and World
War II had a deep impact. In turn, the threat of atomic war
and the social movements for civil rights had a deep impact on
our generation. Garrison's generation carried the consciousness of the Civil War and slavery. It is hard, today, to imagine
a war on our own soil in which in *one* battle (Antietam) there

were as many American casualties as in the entire Vietnam War. Nor can we begin to comprehend a war in which brother fought brother and family fought family.

As the child of slaves, and a member of a post–Civil War generation, Garrison consistently used the experiences of slavery as a basis for seeing progress, for both white and black people. To her, personal history, family history, African American history and American history are inseparable. She herself acknowledged how profoundly the family stories affected her consciousness when she talked about what she had learned "in the silence." These stories were a rich heritage that she plumbed, both intellectually and experientially.

The two chapters in this section are not complete expositions of Garrison's family history. Other stories of her family's slave experiences are interspersed throughout her account. Because those stories are integral to her discussion of a particular idea, to a moral lesson, or to her description of an individual, they fall naturally into other sections. But it is in these first chapters that we fully sense the basis for Garrison's understanding of "oppositional culture" and the historical influences that molded her life.

chapter 1

✳

Remembrances of Slavery

My name came from a family of schoolteachers. A paternal group were teachers in their early days. My rich white grandfather educated his Negro girls. He was a slaveholder. He was my father's father and also his master. I didn't know much about that grandfather. I didn't know him at all. I know his name was Aldridge, but just his name. I don't know the family name—the slave owner's name.[1] That was so far removed from me and where we lived that there was no going back and forth. I just knew these children were there. I knew it through my father who was one of those children. I knew about these girls through him; I didn't know them. I don't remember if I've ever seen them, but there is a side of the family that was in Culpeper, Virginia. They don't have the same name that they had then, but they're a part of that family. They are descended from the girls who married out of that family, and I have seen them since I've been grown—years ago when I first came out of college.

But when they weren't sending Negroes anywhere to get educated, my white grandfather sent his three beautiful redheaded Negro daughters to a school. I don't know what the school was now. It may have been Oberlin. Seems I heard, but I don't know for sure because I didn't pay any attention to that. And when they came home, they had connections. Those Negroes who were born free or freed early had connections all around with each other. Memphis, Tennessee, had large groups of free Negroes and one of the daughters became one of the first teachers in Memphis. After being there for a while she came home and there was a little baby that didn't have a name. She was changing places anyhow and in memory of her life there she said, "We'll call the baby Memphis Tennessee." I suppose it was unusual and everybody came and asked, "Where's Memphis, Tennessee?" So for a long time the name has been a question mark in the minds of people, "Where'd you get such a name?" they'd ask. "Why did they name you?"

My mother and her father, Marshall Thomas, became free as a result of the surrender [of Confederate General Robert E. Lee, April 9, 1865]. I remember him up until I was about ten or twelve. He had a shock of white hair and he was tall and black. He lived in Hollins, Virginia. He died there and is buried there. My mother went to the burial but she didn't take me. It must have been that there was a bit of isolation because the old man had married again, and you know how the children won't go home, won't have anything to do with the new wife. I would go back when I was little and stay all summer. In the fall, Granddaddy would walk round over the place and talk and all that. He was very old. I don't remember the age. I remember more events and more of the things that he was telling me. Time never touched me; it wasn't important—none of that was important to me, only the incidents. They could have been measured in a short period of time, or it could have been a long time.

My mother said that on their plantation, they didn't know anything about Abe Lincoln and that he had issued that paper [the Emancipation Proclamation] January the 1st.[2] She said they were not free until the surrender of Lee. And then the soldiers came through going home, both the Confederates and the Northern soldiers came through, and they told them that they were free. That's the way they knew it. They worked all those years until they said they were free.

Plantation life was hard. Granddaddy had belonged to a slave holder, Harston, in Henry County, Virginia, near Martinsville. That is the biggest city around in that county. I think he owned about all of that county, Harston. Of course they call them Hairstons now, but they were

Harstons. The younger white people of the family still own holdings in Martinsville. They primarily grew tobacco. They had cotton, too, but I think tobacco was the primary thing. In the quarters where my grandfather was there must have been between one and two hundred slaves. Their job was to till that land, see that new ground was cleared for the next crop. Those slaves built their cabins and all. The owners also had slave quarters in other places. So from what my grandfather said, the owner must have had more than any one or two hundred slaves. He must have had a lot of slaves. He must have been a wealthy slave man. I never think to ask the young Harstons about it, but they did tell me that they kept a record of all of the last slaves that were sold on to their place which would include my Great Gran and they said, "Why don't you find out what part of Africa they're from? We have it. Go down there sometime and have them look up the record for you."

Because of the tales surrounding Great Gran I say she was a warrior. She was one of the slaves that was grown when she came from Africa. So I guess the very fact that I knew of my great grandmother created an interest, and I wanted to know about slavery. My mother would tell me about old Granny Roddy as she called her—old Granny Roddy. They'd bring the new overseers in, new white men, and they'd say, "You can whip any of these slaves but Roddy. Don't touch her. If you do, she'll kill you." So we used to like to talk about her because she was big and brave, you know—bad. So that's why I remember her. When we were little we would argue about history. I would say something about her. I always could defend my side by referring to Granny Roddy; she wouldn't let them whip her. She would kill them.

I talked about slavery once to a professor; he asked me if it made me bitter. "Aren't you bitter?" And I've thought about that. You know, you have reactions to things; that's the psychological part of knowing all these things. I remember a story my mother or my grandfather told me—about a woman who had a child. The overseer was the father of this child. He was mean. The woman had been crippled running away from him; she'd hurt her foot on a rock and she walked on the side of her foot because there was nobody to set her fractured ankle. She walked with this limp all of the time. It seemed that this child was born, their child. She wasn't a real bright child, but she was loved by this woman with a love that was terrific. That was all she had, it seemed. I think it was my grandfather who told me, because it happened at the place where he got a whipping. Harston wasn't the master when he got the scars on his back from the whipping. Harstons had bought him from somewhere. I don't know that other master's name.

The overseer got mad with this woman and wanted to punish her, so when the traders came by, Negro traders they called them, he sold this little girl and he knew that would hurt the woman worse than anything he could do. The woman'd come from the field, working the field all day, and she came in looking for the little girl. The overseer was making fun of her. He let her look and then finally he told her that he'd sold the child to the nigger trader, and the woman killed him.

I asked my grandfather, "How'd she kill him?"

My grandfather said she made one step toward the overseer, then grabbed him and choked him to death. It was hardly a struggle. In her anger and in her sadness, she had the strength of two men. She just grabbed him and choked him to death.

I asked, "What did they do with her?" My grandfather never did know what they did.

I used to think about her; I was glad that she choked him. You know, you have reactions to things; that's the psychological part of knowing all these things. You measure; you are the judge and the jury and the executioner—all. You know in your mind. Even with a little bit of training you learn things. Then you go back over it and say, "Now, that wasn't right. I shouldn't have thought that." That kind of change of thinking comes when you are really alone. The ordinary person doesn't have time for that kind of thinking—they have too much to do and too many people around. When you are by yourself a great deal, you have silence. Everything is learned in the silence. Things happen to you, but you learn them in the silence. They become a part of your thinking in the silence, and your acceptance of them is learning. The learning is not out there where all the noise and fuss and everything are going on. It's learning, it's learning from within.

My mother's father was forty-two years in slavery, and I think that's why I have been so interested in slavery. Without knowing it, I have brought over that interest from him telling me things. He fought in the Civil War in place of his master; of course there's no record because in the Confederate Army their Negroes—slaves—Negro soldiers had no records. They didn't get any pension. They didn't get anything, but they were there. He was a strong slave and could handle those sandbags. The slaves who could handle the breastworks [military fortifications] they called them, were sent to take the place of the young white men who didn't want to go. The Negroes who fought with the Yankees got pensions and they have a record there, but there's no record in the Confederate files of any Negro.[3]

My mother said a lot of the Yankee soldiers were just boys who thought it would be wonderful to have this experience of war. But war was a terrific thing and they tried to run away. Their plantation was full of boys trying to run away; they were everywhere. Down in Martinsville there'd be a tattered and torn Yankee boy that would stumble into the field where they were, or stumble into their hut, burning up with fever, hungry, cold. They would put him up in the loft. They had steps to go up there. Granny would make soup out of whatever they had and feed him. She would put things on him to try to allay the fever. She'd have her goose grease and the things that they used. Maybe the next night it would be a Confederate who came. There were plenty of times that one would be in one corner and one would be in another. But whether it was a Yankee or Confederate, it didn't matter. Whichever one it was, he knew that when he reached that Negro cabin, he was going to be taken care of. He'd found a friend. The word would slip back that when they reached that Negro cabin they were going to be taken care of. Sometimes when it was time for them to go, there wasn't anything to give them, and so Granny and them'd make cornbread in a skillet before the fire and wrap some cornbread in a rag or something so they'd have that to eat on.

Momma said, "Children, you all don't know nothing." She'd be telling us, "You don't know what you can go through. And if we didn't know there was a God, we couldn't have gone through this."

All those beliefs were perfected in their religious lives. They knew there was a God through all that meanness, but God was the only thing that wasn't mean. Those masters were mean. Except here and there, of course, like it is in all things. My father's father was a slaveholder. He was my father's master and his father which was common in that time. Those men who had hearts and who had some conscience about things knew it wasn't those children's fault; it wasn't the family's fault that they were mixed up like that. Over in Ohio, white men came up here and brought their mixed children; they bought up Meigs and Lawrence Counties and brought their mixed children up there and settled them on those farms right over there in Lawrence County. For awhile, there wasn't anything over there but mulatto people and white people. Those men couldn't stand what was going to happen to everybody.

Granddaddy [Garrison's mother's father] said the Lord called him to preach. I used to tease Granddaddy, "How did he call you? And whoever saw God?"

I'd tease him with all those questions and Momma would say, "You don't question that. God called him. That's enough!"

So—he became one of the ministers on the plantation, and he didn't work anymore in the field. He kept the Negroes in line with his gospel. On the plantation he didn't preach every week. He preached when the master told him to preach—when the master had something to get across to the slaves. I don't know what it could have been because I don't know the layout of the work load, how it was done. But they had to have a man they could depend on, and I think that the reason he was so well liked among the Negroes was that none of them were ever whipped because of anything that he told the master. There were some Negroes who did cause others to be whipped and they were hated.

I would ask Granddaddy what he'd preach about. And he said, "Preach what the master tell you. You'd go and the master'd be settin' on the porch sometime. You'd take off your hat and stand there and he'd tell you what to preach."

"Like what?" I'd ask. "Didn't you take a text?"

"Yeah, you take a text." And he would say the one he remembered best. He was old then, you know. The one he remembered best was,

"Servants," he would say, "Negroes, obey your master and the Lord, and you'll go to heaven when you die." He said, "They's having such a hard time on earth, they'd do anything that they'd promise me they would."

I'd say, "Well how would you ever know when you were preaching right?"

Then he'd remember other verses. He remembered other things, and he would say he'd preach that and they'd never know the difference in what he was preaching. They were highly emotional and borne down with the work and the woes of slavery.

"Did you ever learn better, Granddaddy?" I'd ask. "Did you ever learn that the Bible didn't say that, Granddaddy?"

"Yes," he said, "there were free Negroes, and they would come. You might have known them before they got free. Some of them bought their freedom; some of them were master's children. He wouldn't let no child of his be a slave. And they'd still live around and they'd get out with other free Negroes who'd come back and who'd learned to read and write. One of these men would come to the field and he'd say, 'Marshall, what'd you preach yesterday?'"

Granddaddy said he would tell him. And then the man would take out the Bible and read to him and tell him what it said. And I'd say, "Could you preach it to the Negroes?"

He said, "No, but I'd tell 'em. I'd sing it." He said, "Master wouldn't know what that chapter said that I'd preached the Sunday before, so I'd sing the Bible to them."

And he had this great bass voice, you know. He said if he wasn't singing Master'd want to know, "Marshall, you ain't singing today?" He would know something was wrong with Marshall.

Granddaddy said, "I've sung half of that Bible that was read to me."

I don't know how it was done. I just know that Granddaddy could sing. And he said that there's a certain way that you could turn—now he didn't know anything about crosscurrents and air and all—but that sound would carry. He wanted to send a message.

I said, "How far was the field?"

"As far as you could see," he'd say. "But somebody heard. All of them wouldn't, but somebody heard."

And he said he'd just clear his throat and let out a long groan like he's going to say something and they'd come alive in that field to listen. And then he'd sing. In order to let him know that they heard him, they would answer with a moan or something they put in. And he said then they'd soon plant tobacco and pick cotton at a rate that you couldn't imagine.

He was communicating to them the correct reading of that text he'd preached on Sunday. He said his folks knew.

I said, "Did everybody?"

He said, "I don't know about everybody."

Some of those early preachers used a chair as a pulpit. They stood behind the chair to preach. In history, their history, the racial history, they're known as chair-back preachers. The relief provided by religion to the lowly living of the slave was something that was a response to a deep-seated human longing. Their call to religion was a reaction to terrific suffering that people have no idea about now.

Before my grandfather went to war, he tried to run away as a young man. Of course, he was severely beaten, and he bore the marks. I used to look at them and rub my fingers across them, and I'd want to know what those welts were on his back. I'd see Momma rub his shoulder, and he would be stiff. He was an old man then.

I'd want to know. "What's that for, Granddaddy?"

"That was by a bullwhip," he'd say. "You ain't gonna feel it. You'll never feel it. Thank God for Abraham Lincoln."

Abraham Lincoln was his great savior, and that's why I don't care what others interpret Abraham Lincoln as being and doing. I've only got to think about those ridges on my Granddaddy's back and they can't do anything when it comes to what I think about Abraham Lincoln. Anything that saved me and those of us who've come on from that, that's enough. The welts on Granddaddy's back were like your finger—ridges, crisscrossed just as that whip struck. I was somewhere and I wanted to see a bullwhip, and I saw one. There was another one with a prodder to it, and that was called a cat of nine tails. There were nine of those thongs on it. The slaves were beaten on their bare backs with those whips.

The master wasn't always in the fields. He'd hire somebody else to oversee, or hire somebody with a reputation that said he could command. Somebody who could break slaves. Sometimes the slaves didn't do anything [to annoy the overseer]. The overseer would just beat them to let them know what a beating was. It was a hideous sort of thing. My Granddaddy was beaten when he was young; he was either trying to run or trying to help somebody, but they caught up with him. Marshall got this terrible beating, but it seems like I don't remember him telling me about any beatings after that.

I was always intrigued with that back. If Momma was going to do anything for Granddaddy, I'd make it in there to see. "Poor old Granddaddy," I'd call him. "My poor Granddaddy." I was always sensitive to people's pain or want. If I'd hear somebody crying, I'd cry, too, and then I'd get mad and fuss at myself. "What are you crying for?" So it was that way; I mean I've had that sort of feeling all along.

chapter 2

✴

Origins

I was born in Hollins, Virginia, just near Roanoke. The family place was there and the house I was born in. My mother's name was Cassie. I used to tell her when I grew up that Cassie was short for Cassandra. She'd say, "Now, where'd you get that from?" and I said, "Well, it just comes out of history." She said, "Well, I'll just keep the name I got, don't bother with the other'n." A younger group connected with the family called themselves Hairstons, but my mother called herself Harston and her father was a Harston. I don't think it was a slave brogue either. I think they did have the correct name.

My father's name was Wesley Carter. He was tall and heavy, fair skinned, blue eyes. I guess the hair was black or dark, straight hair. And he looked like any white man of his time, swarthy, a bit from the sun and rain; and he never was around very much. He was a soldier of fortune, I guess. He mined coal ore and he followed the gold rush in the '90s to the west. And then he came to West Virginia with the bunch that was coming out to open the mines. It wasn't long until he met with an accidental death. So, I never knew him too well or too much.

He was accidentally killed on the railroad. He went down to see his people in Virginia. It was winter. It used to snow—drifts over your head almost. It seems that he must have been struck by a train, and after the holidays when the snow drifts melted up, they found him alongside the tracks. I was small then and I just knew he didn't come back home. I must have been seven or eight when my father died, somewhere round in there. I guess I was seven because we were either fixing to put a school in this place or something. I was so anxious to get to school and get to reading because my father had brought books that he was reading—that he would leave at home, and I wanted to read those books. He had all of those John Henry things,[1] ballads of all kinds and he would read them. My father wasn't buried near us. He was buried at his sister's home. We didn't go. It was a time of year that we couldn't travel. I don't remember too much about it.

My mother never talked about my father much. Most of my talking —that slavery-time talk came from my grandfather, you know. He was there. We lived with him. His name was Marshall Thomas Harston, but he dropped the Harston and named himself Marshall Thomas. We were the family of Thomases that lived down there in Hollins, Virginia. My uncle, Peter, said that he was no Harston. He wasn't a slave. He didn't belong to nobody but himself. He was free and they called him Uncle Peter Free down there. The old people did. They remember Uncle Peter Free. That was his name. They still remember it. My grandfather had four grandchildren: My uncle had two [children]; I believe they died, and then there was my brother and me.

My brother's name was John Carter. When I first was little, you know, he was large enough to go to work in the mines. My mother was always apprehensive and I think she made him so. He left as soon as he could get some things together—a bunch of boys were going somewhere for something—he followed that bunch. He worked wherever he was. His schooling was limited, too. I would teach him as far as I'd go; I'd teach him at night what I'd learned during the day. In his late years he was an insurance man. He was a good worker in his church and lived in Columbus. His principal work was at the steel plant there, Ralston's Steel Mill. He was an old man when he died.

II

family

and

youth

MEMPHIS Tennessee Garrison's life story, as recorded in 1968, is a retrospective account of almost eighty years. This undoubtedly affects her recollections of immediate family, but there can be no question of her mother's important influence. Not only in chapter 3, but also throughout this book, Garrison makes it clear that "Momma" was the person who inspired her by example, encouragement, and support. Her mother kept house for Garrison once she was married and began to work. Without her mother, Garrison would not have been able to manage her home, pursue a career, and maintain the level of public activity that she did—a fact Garrison readily acknowledges.

Garrison's husband, William Melvin Garrison, is not nearly as prominent in her story. He seems almost a reclusive figure, and nowhere does she describe the nature of their personal or intimate relationship. She tells the story of their courtship as a story. He died long before she did, in 1942, just a year after her mother died. Garrison's brother was ten years her elder and he, too, figures only slightly in her life story.

Garrison's mother embodied the contradictions of strong, working-class black women in America. She was intelligent, but did not learn to read until later in her life, and then only minimally. Widowed early in life, she worked multiple, backbreaking jobs raising two children and sending one to high school and college. Yet Garrison did not perceive her mother as suffering or oppressed. Rather, she saw her mother as one who succeeded in spite of the obstacles. For example, lack of education did not prevent her from "reading" the Bible to the Missionary Society or doing a scientific study of pigs' bones.

Garrison always talked of "home" as Gary, West Virginia. At the same time, she understood her roots in the family's land. The story of her two uncles—who were driven from the land by racists who burned their houses—is told matter-of-factly and without any overt expression of bitterness. In fact, she seems to have been angrier about the way she was forced to sell her property for less than its true value. In the case of racism and terror, there is little an individual can do at a specific time and place to change things. But being cheated on a sale, one feels a more personal affront and helplessness.

This comparison highlights one of the important contradictions of racism in American society. On the one hand, many older African Americans talk of segregation as something they "accepted." On the other hand, they often speak with great bitterness of specific incidents when they were humiliated and degraded. In the case of the structural "given," one feels little personal responsibility; in the cases of personal interactions, one's ability to control the situation and exert power is directly challenged.

Garrison's discussion of her school memories paints a dramatic picture of an early one-room schoolhouse in an Appalachian black community. Lacking adequate material resources and restricted to a shorter term than at white schools, early black teachers were still able to provide students with all the important basics. Whether it was with acorns or apples, the lesson got taught!

Her first teacher was more than just a teacher—he was a profound influence on her life. Thus, her own childhood experience in school impressed upon her the critical importance teachers can have in molding individual children and in making an impact on the community. Obviously, this connection affected her own decision not only to become a teacher, but to continue teaching even when other opportunities arose. Later on, Garrison describes how she might have studied law had she had the money, but then concludes that she was more effective in helping people by remaining in the field of education.

chapter 3

✳

My Mother

My mother[1] *had no mixture. Her* strain was pure African, so far as she knew. She was built well and strong. She had strong shoulders and hips and a strong face. She had velvet black skin, soft and satiny. She had keen eyes and all of her features were strong; she had a strong face. She was just as determined as that face was strong, too. I know that now. And she was kind; she was kind to children. There were two of us children in our family, but there were six around the house. Nobody ever came there running away or anything who was turned away. If they didn't have any place to stay, they stayed there. My mother was deeply religious, because her father, I guess, had been a minister. She was also a neighborhood person; everybody in our neighborhood here in West Virginia knew her; that's where most of her home life was. She was a wholesome, good citizen.

She was a Christian. She worked in the church. She was president of the Missionary Society. This was when I was a good size. But whoever heard tell of anybody being president of the Missionary Society and couldn't read all the things a president had to read. But she was determined to be president because she bossed them all anyway. She had skills that they didn't have—all this organizational ability. I'd go to the meetings; I'd follow Momma. The minister would write a note and leave it, and she'd look at it all nonchalant. When the members'd gone I'd read the note to her. Now, when it came the next meeting, she would say, "I didn't have time to do this at the last meeting," and she'd tell all that stuff from the note. She had it down; she was ready for everything. There was one woman, I know now, that was especially a bit wary of how Momma could do that. So, this woman was always saying, "We need a special meeting; we need a Bible reading." She wanted to be president. The next meeting Momma would say, "Sister Taylor says that the president should have something from the Bible to open with and, of course, she wants to pray, I know, so I call on her to pray."

I would get the Bible and read to Momma; that's why I know so much about it—the Psalms especially. I would choose those Psalms that didn't have more than ten verses. At the meeting, Momma would have the Bible down on the table and she would say, "Well, for our lesson we'll read the first Psalm," and she'd stand up there and read every word of it just like it was in that Bible—whatever I had read to her. When I didn't have time, or was afraid she wouldn't get it, I'd only read a verse or two. She'd get the words of my mouth and say, "Will you all repeat after me?" Whatever the situation, she could rise to it in her unlettered way. She conquered her environment and she conquered her personal lack of training and she lived a very satisfactory happy life.

I taught her to read. She wanted to read her Bible, just that, that's all she wanted. And she did. She learned to read and when I went to college, she could even write enough for me to leave an addressed envelope and she would write to me. That was as far as she knew she would get, but she had so much common sense. She had a ready wit and white and black were both friendly to her. They called her aunt as most of the people did—aunt and uncle to the older people. Aunt Cassie. Aunt Cassie was well known all over the place. And to us—to my brother, ten years my senior, and to me, she was everything.

My mother was a worker. She had a hand laundry; she would wash all day for fifty cents, and she worked for the rich people who had the fine things. There were no laundries; there was no dry cleaning then, and she always had a good job with the rich people. Out here in West Virginia she worked for the coal operators. When she wasn't house-keeping with them, she was the nurse with the children in the yard, or she was doing laundry. After her time there, she would work in the small hotels or boarding houses. When she'd leave there, she'd meet this laundry at home; she'd wash and iron half the night.

My mother was unlettered but highly intelligent. Sometimes when we were at home, she would dress up and she would say, "I put my head up and strut like Miss Grace." Miss Grace was the lady of the house. And bless my mother, she would have been a black Miss Grace if she had had the training and the money to have been so; she was that kind.

I remember that she worked for the McQuails, and I remember a lawyer family by the name of Watts, before we came to West Virginia. I didn't bother to remember the names of the other people. This was a new place and the people were going back and forth; they were moving. One family'd be living there; then somebody new would come down from Pennsylvania; the man that had been there had gone somewhere else to set up another mine. They were just a moving, roving set, both white and black, in opening up this West Virginia coalfield, especially that southern area. The McQuails, the Lincolns were the wealthy people who were sent in by the Crozer Land Company. The Houstons still have holdings in West Virginia. The Jenkins Jones and others—they brought the reforms, and they had the nice houses—and they wanted a good laundress. My mother'd be there. Oh, when I look at the washing machines now, I wonder how she did it. It was the survival of the fittest. She had to be strong. No wonder Great Gran survived the Middle Passage;* she was unusual; she had to be. And my mother got some of that strength; she had to, she was still strong up in her nineties.

I think I got mixed up where that strength was concerned. My mother'd say sometimes, "You mixed niggers are no good." She had quite a sense of humor. The things she could say. Why, when she was old and couldn't work, you'd think there were a half dozen people in the house. There wouldn't be anybody but ourselves. Sometimes, in her late years, the teachers with whom I taught at Gary would come by. "Come on, let's go by," they'd say. I had a love seat in the kitchen, so while I was getting supper I could hear what was going on. They'd come by and would

*Second leg of the voyage of a slave ship bringing enslaved Africans from West Africa to the Americas or the West Indies.

be talking to Mom. She'd ask about things and she always had something of value to say or to tell.

I remember some friends of hers were having operations and she said, "What they have to have all this cutting done on them for?"

She'd been complaining with a pain in her side and my husband said, "You got a pain in your side; you may have to have your appendix removed."

She said, "No. I ain't going to have nothing removed. I'm going to take all these things to God. Give me back to him. I'm going to take the appendix back."

He said, "You don't have any teeth." She didn't have any teeth then.

She said, "I didn't come here with nothing but gums. I'll take the gums back." Well, you know, that was an occasion of fun.

And she had a teacher friend who would tell her everything. He would come to visit, and he used to call her his cousin, called her "Cuz."

He said, "I'm going to school next year. I'm going to Howard and I'm going to study medicine, and this is the first book I'm going to need." So he showed her the book.

She said, "What's that book for?"

He said, "It shows the embryology of the pig."

She said, "You're going to take medicine to doctor a pig?"

He said, "No. In certain stages, the embryo of a pig is nearer that of a human being than any other animal."

"Oh, well, sir," she said. "Whatever that means."

She was eating her supper. She was eating a pig's foot; she liked things like that and I had cooked it for her and she was eating it.

She said, "Since you're going to do all that, you can start right now. How many bones in a pig's foot?"

This was just like her, to come off on something like that. So he became alert.

He said, "Well, I don't think this book tells that, but I have a book at home that tells it and I'll bring it to you tomorrow evening. I'll tell you tomorrow evening how many bones in that pig's foot."

The next day she cooked that other pig's foot and she ate it, and she took every bone, every one of those little bones and put them in a dish and set it on the top of the frigidaire. Well, he came as usual; she was a good cook and she had gotten supper.

He said, "I hope you got some pie for supper."

She said, "Yes, I do. I thought of you and I baked some pies." So she said, "Let's get to the pig's foot. How many bones in a pig's foot."

He said, "You know, I couldn't find it anywhere."

She said, "Well, how you going to study anything right when there ain't nothing in the book about it?"

He said, "Yeah, but there are other books that have it. I just happened to have the books that didn't have it."

She said, "Well, that's all right. I know."

He said, "Well, how many bones in a pig's foot?"

She said, "Twenty-six."

I believe it was twenty-six that she said.

And he said, "Well, I guess that is right. It seems to me I've heard, but how do you know?"

She reached up and got the dish and said, "Here they is. Count them."

And you know, the teachers and everybody teased him more about that. They had a lot of fun with him about that. I didn't know she'd done that, but to me that was the cleverest thing. But she—in her not knowing —that had come to her. She had thought of that; she had cooked that pig's foot and counted those bones and put them there, little foot bones. Momma loved the pig and she had eaten all of that foot and there wasn't anything left but the bone. So to me, that was clever. I think about it now, that somebody'd think of things like that.

She could get the best of any situation like that. I used to remember the things she would do and say and we would have a lot of fun about it. They'd come, those who were my friends would come. For those who spent the night with me, and for those whom she liked, she'd fix something special. After she passed, people would come to visit and they'd start talking about Momma. They'd say, "You remember so and so," and Momma lived again through them. I mean, she was here again with them.

And when someone passed, she'd say that when she passed she was not going to suffer any, "I'm just going to sleep."

I said, "Well, how do you know?"

She said, "I've been shown in the spirit. God showed me in the spirit that I'd never suffer."

And that's what she did; she slept away, slept away. I heard her and I went in and she just laid her head in my arms. Then she just looked up and laid her head against me and that was it. She was gone.

So all of those things, and my thinking—what motivated me to do certain things was mostly the closeness of this mother. To me she was unusual because other children's momma wasn't like my momma.

Somebody'd say to her, "I have a book. It would be nice for your little girl. You ought to buy a book."

She'd say, "How much is it?" Well, whatever it was, she'd get it. A book agent had a field day at our house.

Sometimes the people for whom she worked would say, "Aunt Cassie, would you like to have this book? If you take this washing home, take Mr. So and So's shirts home and do them, you may have the book." That was it. Those shirts—no sooner said than done. The book was for me.

In the memoirs of the little book that they gave me at her funeral I wrote,

> I had a wonderful mother.
> Her memory will never grow old.
> God gave her the smile of sunshine;
> He made her a heart of pure gold.
> She was a good friend and neighbor
> To everyone she knew.
> Although he saw fit to take her,
> He knew just what to do.
> But to me she will live forever,
> That wonderful mother I knew.

And that was it. I stopped grieving for her. After I got something—I have to get something to hang onto and then I don't grieve. I just stopped grieving for her. I knew she'd been and she'd passed, and I didn't grieve any more.

She died in 1941. She was in her nineties, I believe. We didn't quite know. But she was between—she must have been either ninety-two or ninety-three by the things she would tell and count them up and all of that. I just let all of that go. When I stopped grieving, I let all of the things that I remembered go. You kind of let them go. So that little book and that little poem are all that's left.

chapter 4

✴

My Husband

*My husband [William Melvin Garri-*son] and I met October 5th one year, and married the next October 5 [1918] and did just what it said, "Till death do us part," because we stayed together. I met him in Gary. Our school in Elkhorn had burned, and we were teaching everywhere—in houses and all. The school in Gary needed another teacher and I went to see if I could get that school so I wouldn't have to teach in a house. They said, "If you want to go up there, we need another teacher badly. You go and see the commissioner." That was the superintendent of the works. So, I went up there to see him and I was coming back on the train; there were trains that ran back and forth up to Gary, up to United States Steel. And there was a little tailor shop by the station, a fellow kept it. He came out and spoke to me and said, "You must be the new teacher the children say is coming." I said, "Yes, I just went up to see your man." While we were talking, this man comes up. Well, I didn't pay any attention to him because I thought he belonged to the other group [white people], so I didn't say anything. So the man from the shop said, "Come here, Mr. Garrison. I want you to meet this lady. This is Miss Carter and she's going to teach here." My husband spoke. He was very nice. He was an electrician at the place. He talked and the train came and he put me on the train and said goodbye and that he hoped to see me when I came up to teach. I had gotten a place to stay and everything. That was it. It just started from that.

When Mr. Garrison couldn't go to the [movie] show with me, he'd send my ticket and send me another ticket for a schoolboy so I wouldn't have to come back alone. That way I wouldn't have any excuse for having to have other company, you know. I thought about it afterwards.

The kids would say, "Miss Carter, give me the next ticket, give me the next ticket."

I'd say, "Who wants to go to the show?"

"I do," they'd yell.

Well, the ticket would go all around, so that cut out anybody else. I didn't have any excuse for meeting a lot of other fellows because there wasn't much to go to but the show and to the things that the school had.

And we were selling bonds; we were selling liberty bonds then and the company, United States Steel, was selling them. They had big bond-selling festive dinners. They wouldn't really be dinners, but you'd have everything there to buy to eat. That was all there was to go to, that and the picture shows. The bond sales were raising money for the war; that was World War I. And then, of course, my husband was called into the service before the war was over. He didn't go overseas; he was just in camp here in this country. He wasn't in there long before the Armistice was signed, but we got married in October, the same October of the year the Armistice was signed.

We moved from Elkhorn to Gary. I had my mother with me; she was living then. And we stayed in Gary until I moved to Huntington. Just in that area.

My husband was an electrician. He was a company boss. He'd place men on these jobs. He had his own book [business], his setup, everything, and he was well paid. If there were any lights to be hung, they'd say, "Garrison, so and so and so. We need some men down on such and such a place. There's a whole entry to light up." He'd send men there who could do all that work and he was foreman. He was the only Negro foreman that the company had anyway. They didn't know he was a Negro. If they did know, they didn't care. They didn't bother.

We had no children but we sent a niece of his to school. She works for the government in Washington now. She's a grandmother now; she had a son so she says I'm a grandma. And there were children here and there that I helped through college. I have some at Institute [West Virginia]; one's a doctor up there and another is a teacher in the Dunbar schools, and two more are on the faculty [of West Virginia State College in Institute]. They were my protégés through college. I helped supply clothes and money for the additional things. When somebody would say something about giving to the church, I would say that I tithe, but I would say, "I wouldn't give a preacher all of that money. I don't give the preacher all that." Whatever is good to be done, I use that money for that. When it's out [spent], it's out. That tenth goes to whatever somebody needs—to some child, to helping somebody through school, to sending fifty dollars or something when somebody is in a hard place. That to me is what it's all about, not going there giving that preacher that money. You see, I'm the rebel.

Before he was boss, my husband ran one of those big Jeffreys, one of those coal machines. Those men made money. They could make $700 or $800 a month even when the coal seam was low. He ran those big machines, but that [coal] dust was almost too much for him, and he quit that. Finally he did lose his health. He died in 1942.

My mother died in Gary, my brother died there, and my husband— all died there, and left me there in the house. But I wasn't alone. I had some kids around; the children who lived near me and had gone to school to me. Dr. [Robert] Gunn was one; he had married and I had just lost my mother. There was nobody there but me. So, he and Mrs. Gunn came down and he said, "Don't you want us to live with you? We're going to live here until I get graduated from college and get ready to go to medical school." And they did. They lived with me four years and she went on and taught at Fisk* for a while and got her masters at Fisk. When Dr. Gunn graduated, the dentist here in Huntington died, Dr. Adams, and I sent Dr. Gunn a letter saying there was a vacancy. Dr. Gunn came here

*Historically black university in Nashville, Tennessee. Robert Gunn attended dental school at Meharry Medical College, also in Nashville.

and he bought the things from Mrs. Adams. Then he rented around and then he bought a house; his backyard's right next to mine. When he left my home in Gary, somebody else got married and came to stay with me. And it was like that; somebody was there when I left; there was an old lady up the street and her niece was living with me. She was one of the girls who had graduated and she came to live with me, so I wasn't at a loss for somebody all the time.

chapter 5

✳

The Family Land

When my grandfather became free it seems that he wandered out looking for work. Many of the slaves stayed on the place. Everything was so torn up after the war you couldn't even find nuts. They say if a crow would fly down the Shenandoah Valley he'd better take his bag of rations with him. That's how lean and sparse it was. That part of Virginia was ravaged by the war the same as the other, the Martinsville part. It seems that the slaves got out on their own after so long, and they went from place to place looking for work. Somebody would find work and come back to the quarters and say, "If you go such and such a place, you'll get so many days' work." It seems that they hunted around like that, just half living here and there. Then there were agencies. I don't know whether the Freedmen's Bureau[1] was operating in that part or not.

My grandfather found himself working down there in Roanoke County. It seems that one of the men that he worked for owned land up in what is now Hollins. My grandfather worked for him a long time and then he bought land. How he got the money to buy I don't know, but it was fifty dollars an acre. That's what he paid for it, or that was what he was charged for it. I doubt if he ever paid it all, but it was in his name and the deed was dated 1870, just five years after he'd come out of slavery.

He had migrated from where he'd been enslaved and run across him a place and bought it.

I left Hollins. We moved to Roanoke and then to the coalfields. I'd go back to Hollins to visit and take my mother to see about the family property; she was the oldest one. I had two uncles who left there when they were grown and went to Pennsylvania. They came back and built houses, and the whites burned them down. That isn't known. The town was always ashamed of it, and they would never let you say anything about it: Uncle Marshall's boys' houses getting burned down. My uncles had divided up the land in five acres each, and one morning the last one who came from Pennsylvania was going to Roanoke to market and he looked back and his house was on fire, so he left. They all left. They wanted no part of it, and they died away from home in Pennsylvania. My mother was the oldest one and she kept tabs on everything. When she died, I had it. I sold it. I was the last one. I saw the deed when I sold the property. It was dated 1870. I had the most peculiar feeling about selling the place after that.

There were fifteen acres in that particular tract, but the first tract that my grandfather bought was ten acres, and that ten acres furnishes the water. There was a creek that ran through it; it was called Horse Pen Branch. He had five acres on each side of that creek. He worked and bought it. There is a dam there that furnishes Roanoke its water supply. And of course, they took it from me. I didn't live there and they claimed that they couldn't find the heirs until somebody told me about it. Then after I came there, the company that built the dam claimed that they had bought it and that they had already paid two or three times for it. I've got a copy of the deed. In the old days they didn't survey like the proper surveying people do now. The deed goes by leaps and bounds. It says the land is bounded on this side by this and on the other by this tree and this point.

But what established my ownership was that the deed called for five acres on each side of the Horse Pen Branch, and the Horse Pen Branch runs from the upper edge of that mountain on down into this dam that they dammed up. Then I knew that if they owned the Horse Pen

Branch, they had my land. After I got a lawyer, they decided that they would give me just what they had given everybody else who sold, which they said was $68 an acre—$680. That didn't pay the taxes I had paid on it. I had kept the taxes up after everybody had died. I just knew the property was there and I kept the taxes up.

On the other side there were one hundred acres that were owned by another family. I also had fifteen acres on that side; old man Brubaker had sold it to my grandfather—fifteen acres for him to farm. They liked him. We were five miles from any colored family, and my grandfather's land was just in there. Those old men, old slaveholders, they liked him. He had everything he wanted. The city of Roanoke bought out that hundred acres, that's now the filter [water filtration] plant. That fifteen acres up there was mine, but the city wouldn't buy it. They hemmed me up in there without a road and they wouldn't buy my land.

I knew a man where I was living in Gary who had a doctor brother in Roanoke—Dr. Massie. Dr. Massie was looking for someplace to buy out. He was an affluent doctor and it was building up out there. The finest women's college in the South is right there. Our place overlooked this beautiful college. Mother used to work there when she first moved there, Hollins College. So Dr. Massie said that he would buy it—said, "I'll buy it. You've got a clear deed to it. I'm going to get a road out there if it takes me all my life." He bought it. I sold it to him for $1,800. Lots are now selling there for $3,000. He hasn't been too long getting a road in there, but I never would have gotten one there. So while I think of what I lost—that I didn't get anything out of it like it was worth, somebody did.

chapter 6

❋

Schooldays

There weren't enough whites to have a school where we lived.[1] The whites were the bosses, and the top men. If they lived there, they'd send their children away to school. Some of their families were still living in Pennsylvania. They would come down in the summer with their children and go back in the winter. But the Negroes had nowhere to go.

My first teacher was very much the fatherly influence in my life. His name was Frazier Price. He was a graduate of Virginia Seminary and College of Lynchburg.* That was a good high school, about the eighth grade then. He was an old man. He had worked his way through school; he'd wanted to be a preacher and a teacher. He colored our existence in the schoolroom and in the church. He was the leader and it was the acquaintance of him that caused my mother to desire to do, to be in things, to be head of her Missionary Society. She'd never met anyone like that. She was a little slave girl, you see. I would go to Sunday school—he also taught Sunday school. He would tell his schoolchildren to go to Sunday school and in the schoolhouse we had Bible and prayer. We'd take turns reading the Bible at openings. We all did. All of those children had some

---

*Black institution in Lynchburg, Virginia; now Virginia University of Lynchburg.

knowledge of the Bible. Now, it's a mixed-up thing in my memory because there're just fragments of it, but then it all seemed that one thing sort of fitted into the other.

I first went to school near Elkhorn; the little town was Ennis. The McQuails coal people had this little one-room schoolhouse there. I guess I was about five and one-half or six probably, when I started school. We didn't bother with birthdays. I know now what they are. I project myself back then, and I feel like I did then. We had eight grades—from the little fellows who were having their first school experience to the children who had come from places where they had already been taught to read. We had a lesson every day; everybody in that school did something. We had wooden seats; he had a table for a desk. We had a big stove in the middle. We burned coal because there was plenty of coal so we were warm. We had a dipper in the bucket for water; the water came down from the mountains on the hillside. I can see all of that now. Beautiful living. I didn't have to go to a big fine school to learn. Mr. Price taught me to read. I had my little McGuffey speller. The back is off of it now, but it's just like he gave it to me. I didn't have any books; there weren't any books for sale, but he gave me the speller. He had a switch lying across up there—dogwood. That was for the fellows that didn't think he'd use it because the other children were a rather eager lot, hadn't had the experience of anything else. We were going to learn to read. Well, I think in about six weeks some of us were reading, maybe less. I think I was reading the first week. I already knew the alphabet and all he had to do was give me that little book to start me out and then I went to it. Then I got the reader, first reader, McGuffey's. When I was grown, I was up in Ohio and I bought me a whole new set of McGuffey's about ten years ago. I came across them and I bought the whole set. As a child, I didn't go through the whole set. They changed to another book when I was about in the seventh reader. They changed to Stickney's, I think it was.

Now Mr. Price would take those children—the little ones—we had slates—and he would put something on the blackboard. I think the blackboard must have been just paint, black paint on something. I don't know what kind of crayon we had—stick crayons came after that—but whatever we had, it worked on the board. We'd copy on the slate and learn how to make letters. We'd make our own tablets. We'd save wrapping paper, everything was wrapped in paper; the stores didn't have bags then. The stores had paper in stacks; sheets were sold in certain lengths and everything was wrapped that you got at the stores—after that came the bags and all that. We'd take that paper and we'd make tablets much like the tablets are now, only your momma would take a needle and sew through it to hold your papers together. Then you had a tablet. It was good for you. We had pencils and we had slates; now that was your means of getting your work done.

You started out with your ABC's; everybody said the ABC's in the beginning. That was the nicest thing. You sang your ABC's; you got so you talked your ABC's! He'd have us all to the board and everybody'd go over the ABC's. Maybe you'd have about six or eight or ten over there who could read well; some of the rest of these little fellows could read just a little bit. Then there were some who couldn't read, but all of them got to say their ABC's. Then he would skip and say, "What's this?" and say them backwards. Then the first class would go back and find something to do while he'd take the big ones and read out of the books. I wouldn't be doing anything. I was listening to what they were reading. I had me a school after school was out and I needed stories to tell the children. I entranced them with the stories. I couldn't read from the book, but I'd tell them stories they'd never heard.

One thing, the kids learned arithmetic very well. They were anxious to count. Mr. Price taught us to count using acorns. We'd pass the acorns coming down to school. We'd get a whole pinafore—little apron—full. I'd bring my pinafore filled with acorns and put them in the box. Then you'd go to the box and you could play with as many acorns as you could count; it wasn't too many. The little ones learned how to count real quick, you know, playing with these acorns. I guess the good Lord sent Mr. Price there.

The schools stressed reading, writing, and arithmetic. If you could read, you were supposed to read the other subjects yourself. You had reading every day and arithmetic every day, but you didn't have other subjects every day. Maybe you'd have geography on Monday and something else. Maybe you'd have history one day and all, but during the week everything that you needed was gotten in. When we had work at the blackboards, our teacher could have two classes doing arithmetic. You'd take the book and you'd do the arithmetic in the spaces in the book and he'd mark it, or if you were at the board he'd make you explain. Everybody'd sit down and you'd explain your problem. That was another way that you taught the children; lots of times that child explaining how he got an answer would do a better job of putting something over than the teacher did.

The March that I was twelve years old I was finishing all those books that had grade eight on them. I did that arithmetic; I was doing that square root and all that stuff. I don't know how I got it. All those eighth-grade books—that geography, history, spelling. I was the best speller in school. On Friday we used to have spelling bees. You'd go to the head of the class and if you could spell anything the child already there didn't spell, you'd turn him down. Our spelling bees were much like the spelling contests they have now, only fun, of course. Kids came up pretty good scholars out of nothing. Negro kids. Oh, maybe some of them had school for maybe around five or six years. After the whites began building good houses and bringing in their families, they put up a school for both of them—the white children and Negroes—both had a school—same kind of school, but in different localities. Everything was separated; you went to the same store but to a different church and to a different school.

I'll never forget that first school, or my teacher, all honor to his memory. Later when I grew up I taught with him. At the time he was teaching he was always somebody who knew the right thing. His teaching has had an influence on me. I still remember him years after. He was a fine old man. He died destitute. I saw that he was properly buried, but I didn't live there then. I was grown, married and gone, just happened to stumble upon it. You know how you go back to things. Well, each of the old people lived his own life and each made his contribution. They built maybe far better than they knew.

Another influence on my learning was the people that my mother worked for—the financiers that would come to our town. These men were finely dressed, and they ate at the head man's house, the man who owned this part of the pie. And my mother worked there, in his house, you see. And I came up partially among those people. Wherever my mother worked, I was there. She never left me. When they hired my mommy, they had Memphis, too. So it wasn't a bad life or a hard life.

I was there. I was just a likeable little girl to play with the children. And then I grew up and I was teaching and I was still at that house. The cook would prepare my luncheon for me to take to school every day, and I was out and gone. The family would be in Florida. My mother would be the housekeeper. They knew I was still there. I have been back. They are dead now; the last one died in Bluefield. I went to see her, and she knew me. She said that I looked like my mother; she said there was something about me that reminded her. She was old then; that's Mrs. McQuail. She said that she had read of me in the papers and all that her servants would bring in.

She said, "I knew you were around among your people working and I know what you're doing. I think about the little girl that played around my house with her pretty long plaits, and the children remember you."

I said, "Well, I came all the way here to tell you what part you played in my life. Without you, I wouldn't have been the person I am now. I wouldn't have had the education. My mother was too poor and she only made enough to pay for what we ate and wore."

She said, "Well, I can't imagine what part I played in it."

I said, "You had that magnificent library; I never saw so many books in all my life."

My mother was a meticulous housekeeper, which her daughter isn't. She would send me in to see that every bit of the dust was off those books. They had to be used by the men of the house. I would stay so long she would come to see what on earth I was doing, and I'd be lying flat on the floor. I'd read half the books she'd sent me in there to dust.

I said, "I read—from ten years old—no eight. I read from the time that I was six or eight years old. I read everything I could find, whether I understood it or not. I read English literature; anything that was easily reached and I didn't have to get up in a chair or anything to get, or take chances on falling or not getting the book back when I heard somebody coming. Everything within my reach I read."

I told her, "That's the beginning of my being able to know and to do, Mrs. McQuail, that library of yours in there."

She said, "Don't I wish I had known it so I could've directed you to more things than you were able to pick out."

I said, "Well, it wasn't to be that way. The very fact is that I got it, and that I learned it, and that I made myself a good life and a good life for that mother who had sacrificed everything and who had lived to that age."

When I went to high school, with the memory that I had—I didn't have a textbook—the teacher would assign so much and so much, and she'd tell me, "Now, you go to the library." I was in Ohio then; we didn't have a high school for Negroes in McDowell County when I came out of the eighth grade.

"You go to the library," the teacher would say, "because we don't have that many textbooks, and you get yours in the library so that there will be enough textbooks to go around for the others."

And I'd say, "Oh, I know that assignment."

She'd say, "How can you know it? I just assigned it."

"Oh," I'd say, "I read that a long time ago when my mother worked for some rich white people; they had all kinds of books and I read it then." She'd give me an examination on it. Anything she'd put down there, I knew. So I never had an English textbook, but I was a straight "A" student.

I read because I had nothing to do. It was something else to do. We stayed there at that house, and I couldn't bring little colored children there to play with me when my mother would be working. The family's children were small and I'd help my mother with those children and all. I'd tell them all the fairy tales, and I'd get away from them by saying, "You all go to sleep now and when you wake up, I'm going to have a new fairy tale." I'd make them go to sleep so I could go down there and read. And I'd have a new fairy tale for them all right; I would make up another one. Momma said, "This child is such a liar." I could make up more tales to tell them. And then I had Granddaddy who told me all the Uncle

Remus tales;[2] Granddaddy stimulated my curiosity. I had fun off of the tales; that created a sense of humor in me. Think of a little ole rabbit doing something like that. So I'd tell them all those. I'd always have something and I'd get time to read. It was just something to do. But I remember that when I needed the story, when I needed the memory, it was there.

When the children would say, "Tell us a story, Aunt Cassie. Don't you know any stories?" she'd say, "Memphis will tell you something when she comes." Well, they'd be good and wait on me; we didn't have any trouble with those children; they were wonderful children. They are the men of the family now. They came to see my mother in her late years. She was eighty-five years old and those four young men, four millionaires, came to see her on her birthday. We were living in McDowell County then. I never saw them anymore. I never had any cause to see them, but I went to see their mother and she told me where they were.

I took the uniform examination[3] and got a school to teach. I had a four-month school that year. It seems to me that I started early in the fall and then went after Christmas to Bluefield [State College] for the first time. Then I went back a couple of semesters after that. I had credits from Ohio along with the credits I had at Bluefield. When it was counted, I lacked nine hours, and I let those nine hours ride for a long time and then I went back. In '39 I got the B.S. degree. During that time, I was not without going to school, however. Anywhere that I was, and I was going a lot, I took some courses. I had some credits at West Virginia State, I had credits in Ohio, in Pennsylvania—wherever I found myself in the summertime I would go to school, which made up additional advanced credits. I didn't finish the masters, but I must have had about twenty hours credit. I don't think I'll hardly go through it now. I don't have any use for it. A lot of the practical training I needed I got in the schools wherever I was. Or if I were out of school in the early spring, I'd take a spring term as I did at Ohio University. You could count that as advanced study, but some of it was undergraduate work. I suppose that all that I did after I got the degree would be counted as advanced work. I did enroll at Ohio State, but my brother died in the meantime and I didn't go at all. I was having so much trouble at that time that I never did go. I just filled out the application blank and before I could attend, his death came. I was going to live with him in Columbus.

I enrolled at [Ohio University in] Athens—I think I enrolled there first as far back as 1909 for undergraduate work. I don't think they could count it as graduate work, but I did take methods and child psychology and lab work. You made those field trips and observed those children day after day playing in school and wherever they were. We had this magnificent lab, and Dr. [Oscar] Chrisman [professor of paidology and psychology] was head of it. You worked with a partner. You and this partner took the trips to the schools. My partner was a white girl from Mississippi, of all things, but she was nice; we got along fine and we did good work in the lab. Then a Miss Emma Waite [principal of the Training School] was the head of the methods class. I thought that the reading in that lab school was the finest thing I'd ever seen. We didn't have that here in this state; no such lab as that, and no such teaching. Every method in reading that I thought that I would need, if that method was given in a course, I would take it and was a part of it. That is why I had such a good success in teaching children.

Memphis Tennessee Garrison,
undated photograph
(Courtesy Mrs. Ruth Carruthers)

Ohio University class photograph, ca. 1910,
including Memphis Tennessee Garrison
(Special Collections, Marshall University Library)

William Melvin Garrison,
undated photograph
*(Special Collections, Marshall
University Library)*

Memphis Tennessee Garrison,
undated photograph
*(Courtesy Black Caucus [WV
Teachers])*

Memphis Tennessee Garrison receiving honorary doctorate of humanities degree from Marshall University, 1970 *(photograph courtesy the* Herald Dispatch, *Huntington, West Virginia)*

Memphis Tennessee Garrison, undated photograph *(Special Collections, Marshall University Library)*

Memphis Tennessee Garrison,
undated photograph
(Courtesy Mrs. Ruth Carruthers)

Colonel Edward O'Toole,
general superintendent of
U.S. Steel's Gary mines,
March 25, 1926 *(photograph
courtesy of Eastern Regional Coal
Archives, Craft Memorial Library,
Bluefield, West Virginia)*

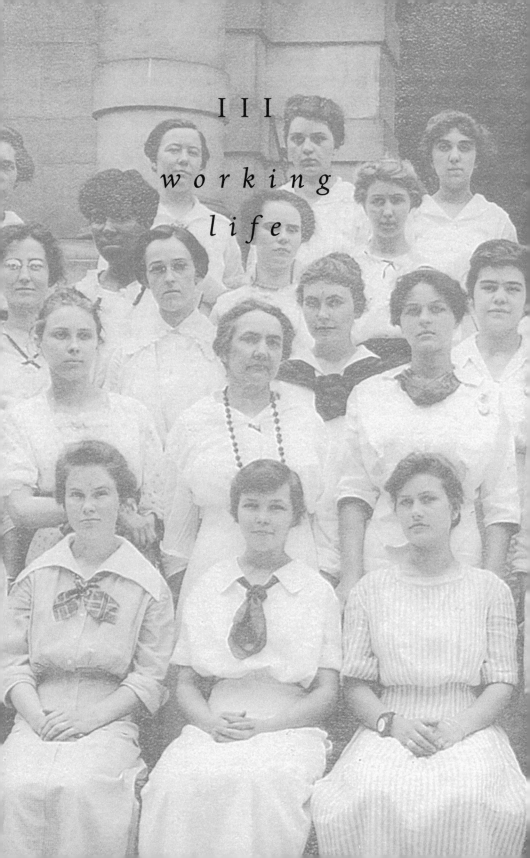

III

working

life

MEMPHIS Tennessee Garrison started her work life teaching and, in many respects, never stopped. At one point her formal teaching career was interrupted by her failure to acquiesce to local politics, but other than that, she remained a schoolteacher and then a substitute teacher for close to fifty years.

She attended high school in Ohio because there were no public high schools for blacks in the Gary area. Following high school she studied at several institutions of higher education and graduated from Bluefield State College in Bluefield, West Virginia, in 1939. As a teacher, she developed an intense interest in children who had learning problems. Long before the days of "special education," Garrison was struggling to develop appropriate pedagogy for learning-disabled children. She was also acutely aware of the relationship between economic status and educational attainment. No one was talking of "school breakfast programs," but Garrison organized her own program.

What is remarkable about Garrison's telling of her efforts is the absence of pity. Not once does she describe the children in a way that degrades them. To her they are challenges —budding flowers that simply need extra encouragement to bloom. And in her discussion of the school breakfasts, she is remarkably sensitive to maintaining the children's dignity and pride. The end result is what is often termed "a self-fulfilling prophecy." She has absolute confidence in the children, and she sees in them only the good potential. The children sense this, believe it to be true, and respond accordingly. Many of today's educators could learn an important lesson in teaching success from Memphis Tennessee Garrison.

But Garrison was more than a talented classroom teacher.

She was a gifted leader and organizer. Perhaps she would have laughed at such a description, and she never claimed such distinction in her story. Yet the facts all point in that direction. When she declared herself as a candidate for the presidency of the black teachers' association, the other candidates withdrew and she won by acclamation. She organized programs and provided the leadership that pushed the organization ahead. Yet her story does not focus on her efforts, but rather on the *content* of those efforts—the important people she invited and the aims she pursued.

It is in her capacity as a company employee that Garrison began her work as a community organizer. Again, she never used this term, but that is what she was, writing for the newspaper, organizing cultural programs, and developing recreational facilities. And this work soon became integrally connected to her political work in the NAACP.

Garrison's life reveals its deepest contradictions in her role as a social worker and troubleshooter for the coal company. Knowing the risks and hardships of coal mining in that period, and knowing the power and wealth of the coal companies, one would expect Garrison to be neutral toward the company, if not anti-company. And yet in many parts of her narrative, she sounds almost pro-company.

There appear to be three major factors that account for Garrison's relationship to U.S. Steel. The first has already been mentioned—that she accepted the given social structural factor and then attempted to work within the personal space afforded to her. In this case, that personal relationship was with U.S. Steel's managing superintendent, whom she fondly called "the Colonel." As an individual, Garrison could do little to challenge the company outright. By developing a trusting and workable relationship with the superintendent, however, Garrison was able to obtain resources she believed would not have been forthcoming otherwise.

The second factor was that of the company itself. U.S. Steel was a giant among the coal producers. It was able, because of its market position, to pay the best wages and obtain the best equipment for that time. Compared to many of the smaller mines, U.S. Steel's mines were safer and the work was better paid. Relative to surrounding communities, then, U.S. Steel appeared to be a more benign operator.

The third factor was Garrison's race consciousness. Nowhere in her discussion of the company does she articulate the problem as a class question. Indeed, her experience is that the white workers and "foreign" workers took the better-paid jobs as their due because they were white. Without class consciousness and class solidarity on the part of the workers, Garrison's main loyalty lay with the African American community and the black miners. And she believed she served them better in her role as mediator and community worker.

These factors, however, do not mean that Garrison failed to perceive the exploitation of workers by the coal industry. But her anger is broadened to include the exploitation of the teachers as well. She refers to the company's failure to pay teachers decent salaries: *It was a stingy thing. They could have paid more because the coal men were rich and it was a coal area.* Again, here the exploitation is experienced directly and seen as a personal issue.

Garrison's stories are often placed in the context of major world events, yet in them she does not explore or develop the significance of many of those events. Her brief description of her courtship mentions her husband's service at the end of World War I, and World War II is referenced in her discussion of the Red Cross and rolling bandages. In contrast, the later chapters emphasize the racial polarization of the country and the ensuing lynchings. *These* are events that have major significance for Garrison. This is an excellent illustration of why "history" is different things to different groups.

For black people, the lynchings at home were more significant than what the Europeans were doing to each other—
a point that many white people find difficult to grasp. Yet
"American history" continues to emphasize our involvement
in foreign wars and rarely discusses the war that went on at
home—the attacks on black people.

chapter 7

⁑

Teaching

My first school in West Virginia, a small school, had a four-months term. In McDowell that was the half of the year that I taught, and I went on back to school [college] for the rest. I was out after Christmas. Then the next year in McDowell, I think, I began the six-months term and then it went to seven, to eight, to nine which equalized it with the white school. Inequality in West Virginia wasn't statewide, it was district-wide.[1] The district was the unit of taxation then. And in some instances, inequality wasn't countywide because some counties had maybe four, five, and six districts each. Equality might vary from district to district even within counties. Then when the Democrats came in in 1932, the school system moved to be countywide, and the county became the unit of taxation. So, that's when things came about equal. There was no high school in McDowell County for Negroes until about 1922. I think high schools started with one year, and then the next year they added the second year, and then added the third until finally it moved up to four years high school in 1926. And then the state educational plan charts changed to the six-three-three plan—six years for elementary, three years for junior high, and three years for senior high. The old eight-four—eight years for elementary and four years for high—passed out. And that was the program, equalizing the schools.

I've never had a child I couldn't teach to read. Some would be slower than others, but they would read. If I taught them long enough, they would get it. I had one boy who was eleven and who had been in school five years. He hadn't been with me five years, but he'd been going to school five years. He did all right in grade two and passed to the third grade finally, and then because I wouldn't keep him in my room, he quit. See, he was a teenager then, and he was sensitive about the other teachers. I would teach him at home; he'd come past my house at Gary sometimes and for a good while I gave him work two or three times a week. He has a farm over in Ohio and he happened to see me in a filling station. He was making waves, knocking folks out of the way to get to me. I saw this big man coming and I looked. "Mrs. Garrison?" I said, "Charles?" And he said, "Yes, Ma'am. You were the finest teacher in the world."

After working with Charles, I still wanted to experiment further so I took every child in the primary grades that hadn't been promoted that particular year in this school. There were thirty-eight of them from the first, the second, and the third grades, and I already had the fourth. I asked for it. Someone told me to try it. I wanted it and they said try and I did. It was a service that I was trying to find help for, and some teacher that I had met at some of these summer schools said that I should try the Horace Mann School at Columbia University. I told the people at Columbia that I would lighten their load if they would indicate on a chart what they wanted. Now, I didn't want them to make out a lot of charts and things. I was trying to find help to see that I was using the right course to grade these children. Then I explained what I was doing. They told me to proceed as I had outlined, and they made some little notes. They told me to make little notations about the education of the parents—that I should find the children with the parents who had at least finished high school to see if they were better learners. Then I was to notice the children whose parents couldn't read or write. I had some of those parents. I did make out this chart. I didn't know the proper way to make it, but the way I was making it was for them to understand the help that I was seeking. They didn't have all of this help for retarded children then. They were put in institutions as persons who couldn't learn. And, I didn't call them retarded because that name didn't figure in my thinking, but I did call them slow learners. They didn't keep up and the reviews had to be frequent. Well, I took those children to see if I couldn't do more than had been done. The teachers were glad to give them up. I charted the children and sent that chart to the Horace Mann School at Columbia University. That was their lab school, I think. I made this chart of about thirty children. I had put on it the mother, the father, and the amount of education they had, how many children were in the family, their economic level—whether they were limited in finances. This was way back in the thirties.

The children responded pretty well. When the year was over, I didn't have any of them who couldn't read. They weren't reading on the same level, but all of them could read something. They would find out that they could read, and the next morning there would be more hands up— "I can read. I can read. I can show you I can read." And the class would come up. I did that with the children until the superintendent made objections to it. She said, "How do you teach anything in here? It's so noisy."

Mrs. Anderson was my superintendent for about four years when I was trying this out. She just approved of the project because she knew that I would follow through; she didn't approve because she believed in what I was doing. She just believed that I would spend more time in school than I would spend anywhere else. "Well," she said, "if you want to do it, go ahead." She didn't understand. I utilized the back of the room. I had the janitor take up the seats in the middle. We utilized the cloakroom and the blackboards, and the tables at the front. The children were in groups. At times, from thirty to forty-five minutes during the day, I'd let a child join any group that was doing what that child liked best. Some would be looking at pictures and comparing the words—slow readers. And I had books made from Sears Roebuck catalogs, from magazines, anything. Sometimes I spent the summer making them. If the child wished, he could work with that group. The child would emerge maybe spelling half a dozen words; maybe there'd be about six or eight in that group. I had another bunch that liked to make things, to draw. If the child drew something, then he'd write the words naming it. Sometimes he'd have to go hunting for the words, and he'd have to go and get the pictures. If he did it quietly, then he could continue. I had another group which was doing their numbers; they couldn't get their numbers, and they'd take those acorns and corn back there—whatever they had, and count. There were bags with all kinds of counters in them—little bags, plastic bags with acorns, beans, corn. Strange to say, when they were busy with that they didn't shoot those things across the room. I mean, it's a temptation to shoot them out. Then there was another group, another little group—two or three of them were children who should have been in special schools. If they would be real quiet, I'd give them a little party over in the edge of the cloakroom where I could see them, but the other children couldn't see them. I've had peanut butter and suckers for them—all day suckers—and they would sit there and they would find something to do. They'd draw or color or something. I told them that if they just wouldn't make any noise, if they'd be very quiet and very nice, things would come to them. Well, now, the time they had! They sucked on that sucker and licked it and looked at each other to see who had done what. The time would be up, but once every day that would happen, either in the morning or some days it would be in the evening. Children were reading books before you knew it. They were asking things; they were spelling. And if I called a spelling test, then sometimes they would take their paper and see if they could spell what I was calling. In that class each little one would say, "Mark my paper, please. Mark my paper and see what I got." It was more of an experiment, a real experiment.

I gave them freedom all day. In the morning they could come into the room if they were very quiet, and they could distribute things for me. Of course, then sometimes I would have more children there than I could use, so I'd send them to the playground. Then they would come back in and we'd have the opening. They did everything; somebody'd open; sometimes somebody'd give a Bible verse wrong. They don't like to do that in the schools now, you know—give Bible verses. But they'd have a Bible verse somewhere; then somebody would say the Lord's Prayer. If he missed something, another would get up and say it. Then they'd sing and we'd sing the songs they liked. Most of them were songs that you did things to—motion songs. Then they would go into whatever we were going to do.

I had the children learn their ABC's by rote. I did that because the time was coming when they would have to use a dictionary. Some people are a long time using the dictionary now because they don't know their ABC's. They can't think what comes after what, and they have a time. You notice people thumbing through phone books, can't find what they want; that's because they didn't learn their ABC's well. Now, while the children didn't have to learn the ABC's to learn to read, they were going to need to know them. If they didn't know their ABC's, they couldn't think right straight—what comes after what, and they'd have a time. We'd say the ABC's; we'd sing them; then after that maybe we would pass out a bunch of letters, all twenty-six of them. Someone would say "A" and the one who had "A" would run up and put it down. Then they'd say "B" and someone would put it down. When we finished, it would be recess time for that group of kids. Look what they had done! Then we'd have a printed "A" and a written [cursive] "A" and they would have to go up and two would be running. And the "B" might have to tiptoe. If somebody had on clod shoes and it wasn't too cold, we'd slip off the shoes and tip tip run so as to minimize the noise because you could, you know, hear the children go. But they'd tip tip; they'd put that letter up. By that time it was time for recess; they'd go get water and go to the restroom and go on the playground for about fifteen minutes. Then they would come in and the class that had prepared their work would turn it in— whether it was English, or it was math, or whatever it was. I had a group of little fourth graders that were slow, well, the third grade, too. I'd have their papers that they'd handed in the day before ready to pass out. We would go over those problems that had been missed.

They'd get an assignment from the board or they'd get it from special sheets that I made. They had little notebooks to keep them in. They'd get so mad sometimes when they hadn't understood about carrying in arithmetic. They'd get it wrong and they'd cry when the red cross mark would have to be on their papers. And I'd have to have all of them to kind of help out to keep them going, or else I'd give a pencil for everybody who got a hundred; I'd give a new pencil. Sometimes I'd have another bunch doing something and if they didn't get a pencil, they wouldn't work; they'd be crying on the desks.

Columbia took the information that I gave, the information that they asked for, and they placed it on a graph and they sent that graph back with the name of every child, and all did well.

From that one class that I had that year I can see the advantage of having these children, these special children taught. It's a wonderful thing that they are doing now with these special children because all of them are not going to remain, mentally, where they are. With some of them it's just like coming out of the shell. Something touches them somewhere and opens up the whole thing to them. But suppose they hadn't had somebody trained to help them reach that point. They would still be useless. So this thing of retarded children, and people helping them—I helped them before I knew anybody was helping any of the retarded children. It came out of the experiment.

Mrs. Anderson, the supervisor, talked negatively about my work at first. She said, "I don't like that teaching. I don't think you're following through what the supervisor said." I said, "Mrs. Anderson, let me go on and when you give the examination, if my children don't make it, then you can blame me, but I'm not afraid they won't make it." Her husband was at one time prosecuting attorney for this county and her children were all born here. She came up when they began putting women in principalships and assistant superintendencies and all. The political climate was good and she passed—she dropped right in the school, working. She wasn't even educated as a teacher; she was educated in one of the select schools for girls. But she was a smart woman; she rose to the occasion; I admire her very much.

Mrs. Anderson liked my success with the project. She talked about it. She hadn't seen me for years, but she had a cook and she asked her about me. "Did you know a teacher named Garrison?"

And the cook said, "Yes, I know her."

Mrs. Anderson said, "I often think about her. We were very good friends, and she's a very fine woman."

I saw Mrs. Anderson later during the political campaign in the thirties. She was with the state and the national campaigns and when she came to my area, I'd go hear her speak. At one meeting, her cook met me and said, "I got a message for you," and she told me that Mrs. Anderson had said, "Tell her to come to see me."

And I did; I went to see her, spent half a day with her and boy, we hashed over everything. She talked about it then. She said, "In my mind, you were a wonderful teacher."

I said, "I think I must have had the same opinion of myself because I never did change; it was no use."

She said, "That was right."

I wanted to experiment and I did.

The children come back now and see me. I've had some from the Midwest. One year, I know I must have had, out of that group, at least seventy-five people that passed by. "We came this way to see you. We heard you moved to Huntington," they'd say. I think all of that has motivated me to continuously do something because I could tell by the responses of the children, even after they were grown, that I had done something for them. I didn't know what; I couldn't put my hands on it, describe, or feel everything, but I knew there was something that had been very useful to them.

Once, I had seventy-two children enrolled. They could find more children to send to me! I'd take thirty-some in the morning and then I'd take the other half in the afternoon. I taught from nine to twelve and from one to four. It was like a double session, but the children in each session wouldn't be the same. One bunch, the little ones, would go home, and the others would come at noon. I always had the problem of having to keep some of those little ones from the morning because the big children who had to come in the afternoon were supposed to take care of them at home. So I'd have to be bothered with some of those little ones, too. They could go out and play until they'd get into something and I'd have to quit teaching to go get them.

I had two children whose parents were churchgoers, and they had revivals two or three times a year, or they'd have midweek services. The children would go to church with them and they'd shout and beat tambourines and like that. You know, it was part of the service. They'd come to school, poor little things, and put their heads on the desk and go to sleep before you could get the class started almost. And you know, I let them sleep. I let them sleep right there and then when they'd wake up—they hadn't had any breakfast sometimes—they were hungry, and I'd let them take their lunch and eat a part of it at recess. "Take your sandwiches with you," I'd tell them. I'm kind to children. I think I do a little too much for them. I have a feeling for them.

I don't know where I got the philosophy of being kind to children. I like them, and I like for people to respond to me, to what I'm doing. "Well," I would say to myself, "What is it? Do you like praise?" Whatever it is, I like for people to respond. I like to be noticed, and when I've done something, I know whether it's good or bad. I know when I haven't done it right, or I know when I've been careless, and I wipe that off. But when I have done something I know hasn't been done before, or I've done something better than I've ever seen it done, I want response from people. And I think it was that sort of thing that I'd transmit to a child—that child that had done just fine. They'd knock each other out of the way to get up to my desk to put their papers up there. "Mrs. Garrison, look at my paper. Mrs. Garrison, see how nice I kept it for you." And they'd bring their papers to school in the morning and they'd say, "Mrs. Garrison, I done all of this over again." So I'd say, "Isn't that nice." And I'd say, "It's the cleanest paper. What did you do, wash your hands before you did it? This paper is extremely neat." They'd tear up all momma's paper just to bring a neat paper in. It seems that what I said touched something in them that they responded to; they had to have a neat paper for me.

I think all of my success was because of the relationship that I had with the children. I'd tell the parents sometimes, "You should be careful of what you do in front of the children," and I'd tell them why. I said, "Teachers know what kind of home you have without ever seeing it. I know what you eat. I know where you go. I know what you talk about. I know your whole life." The children didn't tattle. It was just that the things that happened, that were a part of the children, allowed me to determine what they had experienced. I had one child who would pick a fight. Before he could get out of school he was fighting and carrying on.

We'd sit down and talk about it. I would say, "Lord, which one was fussing, momma or daddy?" His mother would say, "It was me."

Then I visited. I'd leave school in the evening, maybe I'd visit ten homes that evening. If I hadn't had my mother home to cook for my husband, I'd have gotten pitched through the windows. She knew where I'd gone. I'd just drop by the children's home. The children would see me coming, "Mrs. Garrison, I didn't do anything, did I?" You know, sometimes they'd think I was coming because of something that they had done. "Oh, no," I'd say, "I just came to see your mother." And then the next day they'd say, "Mrs. Garrison, we were so glad you came by." And sometimes the children weren't at home when I stopped by and they'd say, "Mrs. Garrison, my momma said she had a pot of good greens and you ate some of them."

As a teacher, you relate to your children in their experiences at home, then you relate those experiences to the learning process. I've had children refuse to go to school if they couldn't come to my room. I had one child—and I was later told that he never did finish school—another teacher took him. One of the supervisors in McDowell County said he was too big for my chairs. As long as I had him, he didn't care where he was sitting. I'd sit him in a chair to himself. I'd miss him and I'd look through another teacher's door and I'd see him sitting in the back of their room. Sometimes, he'd come into my room with his book and if I were at the board showing something, and there wasn't a seat empty, he'd sit there at my desk. I never would move him. Now, some people might have made him go, and might have preached to him that he had to stay in one place. Well, it wasn't important where he stayed if he learned what he had right there to learn. I didn't care where he learned it. Learning it was important for him. Maybe that isn't the way it is done, but it was the way that I had success and it's the way I know that I helped those children. I know from what they have done, where they have gone, and the way they have always reacted to me.

When I started teaching fractions, I started early with the little children without calling them fractions. I like apples and I always kept apples in my drawer at school. Sometimes I'd have a whole drawer of apples.

We'd have a long table, maybe twelve children there were going to have an apple lesson that day. They'd draw apples on the paper, then I'd pass apples already cut on a tray. We had little round paper napkins; we didn't have wax paper like we have now. We had little paper napkins or we put the apples out there on a paper bag, anything that would keep them from touching the table. We'd have halves or pieces that we could put together to make a half, or four pieces to make an apple. Well, I'd cut an apple to show them; they'd look at their pieces of apple. Then I'd say, "Who'll make half an apple?" And maybe two of the children sitting there would know right quick, you know, to put their pieces of apples together to make half an apple. Then I'd ask, "Who will make three-fourths of an apple? Three halves make what?" We'd talk through each fraction. Then after they had that, they'd pass by the fountain in the hall and rinse their apples off, then come back and eat the apples. Everybody ate his own apple. That was more fun to them, to come back and eat that quarter of an apple. Sometimes we'd use other things that they couldn't eat. In order to illustrate, we'd use potatoes or anything that was whole. Well, they soon got it. It wasn't hard for them; it was just how you put parts of the potato together to show them. Then when they had to work with figures, around the last half of the third grade, and when they got to oral arithmetic they could do it. When I said, "Who'll bring me a third? Who'll bring me a half of a potato up here?" They knew it that way more than anything else. When they moved into fractions, they told me that they understood them better than most children who hadn't learned them our way. "Mrs. Garrison," they'd say, "we can get this so good, and them new children, they can't get it."

I was also teaching Palmer writing. I had finished Palmer's School of Writing for Teachers; I had my diploma and I wanted my children to be fine scribes. They would stay in at recess sometimes to get those exercises. Then Palmer began to give prizes and, oh, it was on then. Dr. Gunn, here, laughs about it now, about his certificates he got for writing.

As teachers we just had to do those things. Why did we have to do them? I don't know. We just felt like we had to do them. I wanted my children to feel that the learning process was for each child individually. You've got to realize that this had to be done. I know somehow that's what happened. As long as the child thinks of learning as something the teacher's making him do, something he's got to get, something he's got to make, you're going to have lazy people. You're going to have people who are not informed, and people to whom it's a problem to go to school. He's got to do it for himself. You must get that across. That is a fact.

I had some children who could read as long as they saw the picture. Then I had some who all they had to do was to see it, see the start of it and they knew. They had committed it to memory. The method I used for all is a cure for that. I can teach a child to read, and to read well and to read independently. When he can read independently, you don't have any trouble. I tried to tell them that what the teachers give you is 10 percent, barely 10 percent of what you should know. You teach yourself the rest of it. When you have mastered the mechanics of reading, and you have mastered the basic thing of the numbers game, the rest is with you. The teacher may have to explain a principle or something like that, but you do the rest of it. And that's why it is so necessary for people to read; every family should be good readers. Every child should be a good reader. That's where you get it. The teacher does not teach it to you. The teacher would not have time to teach you what you should know. You're led from one thing into the other until you're just overwhelmed with the desire to go on and it comes from that primary grade on through.

I have this manual that I've had a long time. It's out of print. It seems a man started it in Chicago's south side at a Catholic school. He died before the first printing was hardly off. Here and there you could pick up a copy, you know. I was prowling somewhere in one of the Catholic schools —I have some friends who were teaching Catholic children—and once I was in Chicago and I went to their school. I picked up this book, and I said, "Where'd you get this? They're out of print." "Oh, my friend said, "I have a whole set of them. I have the readers, too, but they're out of print." "They were out of print way back," I said. "Could I buy a set?" I think she sold me the manual. No, she sold all of them—the twelve books, twelve readers. That was just the beginning. I'd talk with the teachers at institutes and illustrate with those books. I don't think there was a program anywhere at any institute in those early years that I wasn't on that program—primary reading—my colleague, Miss Carter, and I. I still have one of those manuals; it was the beginning. I developed my own method of teaching after that.

I rewrote the manual and used the things that I thought would meet the needs of my particular group. I knew the methods were sound because I had used them. The manual is the finest way of teaching phonics I've ever seen anybody use. That was my reading method. It's still my method of helping children when they come. Here and there, there's been a dozen or so around town.

I was also influenced by the McGuffey readers with their ideas of good conduct, character building, their well-mannered individuals—people who had values that were workable and were livable. From them I got wonderful stories about kindness to animals and all like that. The old McGuffey reader was more than a reader. I keep a set of them all the time with select things that I want. If there was a child that needed something, maybe I could find a story, in McGuffey's to help.

They allowed teachers to punish children then, but after the first month, the children got to a place where I didn't need the switch. At different times the children would come, and they'd see a switch somewhere for somebody they thought was a little bad. But after that first month, if that switch was still there, they'd put it up, way up in the corner somewhere, tie it up there. Or they'd put it in the bookcase somewhere. And at the end of the year they'd say, "Well, let's bury it!" They'd have a switch funeral or something. There were other things that hurt them more than spanking their little bottoms.

Sometimes I'd have to take things from the children, or I'd make them sit by themselves. Where you have a lot of social activity, a child is heartbroken when you send him to the cloakroom, or when you sit him by himself and everybody else is having a party or something. You never have to punish him again for that thing. You weren't mad or fussing with them all, and the other children would take your attitude. "See," they would say to the child who was being punished, "if you had behaved you'd be over here with us. What did you want to go and do that for?" That was enough. Especially for the little ones. You'd have some bad ones that you'd have to spank, or you'd have a big quarrel with them and then the momma would come after you. That was all part of it, too. Sometimes you'd catch somebody cheating and then momma would come after you and say that you're embarrassing her child and all like that. You could always rise to the occasion. You seldom have to deal with the same problem again, for you'd tell the child, too, what you were trying to do. I still have a relationship with some of them.

When the change came to integration, some of the children found it difficult to adjust. You know, naturally they would. Some of them in the first place were slow; some of them were placed in new situations. And some of them were, I felt, a little behind the grade into which they were going. I took so many of them that I didn't have room to take any more. I'd take them after school in the evening for an hour, Tuesday, Wednesday, and Thursday. I took them as an experiment. I didn't charge them. The parents would say, "Mrs. Garrison, can you help us?" I said, "Send them on, send them on by my house and at such and such a time."

One fellow went to Vietnam—he came home and went back to West Virginia State. When he had been in the fifth grade out here, fourth or fifth grade, he just couldn't do anything. He'd come out of the fourth grade where he was and his father asked me to help him. He couldn't read and he had a speech defect, that tongue just stayed there. And there was a discipline problem. So I took him a whole semester and a half. I took a piece of paper and I made a replica of a tongue out of it and showed him how he'd hold it. Then I took this tongue and I wouldn't even bend it at all, and showed him how to put his tongue in the roof of his mouth. He was saying that "ting" meaning "thing," and I showed him how to take that tongue, curl it around and let his breath come through. "Uh, uh," now say it, "uh, uh." And he'd put his tongue up there on his lip and we'd practice maybe a whole thirty minutes; we'd practice where to place the tongue. Then he'd do something I taught to him. He'd say, "Wait a minute, let me see which place I put it." I mean, he became conscious of it and he tried so hard. The first 100 he ever made in spelling, he ran all the way from that school to my house. He was out of breath when he came to that kitchen door to hand me that paper, handing me the paper that the teacher had marked a hundred on.

Now, the young man and I laugh about his time with me. He says that first hundred is what got it. "Then I knew, that's when I knew," he said. "That first time I had a hundred."

I taught approximately thirty-five years and five years special when I wasn't confined to a classroom routine. I didn't do it as a substitute teacher; I had an understanding with the superintendent and the principal that I wanted to take the special classes. I continued doing the special work all the time without any fanfare about it. After Mr. Justice [McDowell County school official] left there, and I couldn't follow through that year, I just went back to grade work.

In addition to the thirty-five years, I substituted. For fifty years, I've done some kind of teaching. I've substituted in three states. I got a tri-state certificate. I was down in Ashland, Kentucky, four or five years when they needed a substitute; I was across the Ohio River from Huntington in Sybene when they had the school there. Mrs. Spencer who lives in Huntington was the principal. For three or four years, I was over there. And I helped both of the black schools in Huntington. I haven't been in any of the white schools as a substitute.

I think it was worth it and more because I was dealing with human beings, with their souls, how you go down inside of you. I have no regrets about my life as a teacher. Some people say I wasted my life in the schoolroom. I should have been doing thus and so. I don't have any feeling like that, and yet, I wanted to be a lawyer. I just wish that I could have been; I wanted to work in juvenile court. My mother couldn't wash enough clothes for me to be a lawyer, so I had to take what I could and help.

I thought I might study for the law. I had two books when I started out. Bryce's *American Commonwealth* was one of them. That's what they used to start out their study with. I got it out of this millionaire's home, this coal operator. It was one of the first two books that I bought maybe the first two years that I taught. Maybe I thought I'd read it as I went along, but I just became engrossed in teaching and pursuing teaching work, going and being with people. Wherever I was, whoever and wherever the people were that I lived with, I'd hunt the teachers. You hunt for the people that you want to be with. Whoever you can be with, you are a part of that. One of the girls said, "Why do you associate yourself with them?" I said, "Because they're the ones with whom I have something in common. I get in a crowd of lawyers or ministers or something and there wouldn't be so much that I had to say to them."

You relate to the people and you get suggestions from those people. They'd say, "Did you ever try thus and so? Let me give you this. I'm going to send you that." So I was with teachers and it became so much a part of what I wanted that when I got to a point that I was able financially and had the time to go and take law, well, I didn't want it then. There was nothing that I wanted. The fact of it is that law is such a taskmistress; she's hard on you. You've got to spend time and you've got to have a photographic memory almost to be able to reach out and get the information as you want it and use it. It's not like using a Webster's dictionary that you can take out and take two minutes to look something up. You've got to have some things right at your fingertips at all times. So, I said maybe I went into the best thing after all. I could make my way along with help and encouragement in the things that I did. I had to take it like that. So I don't think that I have any regrets.

I couldn't keep up with as many children as I had over the years and as many things as I did, but I felt that I never failed a child, that I never had a child I hadn't taught something. I would always say that the basis of my teaching is the belief that you haven't taught until you've taught every child. Not that you've taught every child everything, but that you've taught every child something. I still believe it.

I don't have any regrets about teaching. I wish it could have lasted longer. Any teacher, I think, who has taught and been near little children and sat down with them, becomes a little child again. You take that little hand and show them, "This is the way you make it." The feel of that little hand under your hand did something for you. You felt so related to that child. If something happened, you'd study half the night to get it. You'd go to summer schools and take it so you could learn it. If there was some principle of math that that child needed, that it had been slow getting, you felt like you needed to go and get the method to help; you needed to go and see what others were doing. And you'd go. You were compelled to teach, and your children were compelled to learn. It becomes so much a part of you. You give to them. You'd sit in the seats with them and take their little hand and say, "Now, you hold your pencil like this." Then you'd say, "Now show me how you hold it." Then he'd take your hand. You sit there.

Living has been great for me—the experience of living. I used to be able to sit down and lose myself in thinking of some little girl who did something. What she said or did. I could feel one take out my hand, stretch out my finger like I had told her to do. "Put your finger out here. That's it." "Now I got it," they'd say. "Now, you sit over there and watch me." Or, "How'd you fix this?" they'd ask. The funny thing is that you just needed to do that once. If you had to do that every day, you couldn't. You'd do it once. You sit down with that child once, with that nearness and he can do it. He'll say, "I can't do this." But you know he can and if you don't bother to bother, he doesn't. That is the process of learning how to do a thing. Now, you can use that in anything; you can use that in something you want your children to know at home. You can sit down with them and make them know a certain thing or a certain principle. You'll know when you succeed, and they'll know it, too. They won't do it sometime and they'll make out like they don't know it, but you can take your children and teach them.

I wanted ten children of my own. I knew that I could rear ten good children. All I wanted was for them to have good eyes, nose, and feet and all that stuff, and a place to live and something to feed them. I knew I could teach, and I think I put all of my energy and all of what I had into teaching the children who came under my teaching because I knew I could teach ten fine children of my own.

Momma would say, "What in the name of God does somebody as poor as you want with that many children, I just don't know."

"They won't be poor. They'll all be beautiful. They'll be smart, all ten of them," I'd say.

My husband used to put his head in his hands and look away. I don't think he was quite so sure they were going to be smart and well fed or any of the things. But it would have been all right. We both liked children. I used to say that I was going to adopt them. "If I don't have one, I'm going to adopt them."

Then my mother would say, "God in his own time will fix things as he wants them."

We didn't have any. We didn't understand, but we didn't rebel. Maybe I would be a better teacher than I would be a mammy—you know, the old people called you a mammy. That's the way it is, I said to myself, and that's what you are—a teacher. So stop worrying about the other.

I think my whole heritage, as lowly as it was, has been rich. It has done something for me to know that. In all these years, these eighty years, I think the things that have sustained me are my attitude toward what I had to do and my love for children and for people and the acceptance of certain things. That has made me. If I am anything, all that has made it possible. You have an idea; that's all anything there is ever was—nothing but an idea. A house isn't a house; it's nothing but an idea—an idea made visible so we can see it. Within you, you have ideas. I followed through with my ideas, with my whole curriculum for about thirty-five years. I had the results, and I used my own ideas. When I stopped teaching, I went into political work, I followed through.

chapter 8

Participation in Teachers' Organizations

I was a member of the West Virginia
State Teachers' Association (WVSTA), the organization for Negro teachers,[1] and I served a year as its president [1929–30]. Negro and white teachers would meet in their separate meetings in the separate counties, but
sometimes in the state meetings, they would meet together. I remember
we'd meet at Welch at the high school. Wherever it was large enough,
the Negro teachers sat to one side of the room, and the white teachers
sat to the other side. All were in the same room and they listened to the
same speaker. The speakers were white and they would bring questions
and information pertinent to the course of study in the school. These
were largely rural schools; consolidation didn't start until later. The first
consolidated school in McDowell County—Negro—was the Keystone-
Eckman Grade School. The others were just one-room schools or just
one room with two teachers in it. Some places where the larger companies had more people had three or four teachers. As the companies grew
and people kept coming in, the teachers, of course, came also.

In time, about 1929–30, there was estimated to be about 1,100 or 1,200
Negro teachers in the entire state. The meeting at which I was selected
president of the WVSTA was at Bluefield. I didn't come for the night
meeting—the first night—but I was there the next morning for the
meeting. Posted out in the hall was who was running for president—it

just struck me about the election, something that I had passed in the hall. Then I began to announce that I was going to run for president. I was unanimously elected. Three or four other persons said that after it was announced who was running, they just pulled off. Among the others were Dean Whiting,* and another fellow, Barnett,** who became the executive secretary. I think there were three of them, but nobody ran. They said, "Well, Memphis wants it. Let's make her president. She'll be a good one."

So my first meeting after the election—I had held an executive board meeting to formulate programs for the coming year—was held in Clarksburg at the school. All schools were separate Negro schools. We'd meet in the same town as the white WVEA would meet, but we were the West Virginia State Teachers' Association, and they were the West Virginia Education Association. They were the white group. We both met in Clarksburg. I had been to some Ohio meetings—I went to some of the meetings up there during the years that I would be out of teaching—and everybody met together up there, black and white. I had met some of the professors who spoke at those meetings; they had come down from the universities; some were sent there through the National Education Association (NEA). I met a Cornell man, and a man from Ohio State and all of these fine professors. I loved their speeches; I bought their books with their speeches in them. I still have some of the books with the speeches of those early NEA people in them, and I knew some of them.

Before we went to Clarksburg, I met with the committee of the WVEA and found out who the in professors were. See, we didn't have money to bring the professors. All right now, I picked out the ones I wanted and I said, "Will you tell me when you are going to use him and help me to get him on my program that afternoon?" That exposed our teachers to a broad scope of people who were highly trained. Everybody said that we had a wonderful meeting. John Davis† came, and Caliver†† came from Washington, and, oh, I was walking on air. I was ten feet tall

*Gregory Whiting, dean of Bluefield State College.
**Leonard Barnett, principal at Washington High School, London, West Virginia.
†President of West Virginia State College.
††Ambrose Caliver, consultant regarding black education; appointed Specialist in Education at the U.S. Office of Education in the 1930s.

when they said the meeting was fine and a success. I still have the program. I had teachers from Cornell. They allowed me to assign the subjects. They spoke on them. They really spoke—it was wonderful. Of course, sometimes during those times some of the teachers from the white group came with the professors and that made it nice.

When my time was up, I became chairman of the board and I still was instrumental in helping them to formulate their program. The organization was nearly forty years old then, but all of the previous presidents had been men. Then it went on. I believe that up until the time we merged with the WVEA, there were about four women after the time that I was president. I could have gotten the presidency again anytime that I wanted to run for it. I didn't want it anymore. I think it was good for the others to come on in and see how much work you have to do, lying awake at nights trying to formulate something. My program was nice, they said.

And then the WVSTA merged with the WVEA. Later, I was visiting in California when Mr. Reeder*—he was a WVEA man—invited all the past presidents of the state education association as guests at a state meeting, and he didn't invite a single Negro. Well, I was away and I wondered why they didn't eat him up in my stead. When that meeting was held, I was still in California. I stayed out there late that fall. When I saw that program, boy, I wanted to go down to Charleston and tear his office down. Negro teachers and the WVSTA had been a part of education in the state. We didn't have to fear what the WVEA thought about us because we were separate. That was the way it was. All of the state's education didn't have to be under the WVEA name. He had a right to recognize the people who had carried on the educational work regardless of the group they were president of and whether they had taught Negro children or white children. Well, they wouldn't let me say anything to him. I'm lucky I didn't. I did send him a letter. I never did get to take my objections out on him in person, but I felt them.

In 1931, right after I was president of the WVSTA, I went right into

*Phares Reeder, executive director of the WVEA.

the vice presidency of the American Teachers' Association (ATA), which was the national Negro association. I think a man from Kentucky ran, and me, and someone from Indiana. We were meeting at Virginia State College in Petersburg then. I don't know how many Negro teachers were in the United States at that time, but most of them were in the southern tier, and a few in New Jersey.

All the schools, all the way from the primary schools to the colleges, were members of the American Teachers' Association. That was a national body and they had big meetings; they had quite a program. After a while they divided into groups; for example, the college presidents would come to the meeting, but they would have their own group. The elementary teachers would have their section; then they'd have the high school teachers, and the college people; they'd also have the other personnel— the registrars and deans and all.

At the meeting there would be lectures during the day and at night they would have their entertainment. I still have the first page of a lecture given by Mordecai Johnson [President of Howard University]. I sat down and took notes on him at one of those meetings at which he talked to all of us. The subject was something about teaching the disadvantaged. When I went to the meetings, I wouldn't miss a lecture, and I wouldn't miss a mass meeting for anything. I could always be found at those meetings. I wonder now what made me so interested in them. Maybe it was simply that I was used to doing things, but I was there; I'd be found there. If there was something that I wanted to know, I'd sit there and almost write the speech out.

We merged with the National Education Association. A colored girl [Elizabeth Duncan Koontz] became president of the NEA the year that the ATA merged with it [1968–69]. They had worked on it for ten years, though. There was an NEA-ATA Committee working on that. This group of Negroes met with that group of whites, and they began to lay plans and present them. The state bodies merged before the nationals did. It took the national organizations a lot longer because there was more of everything to consider.

On the local level, I was involved with the McDowell-Mercer Round

Table. It was an association of Negro teachers that met once a year. Teachers from two counties came together and first formed the organization at Bluefield State. We picked our officers from the two counties. I think that we dissolved those meetings about the time that we went with the state group. The changes that had come made it not necessary to have those additional meetings.

I also served as president of the Bluefield State College Alumni Association for about four years. After I was president, I became the secretary-treasurer for about the same length of time. At commencement time, the alumni president had charge of alumni activities and the programs —visitors coming back and all like that. The alumni program of the school was under the auspices of the president and a committee; I liked all of the activity and my mother was standing right there behind me so that I could dedicate myself to what I needed to do with the school and all. And when the fiftieth anniversary came, I was one of the speakers. My subject was "Bluefield State Faces the Future."

chapter 9

✴

Beyond Teaching

I taught my first year in a one-room school. After that it was from two teachers on up to eight and ten. And during that time, I became principal of one of those schools. I had three teachers under me. All of these were elementary schools. That was before they changed the school organization to the six-three-three. It used to be the four-four. The years that I was principal of that school, they hadn't begun changing. Later, I had the six-three-three. Then I had the six grades only and I had myself and two other teachers. You got an extra five dollars on your salary for the two teachers you had by being a principal. It was a stingy thing. They could have paid more because the coal men were rich and it was a coal area.

I also wrote articles for the newspaper. I got a little boy to sell the *Afro-American** and I wrote for it awhile. I sent in the news from our area, and I wrote some articles for the *Welch Daily News,* the white paper. I was twelve years writing for them. I wrote the history of Negroes in McDowell County for them and anything else they wanted. If they wanted an idea on something that was going on, I would write it. I know the picture *Hallelujah!*** came to the theater and they didn't want to

*Black newspaper published in Baltimore, Maryland.
**First all-black feature film by a major film company (MGM, 1929).

have it for awhile. Then they talked about it and somebody preached about it and finally they said, "Memphis, you'd better write something on it." I'd also write up our Ninth of April programs[1] every once in a while. I'd say, "Here I am again on the ninth of April with my history." Most of my history, most of the history of the Negro was made in the house of bondage, but history right on. I was even conscious then, and I would write something. Each thing that happened like that, they would ask for a piece for one of their papers. They would ask the coal companies to finance the newspaper because it would provide news. People were getting more literate and all like that. Improving the schools would be news for the people of the coalfields. They were improving the all-over picture, and the country was getting a new image of the coalfields. It was no longer primitive; we were moving up. And the companies would sell newspapers. I think at first they would put them in the company stores and you'd pick up your paper and pay; and then they began to move in and get carriers. When they would ask them to put carriers out, most likely somebody would say, "Let the colored people find some carriers and let the colored people have some news so they will continue to buy the paper when they see the news." So even if we had a white carrier we'd still have a correspondent among us. I just kept at it until I got into something else; I was tired, but for about twelve years I was a correspondent. I got the magnificent sum of $12.50 a month. It paid for more than my pencils then. It was a nice little rake-off.

And then all of those companies had theaters, movies of all kinds and it was also the beginning of a few Negroes in the movies. Silent pictures were on then and they'd play a piano during the movie. You couldn't always pick up the mood of the picture because the player didn't know what the mood was. But people would crowd to a movie where there was music. It made it nice and relaxing. So I got to play for the theater there at Gary,[2] and then for a year I had a dressmaking shop down about Northfork, about six or seven miles away. I played for the first show every night those two years. Then I'd come back and sew 'til about midnight. I've forgotten what I got a week for playing, but it was pretty good. Come seven o'clock, I don't care what I was doing or making or fixing, I'd quit and go play that two hours for those silent pictures. I'd play for the show, and the kids would be waiting. They were my fans. The piano would be down front and they'd fill up those two front rows. Dr. Gunn gets a kick out of laughing about it. And I'd be playing, and if I didn't have the mood of the picture, one of them would get the word to me. "Those are horses. Tell her the horses are running," and I'd go into that. And if there was kissing, the kids would say, "Tell her they're kissing," and then I'd play some soft music. I could see all of the picture and play, too, but sometimes I wouldn't know the pieces well enough to play them and I'd have to look at the music, but I didn't miss it. The kids would keep me informed. It's very pleasant to remember those children.

The early school term in McDowell then was from seven to eight months. If I had a seven-months school, I had a long time for sewing, and the merchants in the little towns all sent their work to me. In addition, I'd make garments for people, and then after a while I didn't have to do any of it. I got married and, while I still taught, I had more security. I gave up the dressmaking shop.

I also stopped playing. I don't know what happened, but I stopped playing and a lady, for whom I sewed, came to the house and I said, "Why don't you play for the show? I'm going to quit." She was white, the wife of one of the engineers. She said, "Do you play for the show?" I said, "Yes." "What do they pay you?" she asked. I think I told her $15 a week. I think that's what it was for five nights. She said, "Well, I should have had that all the time." I wanted to punch her in the nose, and I said, "What did you say?" She caught herself. Afterwards I met her over at the post office or something and she said, "How do you like my playing?" I said, "I haven't heard it." "You don't mean you haven't been to the show since I've been playing," she said. "I do mean it," I said, "and I'm not coming." And she said, "Why?" "I don't have time to explain it to you," I said. She came all the way to my house to see what she had said to upset me, and that's what she had said to me, "She should have had it all the time." Oh, but we became good friends; she didn't mean it like that.

And those were the things that kept me down in this coalfield. I didn't have anything to leave for. If I wanted entertainment, there was entertainment of a kind. If I wanted to work and get money, there was money and work. There was teaching, and if I wanted a vacation there was a husband who had a good job with the company and he got two weeks' vacation. My life was filled with activity and it has been that way with large groups of Negroes who have come out of there and gone off East, South, West, and done well. People'd say, "What're you doing down there in those mountains?" Well, they'd say that to me as if you were coming out of the jungle or something, and I had so much to do, my life was so full. These mountains have been full of everything. I'd teach all day; I'd go home. Momma'd have supper ready. I'd stretch out and maybe my husband would come in going somewhere—the club or something. He would have dinner and go off to work, or back to do something with a group of men.

I decided to run for the school board. The Democrats said to me, "Memphis, if you run for that school board, you're not going to get it."

I said, "That's what you think. What do you bet that I don't get it?"

"Well, how you going to get it?" they asked.

"Because such and such a group is for me," I said. "The company's for me. I'm going to get it in that district if I don't get it anywhere else."

I won the nomination in the primary over four other persons. I got the highest number of voting in my own party. I always think I have a chance to win. And I don't take all the votes. If nobody voted for me, I don't count it that I've lost the votes. I said that to somebody and they said, "Why?" "Because," I said, "somebody sitting right there knows they should have voted for me. Just certain pressures kept them from it. I haven't lost. I have those people right there who know they should have voted for me. And the time will come when they will vote. I haven't lost for one reason or the other. They were pressured into wiping me off. I never lose." I was the only woman and the only Negro running, and I ran a pretty close race in the general election.

One of my other jobs was as a welfare worker for the company itself. I was doing substitute teaching that first year and that's why they gave the welfare worker's job to me. I went in and said, "The Democrats have pitched me out because I ran for the board."[3] And they said, "Tell them where to go and we'll give you a job." I stayed on the substitute's list because whatever I wanted to do as a welfare worker, I could finish it when the teaching day was over. So, I had two jobs. I would teach—usually I'd get about five months' work. They allowed you to substitute teach a hundred days, that's about five months out of the year. Sometimes, I wouldn't have that, but most of the time I'd have that. Even if I could teach more than that time, I wouldn't want it. I wouldn't have to.

I had gotten in bad with the county. Mr. Bryson, the superintendent of schools, said I'd been politicking too much. Well, I hadn't been politicking, but it had been reported that I did. There wasn't any politicking going on. I hadn't been making plans for the coming election. The Democrats were just getting in then. They were slaying Republicans right and left, and I was still a Republican. They said, "If you want to keep your school you've got to register Democratic." Now, what'd they say that for? I might have voted for them if they'd said vote for so and so, but when they tried to pin me down, that was it. I never did. The company's welfare worker job was given to me because I had no teaching job; I hadn't registered Democratic, well—maybe they would have denied this if I told it. The board itself didn't tell me, some of my friends told me. I got the message. The message was loud and long coming from the board.

Some of my friends said to me, "Memphis, now that the change has been made, they are going to put you out this year."

I said, "For what?"

They told me, "Oh, you don't have to get out. Go on and register Democrat."

"Did you register Democrat?" I'd ask them.

"Yeah, I registered," they'd say. "Now you go ahead. You don't have to vote Democratic. You can vote for whom you please. You don't have to tell them, but go on and register and keep your school. That's better than being the only Republican left in the county."

"Oh, no," I said, "I'm not going to register Democrat. I'm not." I was stubborn.

The year that I became the company's welfare worker was in the late thirties—somewhere in the thirties. They gave me the welfare job because I didn't get appointed as a teacher. Of course, when I didn't get a school, that made my company mad, so they upped my salary above the teachers, and I worked for the U.S. Steel Company. The schools weren't going to hire me for the fact that the teachers were not to take part in political work, and they said I had done this. Well, I hadn't but I understood what it was all about. It was to get at teachers. The Republicans had been in office forty years and that's because they utilized all their know-how. The teachers were the key people, so the Democrats were learning fast. They were getting the key people on their side. And when I didn't go to their side, they took my school. They said that it didn't have anything to do with politics, but it did; we knew.

As a welfare worker, I made my own program. We didn't have any recreation there for the people and we got together with the schools, the churches, and the children to create some—it took the whole community. You see the white people had a country club; the Negroes couldn't go to it and so we got together and found a place that the company had on the highway, and we began to plan a place for Negroes to go. We had a swimming pool. The kids took mules and scrapers and started making their pool. Then the company sent a bulldozer for the last part and put in the concrete. And then another group built a pavilion; they cleared the place and made a picnic ground. It was fortunate that we had this stream running from the top of the mountain down to the land on down into the little river. It was across the highway. They sowed grass and they had orchestras and dances and in the day they had roller skating. I bought up all the roller skates that the white people had left over at their skating rinks in the county, enough roller skates for those kids. I would take kids in the car and go hunt the stuff. That was part of the job of this welfare worker.

I brought in entertainment for these underprivileged people who had come up from the South, from the cotton fields; people that had nothing. I brought to these people the outstanding Negroes of the day. I brought them to that coal mining camp. I'd plan it all and sell tickets, but I didn't always make enough to pay the expenses. I'd tell the company that I lacked so much and so much, and they would pay it. For twelve years I brought outstanding Negroes. It became so popular that all the people, all the head people would come themselves. The engineers, they would come to see. The Colonel* would say to them, "Memphis is having one of her colored entertainments tonight, do you all have tickets?" He would ask that himself. He wasn't an educated man, but he was a labor man. He was another John Lewis** in his way.

For twelve years I brought upstanding people from around the country there. I brought lecturers. I had Matt Henson, the Negro who'd gone to the North Pole with Peary. I had musicians. I even had grand opera. The last one who came was a grand opera singer. The white people would laugh their heads off when we'd bring the grand opera singers to the coal mines. I said, "Well, the miners can hear sound; they can hear noise, and if some of the words are on the program they can tell what the singer is saying even if they don't know why." It took so well that even after I quit bringing them, the company brought Red Path for a week in the summer. Red Path was a series that brought in top politicians, top educators; that's where I heard Ruth Bryan Owen. She later became minister to Denmark. She was the daughter of [orator and politician] William Jennings Bryan. She was a lecturer and she came. Then they had stage plays, theater, under a tent. The company would help them erect their tents; they brought their own tents, but the company would furnish the seating and the labor to take care of that part of the work. Red Path never had a Negro in their group, and I gave them the name of a Negro quartet. They used them and it was wonderful; it was new to them; it was new to the manager and he said he was going to try to take them to the other places. There's no need for the Red Path any more what with the television, with radios, with all the means of communication now, there's no need for that.

Among the other things, I worked with crippled children until I got sick. There were all types of things that I had to do for them. They'd set up in this big American Legion building and turn those tables into beds. They'd put sheets and plastic cloths and all on the tables and use them to stretch those children out on. I think we serviced something like two hundred and some crippled children when it was clinic time, and oh,

*Colonel Edward O'Toole (1866–1940), the son of Irish immigrants Edward and Margaret O'Toole, was supervisor of the Gary mines.
**United Mine Workers official.

boy—. I started out keeping the records, but I could hear too much. When I'd hear something, it annoyed me and I'd have to go see. Somebody'd say, "You're nosy. Go back and sit down." I'd say, "No, girl. I've got to see this before I finish that report." I finally had to get clear out. I'd hear this noise and I'd go in there and there would be a baby lying on that table, deformed, one eye or something, twisted and all. It was awful. Just a noise, that's all they could make. Just a little vegetable, and then they'd say, "That child comes from the top of that mountain and the father of the child is also the father of the mother; it's his child." Those people lived in those out-of-the-way places, those mountain places up there. It would be pitiful. It was too much. I couldn't take the suffering of those children. I'd dream about those children; when I started dreaming about those children, I started staying home. That crippled children thing is a terrible thing. They would bring those children from the tops of those mountains to the clinic; and you have never seen—I had never seen human beings in those conditions; you have no idea. You'd hear something like a dog howling and you'd wonder what it was and find out it was a child. I had too much sympathy for the children. I'd end up sick, so I had to stop.

Sometimes I would talk to the women about cleanliness. The county was beginning to have some health people. I had Red Cross and then in wartime, I had the sewing room. I had the knitting classes where you'd knit and sew sweaters for the soldiers. I would have clubs and the county welfare organizations would send somebody. They'd help in Red Cross; they would help in making things for needy children; they would help in cancer drives. The county got credit for all of that because they would get this material together and all. I would get credit for it, too, for it was a part of the company's duty to keep things going through the county— to be a part of the county setup. Other than that, I was pretty busy with the work because sometimes I'd have problems to settle that would cause me to have to go around two or three days to get something straightened out. I had that mother at home or I couldn't have done it. My husband and I would meet at home together. He'd be coming from work and I'd be coming in from somewhere. He would have pitched me out on my ear years before if it hadn't been for my mother. I wouldn't have had any home but for her. I'd say to Momma, "But for you it couldn't have been." And she always felt so proud of herself and so glad to do it. My husband would say to me, "Stop conning your Mom." And I'd say, "She *is* doing it."

I'd also settle disputes. I put down things that were starting that they didn't want. In the mines the men worked side by side: white, foreign, Negro. The Negro would have a foreigner as his buddy. The foreigner would load on that side of the car, and the Negro would be over here. They did everything together; they'd sit down and eat together. But when they'd leave the mines, they'd go on their separate ways, and you didn't see them together any more. Well, sometimes there would arise differences that were a little beyond the boss men if a Negro was concerned. The Negro wouldn't feel that he was getting a fair deal. So the Colonel would say to me sometimes, "I'm going to let you see what you can do with this situation." Well I did do. I knew everybody. I taught everybody's children at some time, either in that first grade or later on, and I'd taught all of them. So, it worked out well.

This has always tickled me. I went to a house one time to see why this man didn't go to work. They were trying to get a certain amount of coal; the companies were pressuring them. They were near the end of what they had to do and this man didn't go to work. I went to the house to see why he didn't go to work. I heard them fussing, heard the noise before I got there. The door was shut. I could hear this loud talking and I kept going because I had to see him, and I knew he was at home. I got to the door and they didn't hear me knock, and I knocked again and opened the door. About the time that I opened the door all this stuff came down on me. He'd thrown a can of baking powder at his wife and it hit the door just as I was coming in. I was just covered with all this stuff. I said, "Lord, what . . . ?" "Come on in, Mrs. Garrison," he said. "This woman here makes me so mad." They looked at me again and I just stood there and looked at them and he made all kinds of apologies. But he laughed after that, and I went on back to the office like that. They flipped, honestly. They never had as much fun off of anything. "Memphis had a can of baking powder thrown at her, you know. She's doing a good job." I never lived down the can of baking powder. It was a lot of fun.

My welfare work was after school. I didn't have any hours. I'd just as soon go any time if there was something wrong, or if there was a fuss or fight between two men who'd been working, the white and the Negro. Maybe they had stopped working and the question needed somebody to find out about it without seeming biased. Why, I'd just as soon be there at 9:00 at night. It was a thing of making it right and it was a thing of moving into a situation with the least friction, the least racial tension.

I started a school—a branch like the branch of Marshall [University in Huntington] that is up at Williamson now. Ours was called something else. I don't remember just what the proper name for it was. It came out of Bluefield [State College]. They didn't have anything set up, but the teachers were sent there to our community. Once a week, teachers came up from the college, and the teachers of the district who wanted to renew their certificates, or make extra credits would come that night and take lessons. Finally, the Colonel came over once to see the results, to see what it was all about. He found that the teachers were improving themselves, so he paid them. Because the teachers had to come from the farthest end of the district, he let them take Monday afternoon off. If they were that anxious to learn, they wouldn't have to travel at night to the danger of themselves. They could teach half a day on Monday, and take the other half of the day and come in for teacher learning. Nearly every teacher in the district enrolled. Bluefield had to send about six teachers down there on Monday afternoon. Monday was the day that the College didn't have classes, so it hit very well for them to come. And for years we had that, perhaps eight or ten years—the teachers from Bluefield College who came in. You would take the six hours or whatever it was to get your renewal or whatever you wanted. If it was history or social studies a teacher came in for that. If it was math—a math teacher came. We could use the lab if it was any science or biology that you wanted to take for your college degree. And they came and that was the first one they had. After that some of the other schools like Kimball and the other districts started it. But Gary had it for a long time—for their district, supported by the U.S. Steel Company.

Although I was teaching while still being the welfare worker, I did keep that job for a number of years, which was very good. And I found things to do. Working for a corporation is a setup. Unless you got into it, you'd hardly believe how smoothly it can work for so many people of so many different backgrounds and groups. The people in industry have a setup. I guess everybody knows it now because it's well organized; they have a setup that you would hardly believe possible.

Whatever salary teachers were getting, I'd get a little more. So I was well paid for my loyalty to the company. Then my husband lost his health; he had a heart condition. The company opened up a poolroom for him in the Negro restaurant; the basement part was turned into a poolroom. We had lovely bowling alleys, duck pins and all that. We had a ladies' bowling league and four pool tables. They gave him that because he was an excellent worker; he was a man with men. My husband could work more men than anybody you ever saw; and he worked just as hard himself.

When he got the poolroom, the company said to him, "Now hire who you want." They were wonderful. The rent was nothing; the lights were nothing. It was fine and when he felt like it, he'd go. He hired men enough to do what he wanted and he'd just oversee the whole thing. Then my mother came there; she was old then and she had to have help, so sometimes I couldn't go see about what was going on at the pool-room and how they were coming with the working. My husband would take the car and get the men and go, so the poolroom came in handy. He had something to do so that he didn't brood. Oh, he had so much. He didn't live but about a year after that. He didn't die of a heart condition. He had pneumonia, was dead in three days.

So, then I ran the business. I kept that poolroom ten years. I couldn't go there regularly. I'd go there and check things. The men ran the alleys, and I just put one man over them. All I got was what they put in the cash register, but I know that anything that kept four men working made money. They'd go at ten in the morning and work till midnight. I just got what was in the register, and then I paid them out of that, but they were fat cats. All of them were fat cats because I know what they did.

After my husband died, the women stopped bowling because they were afraid that I couldn't take care of the situation. I didn't know who they were. So the men got up a bowling club. I just saw to it that things were kept up, but even at that, it was good. I sold out when I left, not the building, just the things that were left there.

I started working for the company somewhere about 1931 or somewhere along in there. I worked until 1946. Then the political picture changed to the fact that unions were coming in. That made a difference in the whole setup—everything. I didn't work for them any under the union. The union came in and they were organized and I wasn't any more a part of it after that. They had new people and a new setup of rules for the laborer and the whole picture changed. Any role that I might have had was either obsolete or it was taken over otherwise. I knew that it was time to quit and when that year was up, that was it.

IV

*life
in the
coalfields*

PERHAPS nowhere else is Garrison's racial pride clearer than in her discussion of the role of black people in the coalfields. This is understandable in the light of historical accounts of mining that have largely ignored black miners. At the same time it is important to remember that Garrison's recollections are based on her experiences in the southern coalfields of West Virginia, where large numbers of African Americans were employed. Other areas, such as northern West Virginia or eastern Kentucky, had far fewer black workers.

Garrison echoes a theme argued by many black intellectuals[1]—that without the slave labor of the Southern black worker and then the cheap labor of the black industrial worker the United States could not have attained its position as a preeminent world power. Yet when one reads economic history, it is almost always told as the triumph of the rich white man whose business decisions created the wealth of this country. Garrison would snort at such a rendition of American history!

Garrison's description of the labor of these black people is both factual and literary. When she says *without those coke ovens the wilderness would have been a dreary dark howling wilderness* she is suggesting that it was the African Americans who brought "light" to this part of the country. In other words, it was more than a question of labor. Their contributions in building community were as significant as the tons of coal they produced.

The early coal towns were ethnically diverse, as Garrison so clearly points out. Her observations of intergroup relations in the community are insightful, but clearly reflect her standpoint as a black person. She disputes the image of all Appalachians as white and of Celtic descent. Indeed, she speaks disparagingly of the "mountain people," who would more likely be seen as fitting the "hillbilly" stereotype.

Although racial separation and segregation have been seen as a "natural" consequence of mixed communities, Garrison's account contradicts this perception. She argues that in the beginning there was little, if any, social segregation, and that came only later. Of course, her recollections of the beginnings of the Gary community are those of a child. Yet children are often more sensitive to social boundaries than adults.

Religion is another topic on which Garrison's analysis contradicts commonly held beliefs. Rural Appalachian "Bible Belt" fundamentalism has characterized descriptions of the region's religion. Yet Garrison's discussion suggests a highly sophisticated and comparative view of religion. She never questions the basic and fundamental values of the church, but clearly sees its social role as something separate. And it is in her discussion of the functions of the black church that we most clearly see how and why those churches eventually became the backbone of the modern civil rights movement.

It is in chapter 13 ("U.S. Steel") that Garrison's attachment to "the Colonel" is plain. She respected and admired the man, as a man. She developed a close working relationship with him that included a high level of trust. When the union started to organize in Gary, he called on Garrison to be his eyes and ears. She played a role that one might characterize as "company spy"—a role she acknowledges in this account (without using those words). Yet there is no evidence that she lost the respect or support of the black community as a result. Her motivation was to protect the interests of the community, and she perceived that the United Mine Workers of America was not able, or willing, to speak to the needs of black miners.

This does not mean she was naïve about the power of the company. Indeed, in her discussion of feudalism, she acknowledges the total control, including that over the

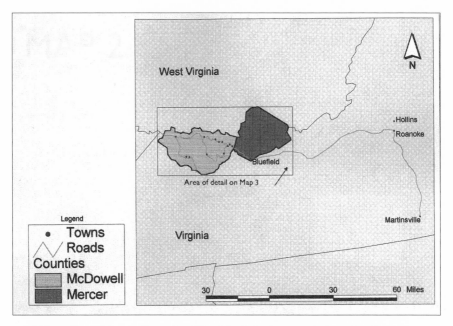

2. McDowell and Mercer Counties, West Virginia. *(Cartography by Neil Cadle, 1999)*

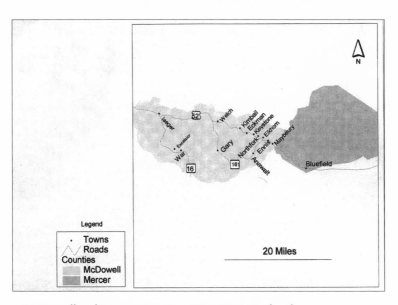

3. McDowell and Mercer Counties, West Virginia, detail.
(Cartography by Neil Cadle, 1999)

4. Southern West Virginia Coal Towns and Railroads, ca. 1914–1920.

The railroads and coal towns were built in the hollows closest to the rich coal seams in southern West Virginia. This map documents the density of the population at the time these seams were being opened up. Most have now been exhausted, and the towns they spawned have disappeared. A 1999 official highway map of West Virginia shows that in McDowell County alone, forty-six communities that were on the older map no longer exist.

churches, which the company exercised in the coalfields. But again, she accepted that as part of the social structure within which she had to maneuver.

In the same way, Garrison saw the union as part of the social structure. She made little distinction between the company union and the United Mine Workers—again, because of her experience with U.S. Steel. It was probably not clear to her that often the companies resisting unionization bettered conditions because of the union threat. Without the union to make the threat there would have been no incentive for U.S. Steel to improve the lot of the workers.

chapter 10

The Coalfields

We came to live in the coalfields
when I was very small. Negroes built this coalfield; that's it. They did
more than any other racial group in settling these counties that became
the rich industrialized places. They laid the tracks, opened the mines,
felled those trees, manned the sawmills, built the first crude huts, and
provided the coke yard forces. That's before I came; that's a part of the
historical setting, before I was born, I guess. But because the coalfields
were opening, my father came around '87 or '88, but that was before I
was born. The people who had security, who had good farms and things
like that weren't moving out here. It was the people who were having a
hard time trying to make a living who came.

The foreigners were the artisans; the Italians were the first ones, they
cut that stone and built the coke ovens. They didn't have to have stone
casts, you know, to build them. They could measure what kind of stone
they needed and all like that. And the coke ovens—without those coke
ovens the wilderness would have been a dreary dark howling wilderness, but with them, it was just like daylight all along the Norfolk and
Western Railway. All of the towns were built along the right-of-way of
the path, and the right-of-way of the path was in the midst of where the
engineers knew the coal was, on either side of the valley. They used to

say that they knew that in that valley was enough coal to last a million years.

The making of that coke and the loading of it was all done by Negroes. It was too hot for anybody else. Way up into the 1900s there were still a lot of Negro coke yard bosses. Those coke ovens were something else. We had a mild winter because of them; there'd be a row of coke ovens all up in flame, all up and down that highway for hundreds of miles. The men pulled this coke. They had long things that looked like paddles, made of iron, huge paddles. They'd pad their hands with leather because they'd get hot. They'd water the ovens down; they had a hose all along the coke yard with running water; the hoses would carry it from the wells or from the river. They'd knock the doors out after melting and burning the coke so many hours. The ovens were red-hot, and, oh, the flames would be high. Sometimes the whole sky would be lighted up. You could see for miles if you were from the mountains. It was a beautiful scene with the moon and the coke ovens together. We'd have all kinds of games, playing and staying together until they'd make you go to bed. They don't have coke ovens now; it's been forty or fifty years since they've had coke ovens.

The first mine that opened was Maybeury. They loaded the coal there in wheelbarrows and wheeled it to a makeshift tipple,* and dumped it in a chute. The coal went down into the cars; that was the beginning of the coal industry in McDowell County.

The McQuails owned the place where we lived and my father was a contractor in the mines. They'd let a Negro man take a section of the mines; he'd hire his own men and work it; they'd pay them for it and he'd pay his miners. I don't know the business part of it. I only knew that my father had lots of money because he had the money to pay his men with and the company didn't have any responsibility for those men. He was the one who had to get that coal out and get it in those cars. Mules used to draw it to the tipple for a long time and then they put the little motors on.

*Structure in a mining area where coal is loaded on railroad cars or barges to be transferred to sale or processing points.

We had a spring and we lived up on the hill—the families did. Four or five of them would come together at the same time that my mother did and we'd go down to the spring to get water and bring it up the hill. While we were getting the water, we'd see the men moving steel. I'd never seen such hammers and I'd never seen that many men work together. They'd bend over to get that steel and they would make a sound and they'd grab the steel and they would chant in unison and move those long rails. Just a few men would do it. I don't know how it was done, but just that it seemed that the sound was helping. Something in the sound gave strength to those men to move something that if they were just going to pick it up in each try, would have been impossible. And they were strong men, and I don't remember anything but Negroes in those work gangs; they were swinging those hammers to the count and to the songs. How did they have all that breath to sing those songs and use those hammers? It just amazes me when I think about how they were, and remember the things that have gone on that weakened those strong bodies—how disease took hold of them and destroyed them because of the type of living they had to do. I think of those strong men. I saw that railroad for miles, that railroad that they would lay.

I used to sing those work songs, but now they won't come. They'd sing the songs of men traveling. There was one that this hefty big sledgehammer man used to sing. They had to keep sledgehammers especially for him. I wanted to know why he'd got so many hammers. "Well," they told me, "he's the big man; he has to have a big hammer." And I remember him and this voice that came up. And I remember a song that went . . . "Didn't he ramble"—hup! And that thing would go down. "That old John Henry"—hup! It would go down. I don't remember a thing else now; there were things that they sang of that had been done, that they had heard of. I guess they sang the history of the race in that steel driving process, but nobody was there to realize what those men were doing. They didn't understand those labor songs, what they meant to labor around the world. You know, Paul Robeson came on in late years and he began singing songs in places where they wouldn't let the men go and talk, and the songs had to do with the living of men, the labor of men and all. And I think that was the same thing that those men sang of earlier. They sang a history of the people in pounding that steel and laying up those rails. Now they had a different tempo to move a rail because they would go faster. "Hup! Hup! A-hug-a-hug!" I remember that the time, the tempo of that, was not the tempo of the steel drivers. But they got it done, and it was beautiful.

The people used to come down from Pennsylvania—the men who'd invested in the mine. You'd see them around. The town was small—a village where everybody could move around in. We were curious little children. I always had a gang going somewhere and we would see them. We could move around among the steel drivers. The visitors would stop when the men were moving steel. They would stop and go where the men were. Now I know what those men were listening for. They were trained men and they were college men. They were financiers that would come and they were listening for the songs.

At first, everybody in the coal camps lived where they could get a house; everybody was too poor to be hostile to one another. At first we lived together—you lived in this house, we lived in that house, the next one lived in that house. At first when the places were new, when they were starting up, that's the way they lived. I remember that because some white woman lived in the next house from us. She had four or five children, but they, the whites, moved more than we did. We'd stay in that place maybe four, five years before moving. During that time, you could have a half dozen white families in that house next door. They moved and they moved. They were a kind of farming kind. They moved up in the mountains. They'd find them a place up there where nobody was going. They just moved intentionally to the mountains. They didn't have to pay rent there; they'd go up there and clear them off a place, two or three acres, and say, "This land is mine, now you try to get it." That's what started the feuding, you know. "You try to get it. I cleared that, that's mine." A lot of them still live up there. There're good people who came out of there; they've been educated and hold good positions and all; they've come off those little strips up there in the mountains.

We didn't live up in the woods. You couldn't get Negroes up in those mountains. They lived down in the coal camps with the white people and many foreigners. Some of the whites and foreigners would lease a place up there and live and come down and mine this coal, but we Negroes didn't move to the mountains. You won't find any Negro up in the mountain living on nothing. You find him down where the action is. I don't know a Negro who goes back in those mountains and works like that. Now all of these were people on the go; they were a migratory set, those first miners, both black and white and foreigners. Wherever there was a new mine opening up and the possibility of better wages, they moved on. And it's still migratory to an extent. I guess that's why the company didn't find it necessary to sell land and let the miners build; they knew they'd be leaving and wouldn't pay for it, so they just rented houses to them.

The first houses were crude. They had sawmills and they sawed their own lumber out and set up these crude houses. I found out about them from persons who were living in them at the time. They told me that the Negroes manned the sawmills and built the first real crude huts, felled those trees. They did more than any other racial group in settling these counties of West Virginia, the rich industrialized places now.

✳

chapter 11

Racial Separation in the Coalfields

When the foreigners came and the
company began building houses, they began separating people by race,
but at first you lived everywhere together;[1] wherever there was a house
you got it. And gradually as they began to build and improve the mines,
more people began to come into the section. The company did it. They
began to have the Hungarians living on their hill and the whites living
over in that bottom, the Negroes living up that hollow. Like that, they
began to separate. And somebody lived in such and such a hollow and
they would say, "There weren't anything but white people living up
there." It was that sort of thing. It was subtle; it didn't look like they in-
tended to do it. Nobody objected. They didn't notice it. They were bent
on making a living, all groups. And of course, this man who was own-
ing the place would say that's the best way to do it. Then of course, the
whites had the better houses because they had the positions of bookkeepers, clerks in stores, all like that. They had fairly nice houses.

If you made more money, your rent was more, and you lived in a
decent house in a more decent or desirable place around the camp.
Churches came into play then. The company would sometimes help the
miners build a church. And they had officers and when they began to elect
officers, you had the Negro constable and it came on up until there was
a Negro on the board of education, and came on up until McDowell

County had a Negro attorney. Now we've gotten to the point that we have a Negro judge down there. He was here to the judges' meeting in the fall. So it's evolved from this primitive sort of living.

I think there were differences in the wages in the mines. I remember what they would pay an hour—maybe they would pay a Negro a little less on an hour than they'd pay a white man. And to justify that, maybe, they'd give the white man just a little edge on them by saying that he was keeping a book or something. But mainly, they were doing the same work, as I remember. Of course I didn't work in the mines, and didn't pay too much attention. My father wasn't hired the same way. He had a contract at times, when he was living.

It seems to me that little boys got a dollar and a quarter a day or whatever it was. I don't remember any little white boys being hired in the mines. I remember the little colored boys. Negroes were drivers of the mules that pulled the cars, and the stable bosses for a long time were Negroes. They took care of those mules. Most of the drivers were Negroes. Most of the mining—98 percent of the mining—was done by the Negro—that coal digging and shooting and loading—until the foreigner came. It was more money for Negroes doing that than anything else until the foreigner began. Those foreigners would work all day and all night in there, trying to get money. They'd send it back to the old country, to their families, either to bring them over or to go back, themselves, and live well. See, the peasantry of Europe came over here. They were just poor farmers and peons and poor people, beggars and all that. It seems to me that I have heard Negroes complain that the foreigners had the best places in the mines. The owners gave those foreigners those places. I don't know, but it seems that I heard later on that the foreigners began to load coal; see, not many white men loaded coal before that. They were the carpenters and the bookkeepers and worked outside in the beginning. But that coal, that coal bit, that getting it ready for market was done exclusively by Negroes until foreign labor came on the scene.

Social contacts between races came when political campaigns would come on. Have campaign gatherings and everybody'd go and there'd be beer and sandwiches and all and everybody hobnobbed and went to that. Sometimes the company would have a holiday for all the men; they'd pitch ball and horseshoes; that sort of thing went on. And whenever Silas Green* and other minstrels would come in everybody went. They sat every which way they wanted because they were mainly children. I don't know when real segregation came and people became so particular that you be to yourself. I don't quite know among us. I know over the country when it started historically, but not when it started among us as children. Seems to me all at once you woke up and you'd been away to school and came back and everybody was different. There wasn't any social life as such between whites and Negroes, not like it is now. I never saw Negro boys and white girls running around together then like I do now. There are more people now and more changes. Maybe this sort of thing could have been then. But there were just certain kinds of people who were in this howling wilderness; people who were destitute; people who had to have something; people who were on their last legs when it came to living. They came here. Men who came were soldiers of fortune, some had money and wanted to come to conquer the wilderness. But I remember all its beauty. I remember. I'll never forget those men, those strong men.

We started a newspaper, a daily newspaper, and to see their names appear doing something kept down payday squabbles and shootings and fussings and things among the miners. They didn't have unlimited lawlessness, but there was some lawlessness everywhere, like gambling. They gambled everywhere. The monthly paydays furnished outlets for those who were not constrained to go to church or to do other things. The gambling could be under a shade tree somewhere, and on the hillside, or in a house, or anywhere. The gambling usually followed the monthly paydays and there would be killing sometimes. They'd get to fussing and then go to the saloons. They had a number of bootleggers who would bootleg liquor back and forth. It was expected. It was a part of the social life of the place. When it got so out of hand and the people— or certain ones of them—got troublesome and ran afoul of the law or shot an officer who was hunting the still of the bootleggers, then they

*Traveling black minstrel show.

would clear that bunch out. They would make them leave. They'd have to go somewhere else off that place.

Another thing that isn't so common or prominent as it is in new places was common law wives. Yes, they came. There were no red light districts, but there were always those people, poor whites and Negroes, who had their share of moral problems. They would come and sometimes as the kids say, "shack up" together. But it didn't last because once a year at some of the places, the superintendent or somebody would visit every house. Later when I was a welfare worker for the company, that became the thing I sometimes hated to do. Anyhow, they would send people around to see. They would ask, "Who lives here?" The answer would be "Mr. & Mrs. so and so." "You married?" the visitor would want to know. "You got your certificate?" If the people could tell a tale and the visitor gave them no trouble about it, it was all right. But those who weren't married and weren't convincing would have to clear out within the end of the month unless they married. So, the company had a nice marriage bureau. Many of the companies wouldn't let them stay otherwise.

The company did it because of the trouble they would have with the men. There was not only the trouble of losing a man's work when it was so badly needed, but there was also the concern for a possible murder. Loose women and loose men, and all of that, could cause problems. In order to avoid that, you had to know what kind of people that you were housing and murders gave the place a bad name. All that could be published by the county court.

I imagine the Pennsylvania-based people, the absentee landlords, got news from that superintendent, that general manager. I can see that it could have been a kind of allover thing.

chapter 12

✴

Churches in the Coalfields

When the churches began to come up, the Catholic priests were very much in evidence among the people, especially the foreign group. They came with the Hungarians and the Irish and all those. Then other churches and the schools came on. For entertainment, the schools had plays and things, but those first times I don't remember. In the early days, I don't remember anything but the churches and the companies having their holidays. The Fourth of July the companies would give the miners beer or all the lemonade they wanted.

The churches would have gatherings. They would invite the associations in, invite the Grand Lodges and then, in a manner, they would make the lodges responsible for church attendance in that the lodges would have the turnouts to get members. They had nowhere to go but the church. And the minister would preach the annual sermon for them. And a lot of people who hadn't been in church the whole year belonged to the lodge; they'd either come to the meeting or pay the fine that the lodge charged for absence; they chose to come. And the churches recruited members by that means, by making the lodges welcome to the church. And any club that wasn't a dancing club would be welcomed to the church. They recruited in that way; in a way it supported the Christian cause. If the activity was at the church, your mother wasn't afraid to let you go because it was all right, but sometimes there were men and women, people of questionable character there. Nobody screened to keep them from coming in. There was the gambler, the drunkard, all of those things. Sometimes the church was a factor in reclaiming those people. The minister would go among them. Sometimes there were young boys who had come to the mining camps, and it was the first time they were away from home. The minister would kind of take those boys under his care. The church was more than just the minister and the preaching on Sunday. Its purpose was to serve—to save people from their sins.

The churches had much to do with the moral living; they would preach this and they would convert people sometimes. They had a lot of revivals and people would come and the church would exhort and they would join. If they were living badly, they'd quit, and if they were gambling, most likely they'd have to quit awhile. The churches were there to take them in if they went back to whatever was Christian and moral. And there was a church in every place. The people put some of their money in their church. After the people had put in their part, they would have their chittlin dinners and chicken suppers, and the sweet potato pie suppers—everything—to raise money. Oh, they had wonderful food at that time. Those good cooks—they were fattening cooks. They'd have those suppers every payday. At the pay window the men would get in long lines for their monthly pay. I can see them now. There'd be some of us there when they left that pay window. They'd get their pay and then they would pay us. We would be selling sweet potato pies or chicken or so. The churches made a lot of money. Then the company would come to them and say, "You've raised so much and so much. What's your church costing?" And usually the company knew the cost because the people were building the church. After the people paid so much, the company would advance $500 to maybe $1,000. They really weren't advancing anything; it was a church they were buying. They would have a lot to say about what kind of preaching you had. The preacher would have to be in accord with the company's policy. There were always those who rebelled against certain things, but the church would have to go along with the company.

Until the lodge halls* were built later on, we didn't have any clubs or halls or anything. The only place we had to meet was the church. And before they built the halls, we met in the basements of the churches, if they had a basement, that is. You couldn't use the sanctuary. You could use the basement for your lodge meetings. But the halls served another purpose beside being a meeting place. You could dance in them. Before that they'd have their parties at their houses. You would just move the furniture and have a big blowout. Just set the furniture all out and dance in the house. And the school buildings here and there; if they couldn't put in an auditorium, they put in a large room where the seats could be moved, and they could have school socials there. All the church clubs would meet at the church because the homes didn't accommodate very many people; the homes were small and humble. People would meet at the church, which meant that the meeting would be brief and to the point because you couldn't have refreshments unless it was ice cream and cake. And then they'd have the church suppers to make money. They'd have the big supper on payday. So many of the men were single men who lived in the shanties, just one-room places, they would be so glad to get that cooking; they would spend money and come buy chicken that they wanted, or homemade pies and cakes. And they had all kinds of food at hog killing time; they'd have sausage and the chittlins started about that time, I remember. Now they've become such a delicacy that the packing companies make a business of it. And just last year, I think it was, at the Waldorf or one of the big hotels, they had this champagne party and served chittlins. They didn't call them chittlins, they called them something else.

For me, the church was somewhere to go. It was there I got some of my religious teaching. But I also got as much out of the school as I did out of the church because my teacher was also a minister; he had trained for the ministry. I used to go to Sunday school—fifty-two Sundays out of the year. My mother saw to it. It didn't get too cold, it didn't get too rainy, and we never had too much to do to keep us from going. I used to

*Meeting places of the secret orders such as the Knights of Pythias.

say that when I got grown up I wasn't ever going anymore. But I did. I went through and became a part of the Sunday school. I started teaching the little class when I was twelve; I read the story cards to the little children who'd go. And later I'd pick them up and the teachers and take them to church. They were a part of the church and they were a part of the life of your community. And with the church, the minister and all, you had a very good idea of what good living and Christianity meant and why it was desirable. As you grew older, you understood that it wasn't the church at all that was doing it, it was what you had accepted. But in the beginning, you accepted all the church offered. It was right. It was good. The church said it and the preacher said it and that was it. I believe that church made you a better person—your character was stronger. I think you had an idea of what you thought you were going to meet as an individual—the temptations that were there for you. The Bible was the history of the Jewish people; it's also the history of the human race, and all of it's there. People don't believe it all, and don't want to hear it all and reject it, but it is said that everything that you need to know is in that Bible. And that was a good beginning and that was all you were able to understand. It started you out, but as you grew older you understood that now you're on your own. Your belief. You.

My mother was a Baptist of the primitive crowd because her father was a preacher to the slaves—their preacher. And on that plantation, I guess if they had anything, it was Baptist, so they were that. I'd go to the other churches that I wanted to go to. If the Methodists were having something, a visitor or a minister, I went. But I am not churched. I think that all of them have an element of good. For ten years I went to Christian Science; I liked it. And I have read of most religions. I very highly prize the yogis and the things that they teach. The Buddhist teachings are fine and the Bible is not unlike most of it And the Koran—parts of our Bible make you think they copied it from that. They have a flood and all that like we have in the Bible, and they have Mohammed who was born their man; he lived just thirty some years, just as our Christ did. It's a counterpart of so much that we have. One of my teachers said to me that I should inform myself of all that, but that it'd mix me up. He thought that one Bible was enough for me to digest, and that it would last a lifetime. It didn't mix me up at all, because to me there is no one thing. Knowing about other religions gave me a greater understanding of what God was and of nature and creation and Christianity. It gave me a better understanding of all that. The Bible, the teaching of the church, the religions and how they are carried out, understanding all of that my study did for me; some of that stuff you can sit and prove for yourself, but I think, in the end, it's what you do with it. That place in the Bible that says every tub must stand on its own bottom—I think you've got to stand on your own belief and what you have done. No one church can contain God. He is it—he is everywhere. He is all. He is in all and through all.

All churches have the right to their belief, and all of them are right to some extent. Do you think there are not going to be any Catholics in heaven? Oh, yeah, I'm questioning heaven now. Since the astronauts went up, one of the little boys said, "Well, it sure ain't up there between here and the moon 'cause they done been up there to see." And then that brings up the question among the young people, "Is heaven a place? Or is it an existence, a condition?" And then you go back to this group sitting there and they say, "Well, the Bible says heaven is within you." Well what does that mean? You hear great arguments of Satan and sage, but you are just where you are. When you finish with it all—the people, the ministers and all who teach—you are still in the same place you started from. Nobody's been to heaven and come back. But the teachings make you broader, make living more pleasant. They give you direction; that's what the church should do for you—give you spiritual direction, give you strength to know that others have done that.

chapter 13

✴

U.S. Steel

I think that it was in the early 1900s
that the United States Steel Company moved in, about ten years after
we'd come to McDowell County. They moved there in a big way and
were an example for the rest of the coal companies even though they
had been operating longer.

Colonel O'Toole was general manager of a whole West Virginia and
Kentucky operation. The Colonel wasn't a college man at all. He was a
big Irishman who had mined coal in Ireland. He'd come to Pennsylvania
and when they wanted a man for this new place, they picked him and they
sent him in. He was wonderful, congenial, white-haired, pink cheeks,
with a ready style; everything was ready with the Colonel. He could out-
cuss anything; I guess if he fought, he could out-fight anything, but he
was a man to be admired. He had children—one was a girl I used to sew
for. When she went to college, I made her college clothes. I don't know
about his clubs, his golf associations and all—or his fraternal associations. I didn't know anything about those, but I used to call him the most
grand totem pole, for he was the general superintendent of the whole
operation for the company. Before I left there, I raised some money for
the church. I had this affair and the Colonel gave money; he had to come
to give them the money; it was the fiftieth anniversary of the church. I
think that his children gave me a picture of their father because I wanted

to run it in the church bulletin. And sometimes I would have plays, little pageants, and I'd have some little fat boy play Colonel O'Toole, you know, and that would tickle him. He would go into stitches. "Where's the Colonel?" he'd say, and I'd say, "My little black Colonel's right over there."

Somebody accused the coal companies of running a feudal system—a writer from New York. He was saying that he was down in the coal-fields of the Guggenheims and so forth, and that he was called in by United States Steel to interview their superintendent, Colonel O'Toole, "a genial Irish chap with twinkling blue eyes and white hair. Instead of me interviewing him though," the writer went on, "he interviewed me." So he went on to tell that he, the Colonel, said that Negroes nowhere were any better off than the Negroes who worked for him down there, not even in New York. The writer put all of this down in this newspaper throughout the country. And the Colonel said that he had the most intelligent of all the Negroes. The Colonel thought that, of course. I had been running a Negro artist series there and the Colonel had never seen Negroes of the intelligence of those people. So the writer said that he was a benevolent feudal lord. The company's slogan was "Safety First." They wanted the people to feel that they were there, that they cared for their welfare. And that's why the Colonel would always say that; he'd tell the people who came to interview him. "Why you interviewing me and my Negroes? I've got the best ones in the United States, Harlem not excepted." He would say that to them and he would talk about the Negro's status in Harlem. He would say, "My people have the same thing; they have everything the others have."

I don't know if it was right to call it feudalism. I knew something of what feudalism was like; slavery was a system of feudalism only the persons were mistreated and owned body and soul. Anywhere that the land-lord is proprietor overall, and what he says goes—if it's almost impossible to get a job without obeying him, that is feudalism. But for that writer, it was satire. I think that it's true everywhere that if you work for somebody and you buck them, it's all over. The difference would be only in the number of people hired. As an individual person, I don't care who you are, if you buck the company and they consider it not in their best interest, and that's true everywhere, they get rid of you.

The company did control the housing and the company store. I guess that's true overall, of all the coal companies. They had a certain amount of power. Even in that, they ruled the political world. In so many places, we knew that when the United States Steel's votes came in, they elected whomever they wanted. If they didn't have it before the votes were counted, they'd have it when the count was finished if they wanted it. They didn't buy the votes, but they got them. They just got them. You knew to put them there. You knew what your company stood for. You knew that they were for the Republican ticket or the Democratic ticket, whatever they wanted. If they were for the Republican ticket straight out, then you knew. They let that be known. And the speakers came, you know. The candidates would come.

The Colonel was a smart man; the Colonel was a man that you liked and the Colonel was a man who had to be heard. The Colonel realized it, but he didn't push his luck. He always made you think that you were doing something because you wanted to. He made you think that you had done it, but you knew, you knew who was doing it. He never exposed his hand, but we knew. If the Colonel wanted it, he was going to get it. You'd know what he wanted by the conversation and you'd do it. You think I'd have been out at every meeting, out at everything that was going on and wouldn't have something to say about the Hatfield that was going to Congress? You think I sat down and talked for nothing? "By the way," I'd say, "What do you think of the coming election? You know Dr. Hatfield's there, and all of us know about the Hatfields. Yes, yes, yes." Any of the persons who were politically inclined or hired in any position would do that. They were out at meetings. The people would just do that. You could pick up what the company felt because you had been with the company and knew what they felt. And everybody who had any power, any job of any note did the same thing. The message was loud and clear. Without your being told, you'd find out. That's right, the message was always loud, and if you didn't hear anything, you started asking. You were wondering what was wrong. That's the way it's done all over. That's the way it's done yet. That's political maneuvering. There were signs of the professional politicians and there were signs of the followers. It was just like it is now.

chapter 14

✳

Miners and Unions

*This is one of the richest soft coal re-*gions in the world and they knew it was fine, but it was in the late years with all the tests that had been made and the surveys that they really knew what a rich vein of coal there is in these hills. And then the absentee landlords, the Carnegies, the steel men, the Guggenheims, and all those people began to stake claims and put in leases before they mined out this first vein of coal. This was a big teeming valley of people.

By the time that my father died, things had changed. The unions had started to come in; the men were on strike and some were just wandering around and the companies were fighting the unions.[1] I know there were union men. I don't know who they were. I wasn't even interested in unions or anything or any information about them. But I remember Mother Jones [union organizer Mary Harris Jones]. She was this woman who spoke in the county road and the miners would leave the premises and go to the county road. That's the only place they couldn't run her out of. They used horses and buggies and wagons and mules to go from place to place in the county and talk in the county road. There weren't any loudspeakers either; they'd go near so that they could hear. And they would listen—there was something that somebody had to say about there was going to be a strike and they ought to have a union and things like that.

Mother Jones was from the west; she had been in Colorado and places around there organizing the men. Anywhere there was mining she was there. She was a tall white woman.[2] She was a laborer; she was with the men to get recognition for labor. It was a good technique to use her. She did not meet with the operators. She kept things stirred up though. You never could tell when somebody was coming in to back her up, you know. I remember instances when she came two or three times. I remember that she was in the section around McDowell County. And then other men began to come in from, I guess, from Pennsylvania, wherever the fields were unionized. They tried to get in here.

They wouldn't allow Mother Jones on the places. I guess they would have beaten her to death. But Mother Jones and her laborers would get in a county road. You know, there weren't any highways; there were just dirt roads around here where all the highways are now. The men could go up to the roads to hear Mother Jones but she didn't dare set foot on the company's property. And with the coming of the foreigner strikes began—the foreigner had such a hard time in his own country, he was a striking man. He was ready for a strike. He struggled with labor for his well-being. But the Negro hadn't had anything, maybe just a little farm down in Virginia, a few acres he was trying to pay for. So all he did was to come and work and half eat and half sleep and sometimes get maimed and killed. Always, there were a lot of people killed in the mines.

And they worked children then. My brother went to work as a little boy of twelve or thirteen, maybe a little older, but he was just a little fellow. And little children like he was had gone to work because their families had come and brought large families and they needed the money; they got twenty-five cents an hour, I believe it was. And they sat there at that entrance and threw a switch for the cars to go up one way and the motor to go the other. And those children would go to sleep or sometimes the car would jump the track or whatever. And sometimes, I remember—I was a little run around, you know—somebody would say somebody got hurt. I knew all the children who worked in the mines. I'd ask, "Was it Richard? He just went to work the other day. Was it Jimmy?" And if they weren't able to say who it was, I was off to see. "Come on, let's go see about it." And they would bring him home on a stretcher ground to pieces. The hospitals were miles away. The doctor had an office with an extra room or two and he took care of him. Maybe little Richard was ground beyond recognition; all they could do was put him in a box and bury him. You had that sort of thing.

They gave the best places in the mines to the whites and they didn't promote the Negro. He still was the coal loader and they'd give places to the whites who could hardly read or write but as long as they were white, they were boss. My brother worked in the mines. He was a driver in the mines after he was big enough. He was a trapper first, a little trapper; then he became a driver when he was big enough to drive a mule and he made out his boss's time sheet and the boss would give him extra money for it. The boss would turn in extra time for him for making out his time sheet. They were good friends. He'd come by the house and they would pitch ball on the sand lot together, like that. From the beginning, little kids, little white and colored kids wherever they were would find each other and play together. They'd pitch ball on the sand lot; they'd pitch horseshoes. There was always some level place where they could play; maybe it was up at the edge of the white neighborhood or at the edge of the colored neighborhood, but they played together.

My mother had a foster son, Luther, and he went to work when he was about sixteen years old, maybe a little older, driving in the mines. He had a mule, a white mule named Charlie, and he and Charlie were pals. I heard about Charlie every time something was going on. Luther served an area of the mines where the foreigners worked. They'd holler, "Hey, buddy, give me a car." And they kept him going, and he said they would pay him extra if he had a car there for that foreigner to start on when he finished the one he was working on. That meant that on payday he was going to give Luther extra money for bringing cars. And the foreigners, well, you wouldn't call them greedy, but they were anxious to get money. They would stay in there and work and they would eat that garlic and onion. Luther would come home smelling like garlic and Momma would make him go out the door. He said, "It makes you strong, and the way they work, it makes them strong." So that foreigner, for a long time, had the best working place in the mines.

Now there was one old man in the community and he had about ten children; his wife had passed; he ruled them and everybody else who came under his influence with an iron hand; he was convinced that there had to be a get together to talk. He saved money to help the union organize. And these union fellows, they worked on the order of, I would say, of the Carpetbaggers. They'd come in and they'd find these fellows and sit down with them anywhere they could. And they would explain about the union. There were three or four of these white fellows who'd get around among the Negroes, you know, and I would see them. I didn't pay any attention to them because I—I just didn't.

And I remember, though, that when I went to get the history of McDowell, I found out that this "old man" had done a great deal of work and saved this money and he gave it to these union men to help them organize. They were going to organize and he was going to be this, that, and the other in the union; they disappeared, money and all, and that was the end of that part of the union.

But from time to time they came. These union organizers came. And the Negroes came and had a part in it. The new Negro came after those first pioneers. They came in transportation lots. I guess the company would lease [train] cars, whatever, but they'd have these transportation cars. They had men to go south to recruit Negroes. These Negroes were laborers and part of them had nothing because of the times. The Negro was unskilled, just out of slavery forty or fifty years; they had nothing. The company would bring those men in as strikebreakers; they didn't know what they were coming to, but the company'd bring them in and put them to work. And they—many of them stayed and that broke the back of the other Negroes.

Very few Negroes would strike because they didn't have anything to strike for. But that white man would strike and what few foreigners there were up to that time would strike. The foreigner had been oppressed, too, in his country. That's why he was leaving; he was seeking freedom. It was class there in his country; he had no status so he came to America for a living and for help—and they would strike and the company would bring the Negroes in, give them jobs and that would break the back of that movement; it would rest for a while and flare up somewhere else.

The foreigners would start the strike; the foreigners didn't come here until around '96. At first mainly Negroes came in, not in large numbers, just large enough. There was a dearth of workers and they didn't get much money. At the turn of the century they had certain things taking place. The foreigners had come in and the companies sent out men to recruit Negroes. They sent their trusted men down in Alabama, Georgia, and the Carolinas, and all down there where Negroes were starving to death.

The Negroes didn't know how to strike. They were just thirty or forty years out of slavery then. They didn't know anything about labor unions. Oh, the particular Negro did. There were around fifty thousand free Negroes when the Civil War ended, but those free Negroes weren't hunting jobs in mines. They were based in urban centers—in the cities —and they were professional and semiprofessional craftsmen. Negroes were fine craftsmen. They came out of slavery times being the best brick-layers. They wrought the wrought iron. The shoemakers had made shoes for the whole plantation. The caterers of the country were Negroes; they could prepare all those wonderful Southern dishes that had gone on, and the people left everywhere to go visit on the plantation when the master had these people who could do that. They were craftsmen; they could weave, and they were out where they were making money for the new republic, for the new country that had come together. So, they handed down the crafts to each other.

Well now, it was the field hands that were looking for work. They knew nothing but work. They were the people who worked hard but there were no more fields to work in as such. Their masters had become poor because the war had destroyed all that they had. These were Ne-groes who were looking for anything they could get. And they were packed together down in those places; that's where they were in those thirteen states. So they began to bring them in. And they did come. They came and they did break the strikes. They'd have that foreigner and that poor white man get together and they'd call a strike and the company'd bring in enough Negroes to furnish their labor. And now the strikers had to see the fact that remains, "If we want to get anywhere, we've got to consider this Negro man." So then the Negro began to come into his own. When a few of the Negroes came in, oh, like over in McDowell County, they came in from Virginia, over in that Tazewell Valley. Over there were rich slaveholders who'd given their children—wasn't hardly any black people over there—the rich slaveholders had mixed them up so. Negroes and whites, you could hardly tell one from the other. The white owner had shared with the Negro owner, and they began to move into McDowell County and ask for things. They were used to things. There came in the Harpers and the Calhouns, those people who began to move in, buying. "We'll buy up this little town." And they bought up the little town of Keystone. "We'll have a store." They began to do things like that. Negroes had a store, a grocery store, a department store, and they had saloons and barber shops, and that began to take place. Then the life of these Negroes who came began to take on new aspects; they began to bring their families and save money. And Negroes had a loan business, and all kinds of eating places. At one time there were—I don't know how many saloons, but that was a business and they owned them.

The Negro was poor and in need and half-starved when he came here. He has a way of camouflaging his real feelings; he can command that for use when anybody less adaptable would be completely crushed. This was necessary to survive. He learned to survive. Then he learned to be comfortable surviving. Then he learned how to boss what he had attained with his surviving. It was an evolution for him, from nothingness, from want, from ignorance on up to where he could stand as a man.

There was no hostility generated against blacks because of their involvement with the strikes. Everybody was too poor, and at first we lived together. You lived in this house. We lived in that house. The next one lived in that house. At first when the places were new, when they were starting up, that's the way they lived. And gradually as they began to build and improve the mines, more and more people began to come into the section. They began to have the Hungarians living up on their hill and the whites living over in that bottom. The Negroes lived up that hollow. Like that, they began to separate, but at first you lived everywhere together. Wherever there was a house in the early days, you got it.

There came in some educated Negroes to the county; this was all in McDowell County. I don't know how other counties fared, but Negroes were faring the same way wherever they went if there was a coal mine. These educated Negroes began to do something about the large number of fatalities in the mines; it was staggering. You see, they only braced the tops in the mines and they used coal oil in the lamps. But the political picture came into view and they began to pressure the operators on the state level. If they got their contracts or if there were certain things they needed, they'd have to do certain things. That sort of thing took place and began to make a difference.

When the NAACP began, it had nothing to do with the strikes—the union. There was a union man always working somewhere in the area even if he had to live in a town that didn't object to unionism, like Welch, and those places where people could buy personal property, like Anawalt. He'd have to live there; they wouldn't let him live on the company's property if they knew that he was for the union. That's why the UMW couldn't make headway. There was no legal way they could push in and say that legally they had a right to it. They came in and would do their work by the persuasion of getting enough people to join to make it effective. And if the company knew they were there (they had to have a place to live and they had to have work to do to get it), the company just wouldn't hire them. But if the union hired them and they lived at some other place, they could come back and forth and visit people and talk, but it couldn't be known that they were union workers.

There was an independent union. [President Franklin D.] Roosevelt was in. It was legal to have a union; you could join other unions besides the United Mine Workers. The company wouldn't say they controlled the independent union; the men were supposed to be in control. The men worked for that company, of course, and the company didn't object to them having a union. They knew what it was all about. The United Mine Workers were trying to come in, and the independent union itself objected. Further, it was decided that under the Labor Relations Board the men were permitted to join any union, and the United Mine Workers could come in. The men could join the United Mine Workers union and they finally did. They dissolved their union. And I don't know how many companies had those same independent unions, but where I lived they had a big one. There was propaganda about the unions. Some of it was anti–United Mine Workers. "You're better off doing this than if you join the United Mine Workers. Them United Mine Workers wants too much dues; they want too much this, that, and the other, and they've got too many hired tough men who are getting top pay. You're better off, you've obeyed the law, you have a union. They didn't say that you couldn't have your union and name it what you want."

The thing of it was that the independent unions didn't charge as much dues to their men as the United Mine Workers did. The United Mine Workers had fixed dues, and the independent unions determined their dues to suit what they thought they'd like to do. They didn't have the question of so many people working up on the top level. They had their offices right around where they were. There were seventeen mines, a whole district down there, owned by the United States Steel. They had seventeen captive mines at that time in that area.[3] Those were the mines that furnished their steel mills; they didn't sell their coal. That went to their steel mills so you can know what a company they had going. The salaries were the same, but they'd be cutting so much out for the United Mine Workers fees, and the independent union would be charging less; that meant that if you were in an independent union, the take-home salaries rose slightly.

I didn't know anybody who ever got hurt or anything in the disputes about the unions. I just know the companies didn't want the UMW on the place and they would tell the men not to have meetings or not to entertain them. When the law [Wagner Act of 1935] came they didn't bother anything about them. They didn't bother anybody when it became the law that they could—that John L. could have his union. Of course, the owners could be punished, you see. The government would have come in on them and John L. would have moved in on them. John L. used to call them fat sons of bitches.

There were no more attempts to improve mine conditions by the United Mine Workers than there were by the independent unions. Actually, the United States Steel was the first coal company in that area to start the safety movement. Anywhere you could see that big sign, "Safety First," you knew United States Steel owned there somewhere. They made a real project of improving and the others began to do it, too. They had fewer accidents; they electrified all of their mines, and they put in electric motors.

I don't know what the setup was for each union regarding the number of hours worked and the pay for them. I was just interested in the law that made it possible for both of them to organize, and nobody dared bother them. You see, you could run them off the place before that law was made. You could dare them to come, and arrest them or what have you. The company's attitude was, and they wanted it understood, that the men didn't have to ask them if they could join the United Mine Workers. You couldn't say that our coal company says that we must do so and so and so. The men could choose. That would be the men's idea. They could have a union. The independent unions had their own by-laws that were drawn up by somebody who knew how to do it. I don't know if any behind-the-scenes work was being done by the companies. To get accurate information on that we would have to bring that question to the state mining department or to this fellow at West Virginia State.*

Negroes joined the union. They felt that a union was more protection, because of the togetherness. They would ask for a raise. They asked together. It was the togetherness that they wanted.

The Mellons and the Carnegies were among the Pennsylvania coal barons. John L. Lewis was right on their heels all the time. He would come down, and I don't remember any violence there on United States Steel places, but there was violence all around the county in different places. Somebody would be killed or somebody'd be missing or they'd find a labor leader or somebody dead. It was that sort of thing in those early times, and over in Logan County, you know, it was a hotbed of union organization—there was a pitched battle there on one of those mountains.** And then, of course, down in Mingo County, there were problems, but the union persisted. And finally in the last election of Roosevelt it became a law that it was right, that a miner could join a

*Probably referring to U. G. Carter, WVSC faculty member who taught mining extension classes.
**Reference to the 1921 Blair Mountain labor insurrection when armed miners set out to march to Logan County.

union, and he was not to be molested by the operator. John L. Lewis and Roosevelt got together on that. Then the unions began to spring up and the operator dare not bother them; if he did, they had jail ready for him. Well, then it began—the big changes in the coal industry.

And then new men came in from Pennsylvania, where the miners were safe. The United States Steel Company was among the last to open up one whole district known as Adkins District. And they bought all modern stuff. The other places had come in around 1900 and begun to build better houses. But now U.S. Steel had the best houses; they had the safest mines. They had the most modern mining machinery and they set the pace. Now they have worked out one seam of their coal. They still have a modern plant there that even processes the coal dust. I haven't been through that tipple; they were just starting it about twenty years ago when I was leaving there, but that's where I lived and worked as a grown woman.

Until I became active as a welfare worker, I knew very little of what went on in the mines. It was then I became conscious of it, so much so that the papers said I was the best-informed woman about the mines in the United States—about the working of the mines. The paper said "best-informed Negro woman." I was the best-informed any kind of woman because the white women weren't involved in those mines. They'd come down sometimes and they'd take them in to see what it was like; there was a superstition that for a woman to go in the mines was bad luck. If one of those women would go in and somebody'd get hurt during the week afterwards, then it would roll. "Keep them women out of that mine. They bring bad luck." I remember one big fellow got his leg broken after one of these trips when they brought some women down and took a load of them in. He began talking about it. Oh, he'd sit and talk about it—how "them women brought bad luck." So, then one of the women said, "Well, any colored women ever go in?" He said, "Then we'd all get killed." And they had a lot of fun. He said he wasn't going to "let no kind of woman in, and certainly not them." It was a superstition; they wouldn't let women go in.

The way I learned about the mines was when they worked out one of these mines in Pocahontas [Virginia]; it was the first coal mine in this area of old Virginia and West Virginia combined; it's right on the border [across from Bramwell, West Virginia]. Well, they worked that mine out, then they blasted it, they cemented it and everything, and turned it into an exhibition mine so you could go through it. The first time I went through, I drove my car through. I was afraid something would fall on me, and I went very slowly and got the literature. They had someone with you to explain it. Next, I walked through a couple of times, and then I could understand what it was all about. I could understand when things happened where I lived, and why they happened. I wanted to know about it because it was all around me. If somebody got hurt and they'd bring them home or take them to the hospital, I'd be the first one at that house, most likely. And I could explain what had happened and nobody ever sued the company. I could explain, or the superintendent, whoever had to notify them, could explain. This was done all over. If I was the person there, it would just happen to be me. I could explain that what happened was a natural thing. I could explain how the mine had been mined down into what they call a "kettle bottom," just like a round sandstone, and it gave no notice that it was going to come out. They could tell, it being worked out, what might happen. The men would take every precaution and even at that, they knew it was eventually coming out. They would get caught and killed sometime. This terrific thing fell out of that mountain down into that what they called "the room" where they were working. It pinned them against the walls; it took hours for them to drill that coal off of them. There were a lot of things about the mines that you knew and learned through that exhibition mine.

And the people who were concerned with the family would see about that family, see how much the man had in the office, see how much work he'd done, see that the family had food, see about those children and everything. If they knew them, I encouraged them to write them something. Just take one day and do it. They might be interested in that. We had no occasion, the NAACP, to bring any charges such as that the company had neglected one family or were kinder to one family. Nothing like that came up. It was done for all people. There were places that weren't so well organized, communities that weren't so well supplied with people to get the least thing, or get the things that were of importance done for the families. It didn't always hold that those things happened, but some of it happened every place. United States Steel made me their public relations person because I was closer connected and I was like Chicken Little. I saw it and heard it and part of it fell on me.

✳

chapter 15

Labor Relations

I was deeply entrenched in that labor situation, but I didn't know it. I'm almost afraid to talk about it now. The company people would say, "This is confidential between us," and tell me something. I wouldn't bother about it anymore; I knew what to do. But I didn't know at the time that it had anything to do with anything else. I wonder that I didn't have my head cut off.

Once two white fellows and a colored fellow were working in one of the places in this mine that was worked out—kettle bottoms or something. There were names for things when you work a place out. So this white fellow was new and his buddy brought him on in. Well, they had a fuss for some reason or another. They had been eating with each other and all. I don't know what occasioned the fuss now. Well, the colored fellow quit or said he would quit if he had to work with them. The place they were working in was the colored fellow's place. He had that place before either of the others came. The white fellow said he'd get him some others and keep the place. The colored fellow said, "No. That's my room. That's mine and I've been working there so long, so long, and I've nearly worked that place out." He wasn't going to give all this up— they paid more in there—to them, and yet he wasn't going to work with them. So they took it to the boss. The boss man said, "I think you fellows ought to be able to resolve your differences," and the colored fellow was daring the white fellow to go in there. He would do nothing in there; they were daring each other. Well, it got so that it was very bitter and then people began to take sides. So the company called me and said, "Come on in, Mrs. Sullivan."* And I said, "Huh, is it something like that?"

They said, "Well, we got something on our hands," and they explained it. I said, "Well, I believe I know all of them. I sewed last summer for one fellow's wife and his little children come by my house to get pieces for their doll clothes. I think I'll start with him first," and I said, "I know that I know my own." Well, I don't know how I knew Carl or how long it took me to fix it up, but in the meantime, they had to start work on that place. The company put some new men in there. Well, I used that as a means of saying that nobody won. The company'd won.

I went back to the men. We found some places for the colored fellow and gave him some more buddies. Some of the foreigners wanted to work with him. He was a good coal loader. Those foreigners are also coal loading fellows. They outwork any white man; they're white men, too, but I mean they outwork any of the natives. Then they gave the other fellow some little outside job. He was pleased no end to have it. And it just eased on off. It just eased out; nobody was bothered, so I scored there. I didn't know how it was done myself. But it could have been a nasty situation.

Then another time some fellow came there, a white fellow. There were other whites who had a house or two in the neighborhood—the Negro neighborhood, like next door. This man stood on the porch and made the remark to one of the other white fellows, "What are you doing living among these niggers? We lynch 'em where I come from." One of the Negro men went in his house and got his gun and came out. At the time, I was rounding the corner, coming over there to see some-one. I didn't know anything about this. And I said, "Where are you going?" He told me what had happened next door and said, "They don't insult me and my family like that." So I said, "Come on. Let's go inside." We went on back in the house and I said, "Well, now, you put your gun up because I promise you that if you put your gun up and go on to

*A reference to mine superintendent J. L. Sullivan.

Welch and shop and do something, I promise you he'll have moving orders before you get back. I give you my word." He went, and I went right to that office and I said, "You're going to have a riot if you don't do something right now. And you can't afford a riot on this place." The superintendent and the head boss left the office and went over there. The man said that he didn't mean anything, said he didn't know they heard him, said it was like that where he came from down in Georgia or somewhere. They told him to pack up, and I guess they moved that night. Nobody asked anything.

Now that was one way of settling something, and that may have been the best way, because when tempers flare and racial situations are bitter, that's what makes riots. Racial situations are the meanest kind. If two white men are fighting they are just fighting each other. Family situations are bitter when they get bad, or the clan situation like the Hatfields [and McCoys]—well, those things are really bad, but I think that racial situations are worse than any of them. Now the labor situation can get bad, too. They killed people, shot them on the courthouse steps when they came to the courthouse to do some things.* They killed those union men down there on the courthouse steps because they'd ruled in favor of the union or something.

They were keeping out the union. They had all kinds of tales about the union, what they would do to keep it out. Union men would come and they say they'd never see them again. I didn't know anybody who ever got hurt or anything. I don't know all the tales that would come. I just know the company didn't want them on the place, and they would tell the men not to have meetings or not to entertain union organizers or anything.

All of the men weren't union men. Anyway, the companies didn't want the union—they fought the union bitterly. They said, "We don't want them here." The company would come to me. They wouldn't tell me there were union men in the area. They would say, "There's a bunch of men at that clubhouse** at such and such a place, and they are union

*Reference to the 1921 murder of Sid Hatfield, "hero" of the Matewan massacre, and Ed Chambers at the McDowell County Courthouse in Welch.
**Residence for single men in a mining community.

inclined. And there are several men that are coming in here to organize a union. Now, you don't work in the mines. You don't have anybody there. You find out who those men who are coming in are. That's all we want you to do." And I'd find out who they were and where they worked. They'd install me in the clubhouse right with these union men who were hiding there and who were wanted. The company hadn't made themselves known to them after I said I'd find out who they were. They couldn't afford to be openly against them because it was pending between Roosevelt and John Lewis. If Roosevelt made it he was going to give John Lewis the law to organize the miners throughout the country. So the company couldn't make any to-do about getting these men out. And the men who were concerned—about sixty-five miners, foreigners and whites and all—lived at the clubhouse. If a new white man moved in, he would be suspected at once. "Say, Memphis," the company people would say to me, "how can you get across to those miners that they're in the midst of this organizing that the union's trying to pull here?" They didn't know whether the legislation was going to pass or not at that time. I said, "I don't know. Why do I have to get the message to them?" They said, "You either get that to them or get word to them that they can hire and they can have an independent union of their own and still obey the law. It doesn't have to be a United Mine Workers union." As much as I could see, the movement was coming up, but they didn't know it at first.

I had a franchise for selling coffee—Haitian coffee. This banker in Philadelphia was trying to help the Haitian farmers come to the United States. I found out that he had the coffee and we had all those people down there who were coffee drinkers. So I got this coffee club together to sell this Haitian coffee and the club would get some of the money to operate on. I asked the lady at the clubhouse to let me serve coffee at her dinner that night free, and I had my help and I had that front. She was so tickled because it was something new. The people were all there—the miners. When they would come up to get their coffee, I'd say, "You live here?" And they'd say, "Yeah." And I'd say, "You got a bunch of union men among you here." "Who?" they'd ask. I said, "I don't know. You find out." You see what I did? I didn't tell them anything. They found out for themselves and they didn't go with the UMW men. Instead, they got a charter themselves and they were recognized. So they had an independent union on U.S. Steel places. Well, nobody knew the how, the what, the where, and they never knew until John L. Lewis—Roosevelt won. The law [Wagner Act] was passed and John L. Lewis was setting up his union, but they already had a union.

The company was trying to keep John L. Lewis out. The men had an independent union. The company couldn't do anything but accept their union because the law didn't say it had to be the Mine Workers. You couldn't keep a man from unionizing. It might have been more beneficial to the miners to join up with John L. Lewis, but they already had their union. They had a charter and were doing all right. Every time the United Mine Workers would raise so much on their coal and all, the company would do the same for the independent union. So it wasn't as if the United Mine Workers were going to get more for that; the company kept right with them. There was really fear of John L. Lewis that was fought in the county for a long time and gradually the Communists began to do it.

At least they did that until the law came. They didn't bother anything about them when it became the law that the miners could organize. If the company had bothered them, they could have been punished; the government would have come in and John L. would have moved in on them. John L. could have his union.

I don't know what brought about the change, but John L. Lewis was making inroads into some of the surrounding places. Some miners were still holding a big part of it—were still holding to their independent union. It got out that I wrote their charter. "Say," somebody said, "who wrote that charter?" They didn't have anybody in the union or in the United Mine Workers who found out who wrote the charter. Of course they knew I was working every which way and they knew I was up there, but it wasn't normal for them to think that I wrote the charter. I don't know who first thought it.

And since I've been in Huntington, Smith Jones who was the principal [of all-black Douglass Junior and Senior High School] here for a while said, "You know, I used to get nervous for you. I used to feel for you. I knew you were going to get your head cut off or your head shot off, running around those mountains. Nothing ever did happen to you."

I said, "Are you disappointed?"

He said, "No, I'm not disappointed, but I was just thinking about what a chance you took."

And I said, "I didn't write that charter."

They never would believe me. They don't yet. I didn't write it. I didn't know when it was written. I just knew they had one. I knew a lawyer and in my mind he was the one that did it, but I never did say anything.

The independent union dissolved itself and they took their treasury and divided it around among scholarships and things like that. I helped them do that because I knew where the scholarships would belong. There were different projects that they had and then they gave so much to the president and the officers and they had a big affair for everybody and dissolved it. Then everybody joined the United Mine Workers. Now since nearly everybody's dead or moved down there in McDowell County, both white and black, nothing's said about it.

In the long run, the United Mine Workers won out. But then the company began putting in super equipment. They had a coal tipple down there worth about forty or fifty million dollars. It does everything—even dig the coal. They got machines and they opened this terrific vein now and I've forgotten how many feet and how many thousands of acres of it that they owned. They keep a maintenance crew there and some people, but most of those houses for those thirteen[4] U.S. Steel operations they tore down and moved to Kentucky or some other place where they were needed. It's still pretty, but they don't have the big place like they did. They have the offices. They don't have the bank. They have the department store; that's owned by somebody there. The company just dissolved itself. If it had been level [nonmountainous], the holdings of U.S. Steel would have been as big as Huntington. There were about six thousand men working in the same mine at one time, so you can see where I could always pull people to have things, to have entertainment.

Gary, West Virginia, August 4, 1903. This photograph, looking south, was taken prior to construction of the main U.S. Steel office and the Catholic church. *(All photographs on the following pages courtesy of Eastern Regional Coal Archives, Craft Memorial Library, Bluefield, West Virginia)*

Last carload of coal from Buckeye Coal & Coke Co., Freeman, West Virginia. White mules were used only aboveground.

Number 3 Works, Gary, West Virginia, viewed from the clubhouse, August 4, 1903. Coke ovens near the power plant occupy the present site of the Gary football stadium.

Number 9 Works, Gary, West Virginia. This photograph shows the mine tipple and tipple row houses on the hillside.

Number 3 Works, Gary townsite, July 28, 1920

Gary Bottom looking toward Methodist Church's parsonage

Gary Bottom, August 4, 1931. Lodge is on hill at right, and Gary District High School, for black students, is below it, at center rear.

Wedding party on Church St. in Gary, West Virginia

V

*political
life*

IT is almost impossible to create a separate category for Memphis Tennessee Garrison's "political" activities, because she was acutely aware of the power dimensions in all arenas of her life. But the activities traditionally defined as "politics" are those for which Garrison is now remembered.

As a teacher, Garrison was following an acceptable woman's role. Yet Garrison clearly challenged gender roles as a player in politics. Still, she makes almost no reference to gender discrimination. Her stories of political activity focus, once again, on herself as an individual, interacting with other individuals—who happened to be men or women, black or white. It is not clear whether this arises out of her failure to perceive gender role limitations, or her dismissal of those limitations as not applicable—for she never says.

The issue of race is clearer. She was acutely aware of herself as a black person, although she consistently evaluated other people as individuals, and not as members of a race. Her discussion of McDowell County politics is clearly based on race, and later on, her work with the NAACP arose from her racial concerns. Only twice does she speak of herself as a black *woman*—when she describes her run for the school board, and when she comments on the description of her as a Negro woman in a newspaper story.

It is in her discussion of loyalty to the Republicans that Garrison's remarkable attachment to principle becomes clear. Garrison's life was guided by deeply felt principles, which stay in place despite seemingly "obvious" contradictions. It is interesting that Garrison felt it necessary to explain, and justify, finally voting for some Democrats when there is almost nothing else in her narrative that she justifies.

Garrison was not a typical "political" person. She was not seeking status or prestige. She was willing to work behind the scenes. She was willing to do the "grunt" work. She was willing to buck the "big boys"—and paid the price. She was willing to hold a high office (when invited to be on a national commission) but revealed no resentment when she apparently was not invited back for another term. Later in her life, when she was questioned as to why she did not seek "higher," she answered: *To me, I didn't have any talent that could gain any more appreciation than what I was having.*

Politics in the southern coalfields were intimately bound to the power of the operators. But although the company was powerful, it was not all-powerful. And Garrison's account makes it clear that the black community understood both the extent of the company's power and its limits. She was a keen inside observer of politics functioning in this period of the history of West Virginia. This was not a downtrodden and helpless black population, but a highly organized and politically skillful constituency.

Garrison's involvement in the NAACP gave her additional resources for political work. She now had an organization that supported her primary agenda. She now had a source of political and cultural education for herself and her community. And she now had causes that transcended the coalfields and placed her on the national playing field. She gives us her view of that playing field—the awed respect she held for certain persons in the NAACP leadership, and the veiled references to those whom she found less than worthy. Like the Republican party, the NAACP became one of her principles, and she gave it her unqualified support—even if individuals within it did not: *The cause you represent overlaps the unpleasantness that comes to you.*

In later references she acknowledges the existence of the "new" civil rights organizations, but makes it clear that their work would not have been possible without the legal staff of the NAACP. And although she spoke with pride of the involvement of the youth and the more militant organizations, she never wavered in her support of the NAACP.

It is difficult in today's society to imagine the terror invoked by lynching. Today's terrorists blow up airplanes or buildings, but they do not infiltrate our own communities and single out our fathers or sons for retribution. Nor are today's terrorists working in complicity with our own government. Yet for several decades black people were subjected to an undercurrent of fear that walked with them all the time—the fear of lynching. Lynch mobs, drunken renegades, or the organized Ku Klux Klan—all could murder black people without fear of serious consequence. Racism was the accepted mode of thought. Those who stood up or spoke out faced severe consequences. Thus, for an organization to begin a national campaign to end lynching entailed a level of courage on the part of its participants that went beyond normal expectations.

What is interesting in Garrison's version of her involvement is the absence of fear. Nowhere in the interview does she indicate the risks she took and the dangers she faced. In the epilogue, Carolyne Brown notes her respect for Garrison's level of courage. But Garrison's voice is simply that of determination to do a job that needs to be done. Whether the sense of fear faded over time, or whether it was always simply absent, is something we will never know.

Her account of the arrest of two poor Negro boys on charges of murder is an example of the "legal lynchings" that were occurring in the South at that time (and, to some extent, continue today). Garrison's response was immediate and typical of her ability to seize the initiative. She dreamed up a way to raise the money for the boys' defense—through the sale of Christmas seals—and launched a fundraiser that eventually grew to become the national organization's biggest.

The NAACP was not just about lynching and national

politics. For Garrison, the NAACP opened a door to black history and culture. She not only walked through the door, but also brought famous people back through that door right into the heart of the coalfields. Garrison's use of her networks to attract black musicians, intellectuals, and political figures speaks to the respect she had earned at the national level.

And it is important to realize that Garrison was not alone. The Appalachian black community produced some of the important intellectuals and leaders of that period. She mentions some but leaves out Carter G. Woodson, the "Father of Black History," who also worked in the coalfields of Fayette County, West Virginia.

The NAACP used Garrison as an organizer, propagandist, and fundraiser. But Garrison used the NAACP to do what she never stopped doing—nurturing West Virginia's black children. Under the umbrella of that organization she was able to reach further than just Gary and McDowell County; she was able to reach the entire state. Her description of the float for the celebration of both the state's birthday in 1963 and the Emancipation Proclamation anniversary is more than a description of a float—it is testimony to Garrison's ability to create pride and build self-esteem among youth.

Garrison had started the Emancipation Day celebration years before—except that it was held on April 9, not the official date. Her explanation of this discrepancy raises an interesting question of who determines historical dates, and how. Garrison's mother said that the slaves found out they were free when Lee surrendered to Grant. So *that* was the day of emancipation. "Official" historians, of course, said the day was January 1, the day the proclamation was issued. Now, which is the "real" date—the day someone signed a paper, or the day that the people were actually freed? Who gets to decide the meaning of history, after all?

chapter 16

✳

Politics

When schools were organized through a district unit, the board of education had commissioners. They debated which teachers to hire and looked after the buildings. Later we moved from a district unit to a county unit—after more progress came—and it's now a county unit. But then it was district. The person who owned the most in that district or the company who owned the most, who worked the most men in that district would be the persons who would be influential. They were the people who had the votes to get what they wanted. At one time when we had school districts, the company ruled that district. For instance, Adkins District was ruled by United States Steel. I've forgotten how many miles were in that district. All of the district boards of education were under the supervision of the United States Steel. The boards were elected on the county ticket, but the persons elected had been picked by company people. In the primary they picked them and they were elected, and they functioned according to company wishes, and the big boss of the company was usually the president of the board. When they were elected, they elected him the president.

I don't really know of anybody who was for the people and who bucked the company and lost everything because of it. It pointed that way, but you had nothing to substantiate it. I went against the Colonel once, and he took my school. He was president of the board. I went to see him and said, "Colonel, what did you take my school for?"

When I lost my school I knew what had happened. I had campaigned for a Negro for sheriff. Nobody ever knew a Negro that they would want running for sheriff, and a fellow in Keystone by the name of Joe Parsons ran. I'm somewhat of a rebel and I thought it was grand that Joe Parsons had the nerve to run. That's what I admired so much, and I think that I spoke for him at one of the meetings in my district. I put it to them. Well, after the election was over and he didn't get it, I got my school back.

The Colonel didn't say much at all about it. The man who was over my school was his nephew; when I went back he said, "Where have you been so long?" I said, "You know where I've been. Your uncle threw me out on my nose," and he said, "I heard about that." And he just laughed, and we laughed about it, you know. And that was all of it.

But Joe Parsons made a good run. He lost the election but he didn't lose his job; he was elected to something else in the county. He wasn't a miner; he was a businessman in Keystone for a long time and then he worked for Baldwin Felts Detective Agency. Then, later, one of the coal companies, the Houston Company that was based at Elkhorn, moved their offices to Cincinnati and Parsons was their man over all that area to see that the men were all right, to protect them. He was a kind of law for that place, and he had a fine salary and the people liked him—black, white—everybody. In the election he had more to lose than most Negroes, had but he was not so tied up that he did lose it. He was independent, even so. And he made a fine showing.

He was bucking everything, the county organization even—the county political organization. He was not a subservient sort of fellow. He knew where he was going. He was about as smart as the rest of them and he had a brother-in-law who is one of the most brilliant men this state ever produced, Harry Capehart. He later became a district judge of, I think, this area. Capehart was born near Guyandotte, and they were West Virginia all. Capehart went to the legislature, two terms, too.

Until [Franklin D.] Roosevelt's time, the late years—Negroes couldn't belong to the Democratic party. Roosevelt was the first Democratic president to win in McDowell County for forty years. The Republicans held it the first time for forty years. Everything was Republican; there were a few Democrats here and there, but they never had a chance of doing very much unless some big Republican liked them and he'd say "Let us let him be so and so." Then he could get in. But the Democrats had their own organization. Negroes did not attend a Democratic meeting. They weren't wanted. I don't know why, but they didn't want Negroes. If you weren't a Republican, you wouldn't be anything. You wouldn't vote. You didn't go to their meetings. They'd ask you what you wanted. And Roosevelt, when Roosevelt came in and was elected, the Negroes helped elect him. They were sick of the whole thing, forty years of that.

I don't think that any Negroes tried to belong to the Democratic party. They didn't want to. The Republicans were doing everything that they wanted done at that time. Or the Republicans were doing everything, most likely, that could be done in that area. This was the beginning of the thing. You know, beginnings always interest me. It's a kind of thing that presents the problems you're going to meet later on. The Democrats began to court the Negro. They began to give him everything. He was welcomed at everything and he was appointed to things. It started with appointments that we'd never had before. In two years in the landslide of '32, the whole county was cleaned out of Republican officeholders except for two, the clerk of the court and another. In '36, everything was wiped out and the Democrats have held the balance of power since.

The Negro supported the political party that he thought was to his best interest and his best interest was the party that was approved by the coal company. Any party, any party that was in power had good support from the coal companies. After the Hoover recession or depression, there were two parties. I mean, there were two parties all the time, but just this one had held power all those forty years. But then it became that it was not so overwhelmingly one-sided; it was a competition; there was more competition between them because the Negro gradually began to change his vote after the Depression. He made friends with the Democratic party. The Democratic party sought the Negro vote then. And some of the men who were interested would sit down with you and say, "What was the source of the power that kept the Republicans in so long?" And they learned who the people were who kept the Republicans in. They learned that the power of the political party was the teacher and they began to woo teachers and fire teachers, too, and they did it. I stayed out for years because I wouldn't register Democratic.

I became a Republican the first time I voted and they were taking registrations. If you were interested in politics, you got out there and helped people register. They didn't pay you for going and getting those names. You got out there for your own sake. There were some rabid segregationists—Long and Eastland*—you know how they all wanted to keep a Negro in his place. They would ask you your political beliefs and there wasn't anything else for me to say but Republican because I had known that you couldn't even go to Democratic meetings. It was normal for me to say Republican, because they were the party of Lincoln and it was normal for me to think Lincoln was the greatest leader because history had told me so, and my mother was a slave. So, we couldn't be anything else. I was like that man they talked about down in Mississippi. After integration he went into some big place where they said that a Negro would never eat. They said if the deceased owner knew it he'd turn over in his grave. And this man went in and sat down at the table and said, "Turn over, Harry." So it was that sort of feeling. The Democrats would have to turn over. Naturally, the whole group would have to turn over. We wanted them to turn over. It was time to make the turn. In the whole place there would be very few Democrats until they learned the lesson of finding out where the strength was. It was like Delilah cutting off Samson's hair. They began to woo the Negroes until they found out where the strength lay. Then they found out. They began to woo them for their votes and they got in. And they are still the majority party in the state now. They were very minority when I started out. The start of it was in the Depression, but they have remained the majority because of what they have done. The Democrats have become the liberal party, and Negroes have come in because they were. They began to give

*Democrat Russell Long was senator from Louisiana (1948–87); James Eastland, Democrat from Mississippi, was appointed senator for three months in 1941 and served as elected senator 1943–58.

better jobs, and they began to give you everything the Republicans gave you. Then they added a little more to put the finishing touch. We didn't lose anything under the Democrats. They saw to it that we didn't because we would have reasoned, "I can get this under the Republicans. I don't need to change." Many of them changed for reasons that they had to change to hold their jobs. You couldn't beat them so you joined them.

I remained a Republican because I wanted to. If I had changed, I would have felt like I was being disloyal to what I had always believed in, and if other people had remained through a lot of things and stayed what they were, I could do the same. When I would think about changing, my grandfather would come up in my mind. When my mother would rub his back—the old man was old then and of course he ached—my mother was there and she'd rub his back for him and those welts, those on his back, those striped welts every which way, ridges just like—I can't think of anything that would remind me of it more than a washboard only they weren't even. But they were those kinds of ridges. I'd say, "Granddaddy, what's wrong with your back?" He said, "That's the bullwhip, Honey, but you ain't going to never feel it, 'cause you's free." I could not think of that and put down anything else but Republican. Anything that had saved me from that, any man who had spoken out against that, who had put his life on the line and died for us, I couldn't forget. Greater love has no man than this, that he'd give up his life for his fellow man. That's all Christ did; that's why when they shot Lincoln, the man who did it [John Wilkes Booth] said, "Now the South has been avenged." And it was the South who put those marks on my grandfather's back. That's history, that's Booth, that's what he said. And I just say that I have to be a Republican. I'm not saying the Republicans are always right, and I wasn't saying that all the Democrats were wrong. I knew a lot of fine people who were Democrats because of their conviction.

The switch came in Roosevelt's first election. I can't say that the company switched, and I wouldn't say that. When you use the term "coal company" you really mean the majority. The entire company wouldn't be for anything, the majority would be. They got the majority to vote for what they wanted, because every man would be what he is. There are too many men to say that each has to be a Democrat and support the party. They understood that there were a lot of people who bucked things, but they were outvoted. If they didn't win they went on, if they could, and kept their jobs and were contented until the next trial came. And it was after the first setup there in the '90s, early '90s they tell me. Of course, you know I didn't know anything about politics then. I learned it later from the people who did know, that after they had got the initial setup and gone up to '96, they had a very good setup so they said. That's when they brought in Negroes on transportation,* those operators did, and the Negroes voted for what they wanted. By '96 the Negro was ready to be voted for instead of doing all the voting.[1] He was ready to be voted for and then came the jobs of constable, justice of peace, member of board of education and they put up Negroes to vote for that and then that sold the Negro on the Republican party, of course. That ended in '32 with Roosevelt.

The Negro was a vital part in changing the whole county, and it was so all over the state where Negroes were engaged in the mines. The mining industry was basically the same. I don't think the company said anything because the companies had been busy feeding all those hungry miners, and I don't think it was so understood that this change was going to be made here with these hungry people. I think they had their choice and they used it.

I worked in political campaigns both statewide and national. I was in a picture with Hoover at the White House in Washington—the first time Hoover had ever had a picture taken with a Negro. And I was in New York. I was at headquarters on the fifth floor of the Waldorf. Mr. Hallanan** came back and named me as a member of the Eastern Planning Board to assist the committeemen, and I held that from '32 to '40, and I was chairman of the woman's committee. I wasn't involved in local politics at that time. I wasn't even in the county. I only knew generally what was going on, but I don't think that the Negroes who were appointed to any position tried to influence anything. When a Negro was appointed

*Method by which men were brought in to work in the mines at company expense, costs to be reimbursed later.
**Walter Simms Hallanan, Republican Committee chairman in West Virginia.

to a position, the politicians generally appointed one that wasn't going to give them any trouble in anything that they wanted to do. But Negroes took pride in those appointments.

I worked with the Republicans, and I was trying to think what my salary was. I think I got all expenses paid and fifty dollars a week, and that was good then. That was clear money for me. And I took leave. The Colonel gave me leave. I took leave of my school there at election time. Those eight years, I was in two locations. I took leave for the semester to carry on this campaign. And that's one thing the Democrats beat my head in with when I got back to teaching. They would say, "You can't campaign now. No teacher is allowed to campaign." I didn't campaign that year. They were punishing me for campaigning the year they didn't put me back. I said, "What'd you all take my contract for?" They said, "You've been campaigning and it's the law that no teacher can be out campaigning." Well, all the campaigning they had done would have been done by teachers. But you see, that's strategy. Then I was put back on the list of teachers and everything worked out all right.

chapter 17

✻

The Depression

The Depression is what wooed the Negro away from the Republicans. The Negro was hard hit by the Depression, the poor white man, too. They got both of those groups. That's what gave them the big victory for Roosevelt. That Hoover Depression was something else. I had little children that came to school in the morning—they walked, you know. They had school busses but not for the children round within walking distance. We didn't have as many hard-surface streets and roads then. The children would be cold and wet. It was raining some, and I'd always see that they were dried off when they got there. I knew that there were parents who were trying. My husband worked large groups of men and he'd give those men extra work trying to help them, so I knew those parents.

There was a restaurant right next to the school; an old lady ran it, and I contracted with her to have a big dish of cereal and some hot bread and butter ready for those children at recess time in the morning. She had cows and milk, and for almost two whole years, at least for a whole year, I fed those children. I never made any to-do about it because I was afraid the parents would be too proud or something so we just called it our recess party. And those little children—I had the first two grades, and I paid for the food myself; the lady wouldn't charge me anything for fixing it. The children would go get it, and each one brought his bowl and he washed it; I had spoons.

Coal production was way down; the men working it had what they called Hoover Orders. I think the company must have issued these Orders trying to feed their men. You'd go to the office like you'd go to get scrip to spend in the stores. You'd get these Orders, so much for the size of your family. And it was understood, I think, that whenever the men did get to work that they could pay it back. So the men didn't think they were being given anything; they were big and kept their pride.

I don't know if they did pay it back, but they had their pride. They kept their Orders, but you couldn't buy everything with that Order. For instance, I think they couldn't buy a lot of pop and candy like people will, you know. That's poor. You could buy potatoes and beans. They had the list made out of what you could buy. You could buy chickens; I don't know whether there was ever any ban on meat, or how much. Some of those people wouldn't have money. I know that those children didn't have enough to eat. And that's one part of my teaching, that I never mention when the children come back to see me. That's one year that we never mention. I never mention it to them, and none of them, I recall, mention it to me. They recall things we've done, you know. We talk just about living around and laugh, but I noticed when we talk about things, we have never mentioned our breakfast, never mentioned that.

Inside of them, now that they're grown, they understand what happened. They were little then and they ate the breakfast, and it was what they needed. Since they've been grown they have known why I did it. They didn't know then, and I have respected their pride. I have never, at any time, mentioned that. Oh, I've talked with the teachers a little about it and they say, "You had your feeding program right there." But I've never mentioned it to a child for fear that I'd hurt his pride. But that was a life saver. Here they'd be just a sitting there as listless, and that hot oatmeal and butter and milk and biscuits and a little jelly or something would come on. I'd almost have to get a switch to make them get in their seats. They'd get so excited. I'd say to another teacher, "Honey, I had a roomful of children; they couldn't move. Now listen to that racket

The Depression / 139

in there." I'd hear the children saying, "Sit down so and so. Ah, you shut up." I would be out in the hall or something then. I said, "Now, that's all the difference in the world in a filled stomach." You see why I'm like I am when you see the experiences.

And why I did it, I don't know. I don't have any explanation for it, but teaching, and that sort of thing helped. I still have it; it's so much a part of me that I get mad with myself for doing it. Why did I do that? If something happens, somebody comes here or something and I'll look at them and if they need a dollar, well, I'm liable to give them a dollar fifty. If that person needs that, I can sense the need. And I couldn't spend it better, yet I get peeved at myself for doing it. It's some kind of compulsion, because we were never hungry. I had one friend to tell me that she did certain things and she says that she can't stand poverty and what it stands for. She said that she'd been too near it herself, in her life. Well, I wasn't near it. I hadn't been near it. We always had plenty of food, always had too much food.

I couldn't consider myself rich. That didn't enter into it. I wasn't rich. When I give, I give for some need. I know that person needs that certain thing worse than I do. I still don't consider that I have enough to be doing it like that. I just do it; all I have ever done in the world is to meet a need. I don't know where that idea came from. I don't know why. I can't tell why now. What set me off was that I got to looking at too many little hungry children. I had forty-two little hungry children sitting there and just from that, I just remember getting it done. I paid for their food and the old lady and her daughter fixed it and didn't charge me for preparing it at all. She had cows, and these big jars—looked like the jars that they have big pickles and things in them. These jars would come over full of milk. They had a dipper in there and little cups would come out from under the desks, little tin cups with little handles to them. They would wash their cups and dry them off on paper in the place and put them back. And I can see those children. I've often wished I had a picture of them, not because they were there but just to see what happened as their little hungry stomachs were filled.

chapter 18

Association with the Republican Party

I campaigned for Hoover; I cam-
paigned for Landon.* I don't think I ever supported Franklin Roosevelt.
I had a cartoon when they were going to run Roosevelt for a fourth
term, I believe, or a third term. It had a baby on it with his hand on its
chin; this baby is looking at this card that says a fourth term and he says,
"A fourth term?" Well somebody put the cartoons out; they were put
out at meetings and people around the room just went into stitches. It
was a lot of fun. They thought the same thing; it wasn't just the Republicans. This baby, in other words, was thinking that Roosevelt was going
to be there until he got grown and wasn't giving him a chance. I liked
the things Mr. Roosevelt did; I liked to hear him speak. "My friends . . ."
he would say. He had a good speaking voice and all, and I like good
speaking; I don't care if it's for or against something. I like to hear what
they have to say. But I don't think I ever voted for him. I don't recall ever
voting for him.

I was head of the Colored Republican Women from 1932 to 1940.
I arranged for speakers for the state—people all over the state. If they
didn't have a speaker for a big mammoth rally they were having in a
county, they would contact me and I would have a speaker there from

*Alfred Landon, the Republican presidential candidate who lost to Franklin D. Roosevelt
in 1932.

somewhere around the country. The Negro and white groups, politically, usually met together at these meetings, so I didn't have to bother about race. The candidates didn't care who they were so long as they were spouting off their virtues and why they should be elected. So, I had some very outstanding people who came in. There was Oscar DePriest who had been a congressman from Illinois. I think he came into the state about that time. He was a great fellow. He was the first Negro elected from Illinois. I had Miss [Nannie Helen] Burroughs, who was head of a training school [National Training School for Women] in Washington, D.C.; and Roscoe Conklin Simmons, one of the greatest orators anywhere, came. He'd run William Jennings Bryan or anybody a race for orations; that he could do. People would sit all night to listen to him. In New York, they sat until three o'clock in the morning until that dinner was over just to hear Roscoe speak. They didn't move. In Washington it was the same way. We stayed there until four o'clock, until everybody got a chance to do things that they wanted to be done. Politicians had come from all over to a meeting at the White House. Hoover was in and they sat there until four o'clock that morning at the White House. The chef prepared their dinner—they sat there until four o'clock that morning when Simmons spoke; everybody sat there to hear him—that was white and black. At seven o'clock we were going to bed. Who cared! Well, I had him to come when I was running for the board of education. And then I had an editor—some editor of a paper. During that time for the campaigns, there were at least dozens of people who were available. That's one of the services that I did render.

Then there were women's clubs—I had a list of those clubs, and anywhere within range, I would go to help them. Sometimes they'd call for the person themselves. I would be going; I had a car at my disposal. I was paid a stipulated salary, not during the election, but during the campaign for the general election or the state election. That election was small and usually the candidates took care of whatever expenses there were. I covered McDowell County once for a candidate, and he got elected. They had put him out the year before. One part of McDowell County that had a heavy vote didn't vote for him, so I was sent in. I made about twelve speeches for him.

Another service was that they wanted women to have their own clubs in the precincts and districts and counties. So most likely I would be called on by the county chairman to come in to assist in setting up women's clubs in the other areas of the county so that they could get their instructions and their meeting places would be near. There are many counties and hundreds of clubs through the state and they got their campaign literature and all through those clubs; so that was another service rendered by the state chairman.

If the election was in November, we started in the summer, June or July, getting headquarters set up all around about as they do now. They were ready to be staffed in late July, and from then on up to the November election things would be humming night and day. The concentration was on the last three months before the election. The Congressional elections didn't have as much work and all—as many things to do as in the general election. That was the one that everybody was a part of. We worked very hard in it. And we worked very hard in the other elections, too, but we didn't do the traveling that we would do in that general election. We would be called to Washington and we would be called to the state office. Something would come up and we would get into that, but in the Congressional election, it was mostly done around in the local areas, and we didn't have the state office and all as we had in the general election.

I also served as a member of the Eastern Planning Board. It was the outcome of a trip to Washington and the White House—we were there around eight or ten days. At the time they formed what was called the Eastern Planning Board; they selected from two to four persons from the states that composed the Eastern area. I think they came from Ohio on through the New England states, up in that northeasterly section. They were to assist in any way that the national committee men requested. We made a trip to Washington—Mr. Nutter* and myself were members from West Virginia. We were also in Charleston several times; we were present as the state Republican organization. They didn't call it that, but the state people met once a year or once every two years. One

*T. G. Nutter, Charleston attorney and civic activist.

meeting was held in Huntington while I was a member of the board. It was all political; if they had something new or something had come up, all the chairmen would meet with us. Or if someone had gone East or if the two members of the planning board had gone to that meeting, we would all be at this state meeting to pass on to the West Virginia group what was the latest thing and what was going to happen and all. We came to the end of the Eastern Planning Board—Mr. Nutter and myself—because the Democrats took over and no longer needed all our little planning.

Politics is really interesting if you want to get down to it and like it, if you like people and like seeing things happen. Sometimes when everything looks like it's just set and it can't miss, you're in for a letdown because anything can happen. That was true of Dewey.* We just knew he'd win when we were going to bed and left Dewey to his own.

I didn't always support the Republicans on the presidential level. I supported whom I felt like supporting. One of the Kennedys came on the scene, and oh, boy, I could rattle on about that Kennedy family and how swell they were and how cultured and what that meant, and the power and all.

And people said, "Memphis, what are you?"

"I'm a Kennedy Republican," I'd tell them. So they had quite a laugh around in Republican circles. No, I didn't deny it. I was.

[John F.] Kennedy was the last Democrat I supported. Of course, Johnson came on; he came in because of Kennedy.** Normally, I wouldn't have supported him. I had a lot against Johnson until the last years—this last time. I found out a lot of things Johnson had done that were very fine, that were outstanding. He was a good man. I know that it is not how liberal you are. You obey the wishes of your party; other than that, they read you out of the party if they want to. You are not an individual in politics. You do the will of your party. You're supposed to adhere to the principles of your party. Well, then, I picked my candidates. I picked

*Republican Thomas E. Dewey lost the presidential election to Democrat Harry S Truman in 1948.
**Vice President Lyndon B. Johnson became president on the death of John F. Kennedy in 1963 and was subsequently elected president in 1964.

the state and I picked the nationals. And I did the same thing under this last election. I picked whom I wanted nationally, and I picked whom I wanted in the state. And there's no such thing as a straight ticket for me. Somehow or other the hearts and goodwill and the liberal attitudes of people ought to be considered, and I reached that point. No matter what party he belongs to, this is a man that I choose, that sort of thing. And I got to the point that I acquainted myself more thoroughly with the people who were running. I went back and got their history, the record of what they had done and from that I determined whom I wanted to vote for. I didn't take what that man was out there saying he had done because most of the things they say are lies or a representation to carry their point. I've always had a feeling that I should do right regardless of what they did. I think if Robert Kennedy had lived, I would have been a Kennedy supporter again. When I saw Robert Kennedy and the things that he had done, I felt that he put his life on the line for what he believed in.

I don't know now whether I supported [Richard] Nixon [for president in 1964] or whether I supported Johnson, because I split that ticket up in so many ways it wasn't even funny. I supported Arch Moore.* I remember because I thought it was time for a change. I thought that Hulett Smith** had let down [Governor William Wallace] Barron's administration. I thought Barron was a good administrator. Barron was a good politician even though he did get in jail, nearly. He was smart enough not to get in.† I thought Arch Moore would be the best man. I liked [James M.] Sprouse. He has his day coming, too. I think Moore couldn't have gotten in without the help of the Democrats; lots of Democrats felt it was time for a change. I like Callebs,†† too. I like the underdog.

---

*Three-term Republican governor of West Virginia, elected 1968 (defeating Democrat James M. Sprouse), 1972, and 1984.

**Democrat, elected governor of West Virginia in 1964.

†After leaving office in 1965, Governor William Wallace Barron was tried for bribery but acquitted; in a later trial, however, he was convicted of jury tampering and spent four years in prison.

††John Callebs, Republican who ran for secretary of state in West Virginia, opposing John D. Rockefeller IV in 1968.

chapter 19

✴

The Negro Artists' Series

I began the Negro artist series in the
twenties. Now where did I get the idea? It seems that I was somewhere
and met some of the people who had a quartet and who had sung at the
schools. It seems to me that we had something at the schools and these
people came.

I know that Dr. DuBois* came to Bluefield around 1918. I just heard of
him. I didn't see him. Around in the twenties I got a copy of the *Crisis.*
That's the first time I'd had that magazine. And in this *Crisis,* it spoke of
all these different people and what they did. The NAACP was behind
bringing all these people to communities. The club was for the advancement of colored people and to bring these people in was advancing colored people, too. Then I knew that different schools had had them; they
had come to Charleston. I would say that this was advancing and the
National Association for the Advancement of Colored People is helping.
That's where I learned it from. I got the idea to get these people from
New York—these people who were available and these people who would
give concerts—I got it from the NAACP. They had already had Black
Patti,** [vaudeville performer] Bert Williams—they already had all that

*W. E. B. DuBois, black educator and writer; editor of the *Crisis,* journal of the NAACP.
**Classically trained soprano Mildred S. Joyner, also known as Sissieretta Jones, was called
the "Black Patti" in comparison with white opera singer Adelina Patti.

there in New York. And then I would ask them for the addresses of these people who were available and I would correspond with these people. Right then, I began to inquire. They wouldn't come for one little place. It wasn't enough money. I had to find five places through the state. If one dropped out, I'd keep trying until I got five. I had the original Fisk Jubilee Singers. I had the Williams Singers. Oh, I had dozens of them for years after. I had violinists, Wesley Howard from Howard University, and Maude Cuney Hare, a Creole musician from New England, and Willis Richardson, the baritone. They also came to Huntington. I had Huntington on the list; I had Charleston and Bluefield on the list. When the opera singer came, West Virginia State College took her so that I could have five places. It's a matter of record how the company backed my Negro Artists' Series and those people who came from year to year to bring some entertainment and culture. I had [radio news commentator] Lowell Thomas for a week. He went to all ten of those theaters that the company owned and we had all the schoolchildren. Black and white came and the company paid for it.

I'd meet people when I traveled in the summer. I'd go to school; then maybe I'd go to New York for the rest of the time. Some of the girls would be going. We'd travel like that and find out who some of the performers and speakers were, then I would have them come down. That went on about twelve years. It made an impression on those people.

I kept a list of all of those people that I had each year. There was one man that became the head of the music department for the Atlanta University setup. He was at Clark College.* We had some girls whom I had taught and they went to college down there.

The first thing that he asked them when he saw them was, "And you come from Gary?"

They said, "Yes."

"Do you know Mrs. Memphis Tennessee?" he asked.

"She was our first teacher," they told him.

"Give her my love," he told them.

De Koven Killingsworth was his name. Every once in awhile, some-

*Atlanta University and Clark College were historically black schools in Atlanta, Georgia. They consolidated in 1988 as Clark Atlanta University.

body will mention him. He's old now and retired. But people tell me, "He says that he knows you. He talks about you." Every once and awhile somebody comes in and says that.

The financial backing for the series came from the sale of tickets. We weren't making anything; we just made enough to pay the artists and take care of their expenses. The NAACP would sell tickets to the people to come. And if I didn't sell enough tickets to the miners and their families, then I'd sell tickets to the head people, to the man and all. If I didn't sell enough tickets, I'd never ask him for anything, but if I missed, I'd tell the Colonel if he asked.

He'd say, "Memphis, did you have enough for your colored singers?"

I'd say, "Yeah," or, "Colonel, I lacked twenty-five dollars."

"Who paid it?" he'd ask.

And I'd say, "The principal, Mr. Moon. He gave me the twenty-five dollars."

"Well, write Moon a check," he'd say to his secretary. "Write Memphis a check to give to Moon to pay the money back."

Then the Colonel would tell me always, "Memphis, when your big colored people come in, bring them in my office to see me. I want to meet these fine colored people."

All of the people came to the performances. Some of those people had never heard a singer. Some of the miners had come from the foothills of Alabama and from all down in the red clay of Georgia. They had come to United States Steel on transportation to make money in the mines and to bring their families and their children. They'd come and listen. They'd come and listen.

Maybe sometime you'd see a lady with a baby and she'd say, "I named the baby Clarice after that pretty girl that you brought last year." The performer's name would be Clarice Michaels or Jones or Brown or whatever. And maybe she was one of those girls who had a solo part in one of those songs that Jeanette MacDonald* and them used to sing. Sometimes I'd have people who were the heroes in plays. And then the pictures came—the movies came. After that, these people saw what others

*Singer who starred in Broadway and Hollywood musicals.

were doing and how they had made it. The saw a whole change, and their lives were changed.

The last artist who came was this opera singer, Caterina Jarboro. She'd never seen anything like this in her life and she wondered how we kept our shoes white, how we lived in a place like this. Boy, she just kind of looked down her nose at me. She was well dressed, and she had sung all over Europe in the finest places, and she had all this training. She was with the Chicago Grand Opera Company, and she had the summer idle and she took these extra engagements. I was laughing up my sleeve at her, too. She didn't bring her accompanist and I had to get one from West Virginia State. We were having the performance at the Pocahontas Theater in Welch. Dr. [Prince Ahmed] Williams from West Virginia State was the accompanist. He had met her in New York, so I had her stop at the doctor's house. It was a lovely home over in Keystone, and I went over to meet her and made all of the arrangements about the theater. Lewis Furniture Company had put these lovely, gorgeous rugs on that stage for her to lie flat on her back and sing the death scene—Aida sealing herself in that tomb with her prince. The floral company had sent flowers and the theater manager was still laughing at us for bringing grand opera to the coal miners. So he charged me $175 for the theater; he had to do without his picture, you see, that night. It was Sunday night. And $400 for her coming was what I had to pay her. Now you know, I had to sweat with all this, but I was just so determined. Then the advertising—the *Welch Daily News* did the advertising—all those cards that they made and those big placards; advertising was a hundred and some dollars. I went all out on that one because that one was at the theater and all groups were coming, all the county was coming. I had advertised it all over the county, you see. Most of the other events were held in the school in Gary, but this one, this was something special! I hadn't had one for a whole year, so I took it to the county seat and didn't have the school have it or the NAACP.

It rained that night; man, it rained! You would have thought it was a cloudburst. Memphis, even the heavens are against you! Even the heavens are weeping. We had this woman's club at this time, patterned it after the woman's club in Welch. They had cultural things for their people and I was bringing black culture to black people. I was going to go over and join them for a while when I was through counting the money. Well, I had money to pay the singer. I had money to pay half of the printing. I didn't have any money to pay the theater. I had taken in around six hundred dollars which had been gobbled up with all the extras, you know, between six and seven hundred—that's a lot of money from there.

I just had the people from close around. Nobody came from out of those hollers and from miles up those railroads at night with a storm like that. They came from Gary; that's seven or nine miles away. And the people in Welch came. I guess I had about three hundred people but that theater holds about two thousand or more. So you know what it looked like. She sang as if the place were full. In her mind she peopled that place out there because she was magnificent. And when the lights would go off and all, she wasn't singing to empty benches, she was singing to people and she had a wonderful voice. She was a real professional. She had to go back at the end of the next week because they were opening in New York at the opera house again. She had brought her costumes just like they were. The people had never seen costumes like that. The mayor, the doctors, the white hospital staff, attorneys, and bankers— they all came. The florists at our club set those flowers on the stage. The singer had a polite little song that she sang and she threw the bouquets to the audience and, oh, they scrambled for them. She had this basket as she sang and she was pretty and as charming as she could be; she was young then. That was the talk of the town for a long time—this opera singer that I'd brought.

Oh, she was wonderful!

So the theater people got together but said not to tell me. They were just waiting for me. I made them the last ones to go to when I paid the bills.

"Oh, I said, I'll see you as soon as I get things—everything straightened out."

I paid it all and I had about nine dollars left, so I wasn't going to see them until the next day. I didn't have it.

I saw Mr. Rogers, the theater man, and I said, "I'll see you tomorrow." He looked all surprised at me being happy about seeing him tomorrow.

I got down there and he said, "Come in," and we sat down. I didn't say a word.

He said, "Well."

I said, "Well, what?"

He said, "Well, you owe us some 175 dollars."

I said, "Where am I going to get it from?"

I showed him that I had his bill. All the other bills were paid. His was on top and I handed it to him. Then he looked at it and he marked it paid and handed it back to me. I didn't try any more. That was it. There was too much work and we lived too far. The people who were willing to work, I couldn't contact them as I should. I had worked myself to death. I had quit everything else. I had quit building everything and was just doing that. I'd neglected my home and everything and was just doing that. That's the only way to get it done. So I didn't do that anymore. About two or three years after that, I had this pageant, "The Progress of the American Negro," and they let me have the theater again.

We had a regular Ninth of April celebration called Emancipation Day. I helped start it. It had been celebrated in different parts of the country, but not there. The NAACP sponsored the Ninth of April celebration, or we said that they did it. They didn't ever hear about it until it was time for it to happen, but they were the ones who powered it. We called it "Emancipation Celebration," and then people said we had the wrong time because the Emancipation Proclamation was issued on the first of January. My mother said we didn't have the wrong time. She said, "The first of January, we didn't know it was such a thing as that piece of paper. We didn't know we was free 'til Lee surrendered to Grant. That's when we knew it; we were slaves 'til the surrender."

We started to call it Freedom Day after we began to get criticism. We had been teaching bad history. The first of January '63 was the time, not the ninth of April '65. So we settled that by celebrating and calling it Freedom Celebration. On that day everything quit; every operation on the place quit. We held ballgames and all kinds of games. There were all kinds of people and speeches—some political; somebody sometimes would set up their campaign at the Ninth of April celebration and would come and speak. It would go on into the night when there'd be a lecturer come in. I had this Negro from Chicago who was the first senator—a big fellow. I've forgotten his name [Oscar De Priest]. There was also a first cousin of Booker T. Washington,* Roscoe Conklin Simmons, who spoke for us. And people would come from everywhere. We had this auditorium and the glee clubs, the school glee clubs would sing. Beautiful! The music would be fine, and I'd let every person have his way. I'd sit back like I wasn't doing anything and watch it, and that was to keep peace and jealousies down.

The pageant was a Ninth of April activity. It brought in money, but the fellow who was managing it finally got in jail a little while about it. All I could do was furnish him the material. I wrote the thing and he took over to do the rest of it. He had trouble, but I didn't because I had done my part. I never did get my script back. I got some of it, but he lost it in the melee. I left it up to them. The pageant was very nice itself. They had three periods in the history of slavery and the Negro. The first was Africa and the stage scene was a jungle. In the background was this pale cloth showing the ocean in the distance. And they were dressed in loincloths—they had more croker [burlap] sacks made up in loincloths. They cut fresh trees that day and they had a sandy beach. They had stuff to lay down to make the sandy beach. The Africans came down to see what had come in on the beach. They'd seen this thing on the horizon. Then here, I had a bunch of white men painted up and they had guns and chains and all of that and while the Africans were sleeping they came and chained them together. And one old woman in the audience stood and she said, "Jesus, I praise, glory hallelujah. Thank God for freedom in the midst of all this." That kind of broke the spell for a while. We laughed at her about it; it was all right that she did it; it was something new. Then they chained the Africans together and this same Professor Williams from West Virginia State College played the music. He had all that African chant, and finally, the white men disappeared to go to that ship and were replaced by their slave drivers. They were spaced with their whips, cracking their whips and marching the Africans to the beach. Now the marching was done over and over; looked like they were moving, but they

*Leading black educator who founded the Tuskegee Institute in Alabama in 1881; he lived in West Virginia for a time.

weren't. It looked like there were a lot of them, but there weren't many of them. A girl taught that slave dance to that bunch. She was a whiz; she was a physical ed teacher and it was the most beautiful thing you ever wanted to see. Well, then it went on until it was the present-day Negro. A young man who had been to Fisk trained all of the speakers; they talked about all of the things that the Negro has come to do, such as [scientist George Washington] Carver and his discoveries, and the singers, and sports—all of it. It was very elaborate and was nice.

The schools would also have exhibitions at the close of school and use all of the children even if they didn't say anything but a little speech. Mommas had them all dressed up for the stage. Before they closed the mines, it came to the point that you could hardly go into a house without finding somebody who was a college graduate. At every Negro home of that place there would be one in that house that would be a college graduate, which I thought was a terrific thing. I didn't have many people to talk to about it or anything, and not many of them had had the experience that I had had in it, but that's the way it was. I made a list once just to see. Out of this group of six hundred people who were hired that lived right in this little area, every home had a college graduate, sometimes two. But they didn't stay because there was nothing to do; they had gone. They had come and gone. Of course, they weren't going back to the mine once they had gotten out, gone to school. They weren't coming back anymore.

It was a new life for those people. I've seen my people come from nothingness. It's been an experience that I wouldn't have missed. They couldn't have given me a place out anywhere else. Knowing what I know now, I would've chosen the same life. People would ask me, "Why do you stay down in these hills? Why do you stay down here in these mountains? Why does a woman like you hang around a place like this?" And I, all I would say, all I can say is that I loved the people.

There was an article, "Mrs. Memphis T. Garrison, Lovable Lady." One of the top newsmen did it. He was sitting there. I didn't know he was interviewing me for an article in the paper. He was sitting there asking about the people down in the hills and he said he'd like to come down just to see the people I love so well.

Ours was one of the best coal mining setups anywhere—that United States Steel thing right here in West Virginia. I used to make big bulletin boards for the company—larger than their picture windows. They sat right in the middle of the town where you go to the bank—the bank, the post office, the church, the drugstore, and the department store—all of it was right there. You had to pass the bulletin board to get to them. On the bulletin boards I would have what the company was doing. What the output was—I'd get it from the office. I'd have miners digging coal in pictures, little stick pictures on there. How many tons this area got out. What they'd taken up for sampling.

In addition to doing those things, I was teaching school every day. My mother was there with me. She couldn't keep house or anything like that, but she could get those meals. We were always well fed and happy; she was an excellent cook. So you see all of it. I couldn't have done it if it wasn't for my momma. She would just beam when I said that. That's all she wanted to hear. That's the thing that took me through; that was the whole picture. I was what she wanted to be, what she would like to have been. If I was having company—there was no hotel for people to stay in, nowhere to stay—she was going to feed them. If they were coming back through our town, they would hunt for my house because of her warmth and hospitality. They would never forget her. All the things that I was doing, it was also she who was doing them—that's what she wanted to be. "Who's coming?" she would ask. "Who's so and so? I like quality folks." That's what she called them—quality folks. She liked to fix for them. She'd put on her big white apron or whatever she had, and, oh, she would be so gracious. She would smile and she would talk what she knew. Talk to them and ask them questions and they would tell her things. She had a lot of common sense; and then she'd get in one of her puns right there and that would clinch it. Everybody just had a wonderful time and they were coming back. So that went on for years, twenty years. So when they said, "Why do you stay down in that place? Why don't you come out where your talent will be appreciated?" To me, I didn't have any talent that could gain any more appreciation than what I was having.

chapter 20

Public Executions

*A man was hanged at the court-*house [in Welch in 1894]—John Hardy. I got the story of John Hardy from the detective who was working there. John Hardy was a gambler. John Hardy was a colorful figure. The sheriff, the people, the judge—all who knew him said he was the handsomest black man that they had ever seen—fine of feature, skin black, tall, well-formed, and dressed in the height of fashion of his time. He gambled. When paydays came, he gambled and he won. He was an ace gambler. He was dressed up all the time and he laid his gun beside him, so said his cronies. The officers who had the story told me about it and what happened to him. He wasn't a drinker. What happened to him to change him from this high-class gambler to where he could murder a man has just been one of the things that changes in human personalities for different reasons. But he killed this man over fifty cents, a small sum of money. And of course, the law came to hunt him and he hid around in the houses at Eckman, that's the place above Welch. He hid around in the houses. The people would feed him. They were afraid of him. The law couldn't find him. Finally, an officer found him and arrested him, and they caught the train to take them into Welch and they took him from one coach to another. Coaches were wide open; he jumped the train and pulled the officer off of it with him. Both of them rolled down the bank and were hurt, and he got loose. And then they finally got him and lodged him in jail. He told them he'd never hang, never hang. He stayed in that jail and watched them build the scaffold, and he said, "They'll never hang me." But they hanged him.

I remember hearing about lynching;[1] I remember it down in McDowell County at Elkhorn. Once when I was a child I came as near being on the scene of one as going to see the rope that was there that had been used. I was with a bunch of children, eight, ten, twelve—and there isn't a hill in McDowell County that we haven't climbed. They wouldn't go if they couldn't find me. "Go get Memphis," they'd say. We went way down five or ten miles from where we lived. We went up this hollow looking for chestnuts, and we came upon this coil of rope, coiled at the foot of this tree with a broken limb. Somebody broke the limb to get the rope down. It was tied to the limb. We didn't know anything about why this rope was there. We thought about cutting it up—"I'll give you a piece and we'll have a good jumping rope." But it was too big for us to take for a jumping rope. We went back home and kept talking about this coil of rope down there.

"Where at?" people asked us.

"Well, it was down in such and such a hollow," we said.

And then somebody said to one of the children's parents, "Did your boy tell you anything about a rope the children came across?" He said, "Yeah."

"That's where they hung Jim. They say they hung him there and left him."

The people had gone looking for him, and they had trouble finding him. Whoever hanged him, got out of the way. But the people did know that they'd hanged him somewhere so the crowd had gone looking for him, and they found him, cut him down, and buried him. They weren't the people who had done it; they were the people who knew that this had taken place. They never knew who did it. And this rope was the rope we had found. Well, we never went back there.

In my time, they lynched a couple of men in Greenbrier County. I don't remember for what cause, but I remember the lynching. And the National Association for the Advancement of Colored People, the

NAACP statewide—we didn't have a statewide conference then—but Harry Capehart, a prominent lawyer, went up to see about that. It was he who introduced the antilynching bill. West Virginia has an antilynching bill. The NAACP did back the law; I mean we did back Capehart.

The NAACP sent Walter White into the South and Walter White was white of skin, you know. Walter White put on those overalls with one strap over the shoulder and got him some licorice and tobacco and spit from here to nowhere and got his southern drawl on. He'd come from up there about Birmingham, and they'd tell him everything, tell him he'd just missed the party. They'd just lynched a Negro the night before. He investigated twenty-some lynchings before they discovered that they had given themselves away. That's why we got the information to move into Congress. You couldn't get your hands on them. They were lynching almost one a day, but you couldn't find out much. Nobody talked. Walter White moved in on that, but in this state, other than those two lynchings, I don't remember any lynchings that were reported.

chapter 21

Finding the NAACP

I first heard of the NAACP around 1918, and then Dr. DuBois came to Bluefield; the president brought him down to see the coalfields. United States Steel was the favorable setup, the best one, so they brought him there. He was the editor of the *Crisis*. Dr. DuBois left a copy of the *Crisis* with the lawyer who was my principal and he brought the *Crisis* to school. It was my *Crisis* from that time on.

Then after I started to read the *Crisis,* I took the agency and my schoolchildren sold it, and they'd give them six cents for each one. I had a hundred copies sent to me once each month. And the children would sell them at fifteen cents a copy, a little magazine. I had ten little agents and they got six cents apiece for each magazine that they sold. They covered all sections. I didn't have to have that many children, but they lived far apart and could take the magazine to their communities. One would live way up on a hill, another would live on Hunk Hill, and another one lived down in the bottom. Wherever they were, they'd sell the magazine. People would pay them. They'd bring me the nine cents, and they'd keep the six cents for selling them. Nine cents was what I paid for them. That year I sold a hundred copies a month through the schoolchildren. Everybody found out about that NAACP through the *Crisis;* that's why I had so many people the next spring to set up the first branch. That was the first branch in southern West Virginia. There were only two others in

West Virginia—Charleston set up in 1918 and Wheeling, I believe, had started one that year. And in 1921, Gary was the next one.

The *Crisis* made me know about the NAACP and that the branches were all around, how far it had gone. I'd heard of it just here and there. The NAACP was for helping those people that weren't having anything. It was for getting those things for Negroes that they didn't have. And this lynching—you see that year they lynched more than three hundred Negroes in these United States. They were lynching a Negro a day, nearly! And this organization was organizing wherever people knew so that they could do something about that, find a way to help. That was the searching, to get the lynching of our people stopped.

And this magazine, the *Crisis,* was the organ of the NAACP. In 1921, I was ready for a branch. I didn't have to get 50 members—I had around 250. I was ready to set up a branch there in Gary. New York sent their field secretary down—Pickens—William Pickens, a Negro who had just graduated from Yale. He came down and we had this big mass meeting and we got the officers and all. Our justice of the peace was president and I was the secretary. All the officers came down and then we began to help the national fight lynching. But it was that sort of thing.

Then we began the Ninth of April celebration with the NAACP; they had a committee. The committee was made up of representatives from all the works and they'd meet together and plan what they were going to have and the coal company would give refreshments. All the drinks—the lemonade, the ice, the pop, the ice cream—and we'd bring our own baskets, like chicken and stuff like that. Every fellow brought his own basket, but all this other stuff was there. The ball suits for the boys, all that stuff you see on a maypole*—they'd give me the goods [fabric] by the bolt for all that. And it went on for a long time. I don't know when we stopped it. I think since I left there they have had something. I was just a part of whatever it was. And I was happy. All I wanted to do was to get out and go somewhere and see somebody and be a part of that. I didn't want to leave there. All that was going on and I had all the help.

*Usually found at community or school celebrations early in May. Colorful strips of fabric or paper were attached to the top of a tall pole and twisted around it in an intricate pattern, usually by children marching or dancing around it.

Children were leaving and finishing college and coming back and it was just fine. The college presidents would come over for the commencements; the Bluefield people would come, and John W. Davis, from West Virginia State. He would drop in for a lecture. And the crowd would be there.

The NAACP went down in the Depression. Those men couldn't find the dollar a month to help the NAACP. I kept a membership of fifty, though; it took fifty to have a branch and it was a dollar a month. You sent fifty cents to New York and kept fifty cents in your treasury. Out of my meager salary, I'd send fifty cents apiece for those fifty people. I sent that twenty-five dollars in 1931, 1932, 1933. They know at the national office. That's a matter of record.

My husband said to my mother, "I believe my wife is off [deranged]."

Momma said, "Off where?"

He said, "Why would she send that money there to hold this?"

I did it because it was all they had. They didn't have any clubs; they didn't have anything. They would get literature from the NAACP and then sit down and discuss it. I wanted to hold on to it for them because they were underprivileged and that's what I did to hold it. I sent it myself.

Momma said, "No, she ain't gone. She ain't off. She's just a little foolish sometimes. You catch her talking that way sometimes."

chapter 22

Local NAACP Activities

At the outset, there was not much to do in the NAACP so far as the local branch was concerned because it was all so new to the people and also the programs for the branches were not as well defined as they are now. When the NAACP came about it was just for advancement. It was just what it said, for the advancement of colored people. He advanced socially, he advanced materially because he could get a good job. And sometimes they would get together and talk about that.

The local branch of the NAACP didn't touch the discrimination in the coal mines. They would talk about it at the meeting, but there was nobody who was able to move in on it. We hadn't come to that time. I was the only welfare worker in any of the mines, and my job came about because I wasn't hired back to teach.

At that time, the year that the branch was set up, which was around 1921, the problem of lynching claimed the nation's attention. For that year, there were more than three hundred lynchings and it became quite a thing to be talked about, and something had to be done about it. At that time there was a representative from Missouri who came in about then or maybe a little later. This man, L. C. Dyer, went to Congress for his lifetime on that antilynching law. He introduced the legislation into the Congress of the United States. It was known as the Dyer antilynching bill. He always said that he was going to get the law passed when he was seated. Poor Negroes who could vote would go and vote for him, and he'd get the office and nothing would happen on that bill. They never got further than voting on it in the House. So we began to raise funds and to move into organizing the states to supply some of the money to finance this bill through, so our main goal was fighting lynching, and it remained so.

Other things of concern were added then. They came up with questions about the schools and the teachers' salaries—unequal salaries, unequal school terms. Finally, we had a group of things pertinent to the Negro's welfare and his status as a citizen. We fought for those or organized to do something about them. Unequal school terms were all through the nation where Negroes lived, largely, but not in the North. Negroes would have unequal treatment from the school systems, especially in the South, which we could do nothing about but talk. The Negro had no voting power; he had no status, and of course, we couldn't do anything more than talk about it. In some places they didn't even allow branches and nothing was tried. There are some places yet that don't have branches. Wherever the Negro is dependent upon the white economy for his living, he dare not join anything that they tell him not to or that they object to. And here in our state and in the adjoining state, Virginia, and on into North Carolina where we had the beginnings of good large branches, they began to move. Where the Negroes had a four-month school year and whites had six, we began to ask for the six. There were places we had six months and the whites had nine months, so we began to ask for the nine. And so it grew.

We advertised the NAACP, and we got the money. We advertised on the basis of our Negro Artists' Series. That could bring people out. We'd say, "The National Association is bringing this." Of course, they didn't give you the money, but if after you counted your finances and deducted your expenses, if you were twenty-five dollars off, the company would give it back to you. Somebody would have to advance the money, though, and most likely it would be me. Sometimes we had a surplus and that would go in the treasury. And we'd send delegates to the meetings to find out about these things, because Negro papers weren't widely circulated. The first year that the branch was set up I had the *Crisis* agency. Nobody had seen it before Dr. DuBois came to visit. The group of southerners who'd come up from Alabama, Georgia, and all down there in the early years of mining didn't know. The church was the unit of meeting then, not groups like the NAACP. Churches—all the way from the holy rollers to the Catholic and Episcopal churches were there and furnished the Negro with the things he needed.

The NAACP was also established in Raleigh County and Logan County. I was in Raleigh; I was in Beckley when they had their first mass meeting; I was there to set up and to see where their offices were. I spoke to them and they were ready to set up. In Logan—Laredo—I set up. And there was one in Mercer County that I set up. Later on, I raised money for a Negro there who was accused of murdering the justice of the peace over there. His name was Payne [Boyd]; I don't remember what the other name was, but I used the branch to help him. They had their own program, but I raised money to help him, and Bluefield was going to help.

He was defended by the late Congressman John Kee. Payne was supposed to have murdered this man and everything pointed to him. Kee defended and I raised the first fifty dollars. We needed five hundred dollars. Kee's son said, "That's all my father ever got was that fifty dollars." I said, "Yes, but your family's gone to Congress on it. You got all the Negro vote in that area for years and years." He came to the Bluefield meeting to speak once and I said, "There's a Kee here today that we have; we will ever remember his Daddy, too."

His father saved this man. He went all the way to Washington and sat down with those records and found out that this man was in the army when this thing happened. And Kee, all of them—Mrs. Kee, all of them, any of them—after that, all they had to do in that district was to ask for it and every Negro was right there to put a vote in for them. One man told me that he voted for Kee, said, "Yes, I'm going to vote for them Kees as long as there is a Kee." I never will forget what he did, that was up in Mercer County. He was up what they call Crane Creek way. He told me that he voted for John Kee and he said he went back home and somebody—some campaign—had given him a cap that had "Billy" on it.

He put on his cap and went back to the polls and "Billy" voted that time. He was telling me, "I put in two votes for him. Oh, they didn't know me with my cap on. I was Billy something." They would tell you all kinds of tales about it, but that was just how loyal they were to John Kee up until he died. Then Mrs. Kee—all she had to do was go up in there and make one speech, and then young Kee—. It's been forty-some years up until this time from John Kee's first going to Congress as a lawyer, to this time.

Our branch meetings in McDowell County would range anywhere from 50 to 150 in attendance; sometimes from 200 to 250 if they were having a contest of some kind. For a few years, I had a baby contest. Everything was gauged towards the children who were coming along in order that they might have it better. I'd have a baby contest and get about twenty babies in, and the baby who brought the largest amount of money, whether it'd be from raising money or from the one-dollar memberships, would get a ten-dollar gold piece. The one who brought in the second largest amount would get a five-dollar gold piece, and the third would get $2.50 in gold—all the gold wasn't in Fort Knox then. It would be quite an affair. The largest church would open its doors and it would be an NAACP afternoon—the National Association's afternoon at the church. The people and the babies and the public at large would come. The mothers and their babies could leave after the money was counted and the contest was over. The rest would stay, and there would be speakers or persons to answer questions before they would leave. Well, now, that stirred up quite an interest until the next year or until it was time to go to the national meeting. Wherever the national meetings were held, we usually paid the expenses of the delegate. It got so that we might not have enough money if the meetings were far. We'd pay what we had. If we didn't have enough and if somebody wanted to put the other to it and go, we'd be willing to send them. We always wanted a representative because something new might come up and we could get it.

They'd come to these baby contests, then they'd go back. That's where I'd get the people to set up other branches. They would call for speakers and the places would begin setting up. There would be a person from Anawalt and the other part of the district up at Jenkins Jones. They'd say,

"We'd like to have a branch at our place. What do you do?" Most likely I'd have the literature and could tell them what they should do. Maybe over in the other district, over in Warren they'd say, "We'd like to have one at our place." I'd tell them, "I'll come to you. Get your fifty people and call me, and I'll come." In that period between 1921 and 1931 when they began to cut into it with the Depression, I'd set up many branches. They'd go down, and they'd tell me and I'd go get them back together again. Most of the time I had my own transportation. I've crawled around those mud roads and got stuck and somebody'd come pull me out. That's the reason my husband would say to my mother, "I don't believe your daughter's got it all." My mother would answer, "Yeah, she's got all she needs, but she's just foolish sometimes."

Charleston already had a branch. They had a blooming one. Dr. Mordecai Johnson, who was later president of Howard, organized it and was its president. We'd be able to get him to come down and spark one of the big meetings that we had at our Ninth of April celebration. The company would close their mines. That night we would have this big program; they didn't come to the celebration during the day. The kids would be there then. I had a maypole, and all that. People would come at night to a big program and the president would preside; he was justice of the peace of the district. He would preside, and I would have some sort of pageantry or something with the kids. Sometimes I'd have candlelight portraits—big frames there and little children who would represent Negroes who had gone before. They'd come and appear in the frame. We'd have a commentator and then, facing the rising sun—there would be a sun coming up and an electric light behind them and a small sheet. The children's faces would come up—they are the future. This was Dr. DuBois, and so and so, and this was the future. The parents would just be in awe to think that their children were going to be something. It was a good wholesome feeling—the whole thing. So then we'd sometimes have a speaker. Oscar DePriest, the first Negro congressman from Chicago, came down on the Ninth of April. He had them all jumping in their seats—the things he could tell.

The NAACP was behind this and people felt that they were attending in order to have unity. They might not have come if I, or some other person, was just having it. They came to be there with the rest of the people and to be there so the company would see how they appreciated it.

And there were other things that the branch did. For instance, if something happened where there was a difference because of racial differences, or if the constable—they had white and colored constables and white and colored justices of the peace—and if there was a difference or they ruled wrong, somebody in the NAACP would take issue with it and call the branch. The branch would send a letter or note letting them know that it was noticed and that it wasn't right. We didn't bring any suits or anything, but most of the time just the intervention—that somebody noticed—made them a little wary of doing things any other way. And then there were some other things that came up about that time— lynching, the differences in schools and education—and we began to ask for representation on everything. Of course, we already had the boards and all; that didn't come with the NAACP; that all came with the company setting up their political groups so as to get what they wanted; that came with the privilege of being voted for. But we began to fight for them to stop giving us the old schoolhouses and old furniture and giving the whites the new schools and new furniture. They'd get around that by promising that the next time they built a school they'd do that, or they'd do it when we had the next levy. But nobody knew much about levies.

The company built the schoolhouses, or the board of education that was based in the district built them. For a long time we took what we could get. The need for more teachers worked out the same way. We'd asked for more space and teachers because it was so crowded. It worked out pretty well. They'd put up a new school in a situation like that.

I don't think the NAACP was noticed by the company except for the fact that maybe they were fighting this thing in Congress, or raising money for that—things that were far removed from the coalfields. Or if they asked for some changes for the teachers—that was to be expected and that didn't bother the company. Or if the NAACP wanted to bring some cultural activity to help the people adjust, why that was alright; we did twelve years of that. After that was over, the company began to bring in cultural activities developed by Red Path. There really wasn't any attention paid to the NAACP. It was accepted. It wasn't objectionable because the NAACP didn't have a program like they have now. It has moved into the militant program of legal action. There was no legal action that I know of brought at that time. They would just object to something— no demonstration—nothing like that. That was no part of the life of that time or of the organization. And the people, the Negro people, were the ones who liked the organization because it gave them a place to go. It was something to do. It was a trip to take and they would hear about that. There were papers to be passed and there were the stamps—the seals to sell.

chapter 23

✳

NAACP Christmas Seals

The seals began in 1927. The first seals were in the Christmas of '27 and that has continued every year up to this time, which is about the forty-second or forty-third year of that. I raised money with the Christmas seals for a trial of two little Negro boys who had been jailed in Mississippi and were released later on through the efforts of a young white lawyer who lived down there. And they traveled through the country. They brought them through here later on, but I didn't see them. I was away, but they were in Ohio and they were in World War II—these two little boys. The NAACP kept a kind of follow-through on them.

Their case revolved around a drowning. It seems that they were all peons—peonage people—poor whites and these poor Negroes. It was in Mississippi where the water backed up; they call it a bayou. The boys had this old piece of board out there playing on it, and it capsized. There was a little white boy, thirteen, and the other two Negro boys were brothers, twelve and thirteen. The white boy drowned. He fought so they couldn't save him and the Negro boys ran away. They found them that night cold and wet in an old house. Both parents were hunting their children; they knew they played together. The children said they tried to save him and couldn't and the white parents believed it until some of the others found out that this child had been drowned playing with little

Negroes. Then they reported that the little Negro boys had drowned him, and the white sheriff came. It was way back out there, way down around Natchez.

I heard about it from Walter White. He had found out about it from this lawyer who had gone into court that morning and had seen these little Negro boys sitting there waiting for the trial and he noticed that they were half starved and ragged and their little shins were burned. They had been tortured with a hot poker to make them confess. So, when he got the particulars, he sent to the national office. Five hundred dollars would be needed to defend them, and all the branches were asked to help. When I got the request, we began to raise money. I was already selling Red Cross seals. I shared doing that in the district and everybody bought from me. I quit selling Red Cross seals and had these NAACP seals printed there at the office and made $516 and some cents. I don't know how I paid that printing bill, but whatever it was, I paid it. I sent all the money to the national. And the people sold through the country—I sent seals anywhere they said they wanted them—one seal or however many they wanted. I sent out a whole lot, but the only ones who responded was the $516 worth. I sent that for the defense of these people; then I started selling seals every year and I set up criteria by which the money was to be used exclusively to defend people who couldn't help themselves—people like these.

I got the idea for the seals from the health seals that the Red Cross sold at Christmastime. The year before, I had sold $15,000 worth of Red Cross seals through the district. The company always backed what I did. To the Colonel, I was a smart gal, and whatever I'd bring the Colonel he'd say, "Memphis, do you think you want that?" "Sure," I'd say. "I want it." And here came the Red Cross lady and she was glad to have somebody to sell the seals through the district. And I had sold. That's more than I had ever sold, because I quit after that. She came to see why I'd quit, and she sat down and gave me all of this talk about how Negroes had more tuberculosis than anybody else and how the death rate had taken them. She just couldn't imagine me selling seals for the NAACP. And I remember that I said to her, "But I found out that Negroes had something else beside tuberculosis—had other problems." So I started the seals and I've never missed a year. One year I personally sold more seals than anybody else in the nation. Everybody bought; some of the white people would buy; when I would send the seals they would send the money.

There was a branch in Keystone, in Kimball, and in other places around the county—in Excelsior, which was another place over in there. I sent seals to all those branches, but most of them I sold myself. I remember a mail carrier in Mobile, Alabama, sent for three thousand seals. They were a penny apiece and three thousand seals would have been three hundred dollars. He sent me twenty-five dollars. He was afraid to sell them after he got them. And a teacher in Florida, Jim Evans—he has since been head of some government—big government post. Jim Evans was also at West Virginia State for awhile. I sent Jim Evans fifty dollars' worth of seals down to his school. I thought he might sell them among the teachers. He sent me the fifty dollars, and in later years he told me that he took the money out of his own pocket and he thought he was never going to catch up on that fifty dollars. But he said that I had sent him that letter telling him that he was just the man for it because I could see that he was a go-getter and all like that. He said I had built up all of that stuff so he said, "I took my fifty dollars out and sent it," and he said that he never did catch up on that fifty dollars. Well, there may have been others who did the same thing rather than let the whole program down, but most of the seals around West Virginia were sold in the schools.

I didn't know what to call the seals other than an NAACP Christmas seal until something special was done with the money, then it became a seal for freedom. For five years, I sold the first seals from my home, and I'd give the national office the money. I had the seals printed up at Welch at the *Daily News* office. Two of the first years I designed the seal, and then Simms Campbell, the Negro cartoonist for *Esquire,* designed one year and a Negro sculptor designed. I got names of other designers from the *Crisis* and then I've had help since, different ones have designed.

After five years the National Association took them over. Why did they let me keep the seals at my house? Why didn't the national office take over before that time was up? Later, Mrs. James Weldon Johnson, wife of the deceased executive director, told me. When I would go to

New York after Mr. Johnson died, Mrs. Johnson remembered me. She had a suite in the hotel where I would stop. She would usually take me to lunch and then we would hash over all of the things and all of the fineness and greatness of her husband and how she felt about this man that we thought was great. I had had the nerve to advertise the seals in the New York papers, the white papers. I don't know who paid for it now. There was no Tuberculosis Association or such then; the Red Cross handled the health seals and the Red Cross was based in New York and they saw this Christmas seal. Mrs. Johnson told me that when the Red Cross saw this Christmas seal they called Mr. Johnson in and wanted to know what was the meaning of this national seal when they thought they had the franchise. There was no franchise; nobody else but them had the seals. So Mr. Johnson's answer was that the association, as such, had no such seal and they had no jurisdiction over an individual who wanted to use any legal means of raising money. So they evaded that by letting me keep them. I didn't know what was going on until years later. When they did take them over, well, there were other seals by that time. The Tuberculosis Association had taken over their sale, and they knew nothing about the controversy with the Red Cross and so nobody bothers because the place is full of all kinds of seals now—Easter seals, and every kind of seal you want—Boys' Town and all of those—Indians, everything's got a seal now and all of them make money. I always wondered why, though— why they permitted me to keep the seals. Usually if it's making money for an organization they see about that money. They thought it was going to be a failure, but it wasn't. The years that I didn't have much money as a result of selling the seals, I'd have a big dance and get the money and send it.

The money was good; it went into four figures, and it got too much for me to handle. I would send the seals out to the people; they would send me the money; I'd send the money to the national office and they would send the receipts so the people would know that I had sent the money. That's why I kept such a good clientele. It was the fact that they knew the national office had the money. I did all the mailing from my house, and all the receiving and the sending. I paid for the mailing. I never took a penny; they have no record that I ever took a penny for mailing. And that's what Walter White said just before he died. In the Negro papers of the nation he said, "We gave her the consent and she went ahead and did all the work herself and never charged a penny because she believed in the principles of the association and that was her contribution."

I don't know how much the mailing ran. It wasn't but two cents a letter then, and a penny for a postcard. I thought that was what I could do, and I was trying to fight this thing for people who couldn't do it for themselves. They didn't have the pennies; the people in the South couldn't work, and the money was going to fight lynching and protect them. This money was for that.

But it just got to be too much; I couldn't handle it. When those seals were going out, I'd take two or three high school kids and I'd stay at school, stay in my room after school until six o'clock—six and seven o'clock getting all that addressing and checking done. So the national said we'll take over and we'll give you some help. That was the year that Roy Wilkins came to us. That was his first year and his duty was to be assistant secretary and take over the mailing of the seals for the national office. And for a long time, for five years, you could get them from the national scrapbook. We used phrases like "I am the seal, herald of democracy," and so forth. That was some of my advertising. I sent my advertising to the national office and they would get out the big advertising stickers and things like that. And then, they took it over all together and I'd just get seals for the state, and distribute the seals in West Virginia. I would take the seals for the whole state and distribute them. I did that for three or four years and the state would be credited for the number of seals sold. We didn't have the state conference for West Virginia as such then. Finally I'd just get seals for the branch wherever I was, so I got less and less of them. And this year the seals grossed $165,876 and some cents. $165,000—I said when they got a quarter million dollars, I was going to quit, but I'm going to quit at this.

The *Afro[-American]** sent a correspondent to see me and they printed the interview in the paper. They had been buying seals—twenty-five

*Black newspaper published in Baltimore, Maryland.

dollars' worth every year. Every Negro newspaper would buy. The St. Louis newspaper took me to task for selling the seals for a penny—by bringing it down so that you could give a penny they thought it was belittling, but after awhile they came around and they bought seals. And the *Afro-American*—every Christmas as long as old man Murphy—the elder Murphy—lived, they bought seals.

And during that time, I kept the *Crisis* agency. The schoolchildren sold it. I saw to it that they got the *Crisis* and that the national got paid for them and the kids kept their money. It came once a month. One of the kids took the agency over, but for two or three years, I kept that going so as to have the magazine. Now I understand that in order to give us a brief or better history, this year the NAACP is republishing fifty years of the *Crisis*—fifty issues beginning with the first year. They will publish every one of them just like they were published through the years up to '59 or '60. I suppose they will be bound.

✳

chapter 24

State and National NAACP Activities

We formed the state NAACP confer-
ence in 1944, and I was state treasurer for twenty-one years, from 1945 to
1966. I went to all of the meetings and until the later years I never charged
for going to the meetings or for serving on anything. That was my contribution. If there was any trouble in the state it was mine. I felt free to
go, and I didn't feel that I needed to be paid. I'd settle disputes and set up
branches and speak for their mass meetings or the close of their branches.
And I extended it into Virginia. The branches in Virginia had come in
during that time—the one in Pocahontas and the one in Marion. I knew
the minister who had set up both of them very well, and I went to him
for his drives, for his mass meetings when he would be getting new
members or starting a new project. Of course, they would give me expenses for that.

I attended thirty national conferences; the first one was the fifteenth
annual conference in Philadelphia. We had a new branch in Gary; I was
secretary and I was getting all this literature and I brought it to the meetings and told them I thought we should know what was going on. The
president also said that he thought we should know what was going on.
He said that we could send a delegate, and inasmuch as I had done so
much organization in the state and the other counties, it would be nice
for them to send me, and they did. We met in Philadelphia.

Wherever we met we used to send people to speak in the churches. The churches would ask for them; they knew they could get them and they wanted a speaker to come in and speak on the national association. We were getting it introduced to the country, to the people. A speaker would go to either white or Negro churches, to Jewish tabernacles, what have you. I don't think I've ever gone to an organizational meeting that I didn't work or speak at some church on Sunday morning. Now, at that time I went to a Methodist church, I believe. It was a Negro church in Philadelphia.

The branch financed my trip to the meeting. And when you'd go and speak at a church, they would take up a collection for the NAACP, for the national work and the speaker took that back to the meeting. The next meeting that I went to was in Denver, and then Indianapolis.

I got inspiration from attending these meetings, and a wide acquaintance with Negroes through the country, and their problems—a wide acquaintance. As a result, I know the best people, as such, the most highly educated Negroes. I know all the best people through the country in my group. Among the white group, I know the most liberal. I don't know whether they're the best or the worst; some were rich, some were poor, some were professionals, some were not. But among them, I know the most liberal white friends that we have through the country. I mean personally, which has made me ten feet tall. I stand tall with the fact that I know them, that I have seen them, that I have talked with them, that I've been a part of the program and that I have been inspired by their help and their interest. Julius Rosenwald built the schools in the South, the libraries and the Julius Rosenwald schools. When he was president of Sears Roebuck, he used to come to our national meetings. He would sit with us in committees; he would be there as a speaker. I saw Clarence Darrow, one of the finest criminal lawyers America ever produced. This man with his coat off and his galluses snapping on his shoulders, this great big hunk of a man with the finest command of legal language you ever want to hear. You didn't know what it was all about, but the fact that he said it made it fine and beautiful and knowledgeable. Your respect grew for him as he talked. He could sit down and elaborate on the most trivial thing and make a classic out of what he said. I sat and listened to that. He defended the first Negro that moved into a white neighborhood; the one who shot out and killed this white man after he was stoned. He was on trial and we backed the trial, and Clarence Darrow defended him for nothing. We didn't have the money; nobody had it. And then when Darrow came to the meeting, there was no place they wouldn't have carried him if the old man could have been carried. But the old man was failing in health then. I never saw him again. I read of him again because he came back to fight the monkey trial.*

There came to these meetings the religious, the professionals, and all the white group; the government men, the most liberal minds that we had. The Garrisons from Massachusetts—Lloyd Garrison was one of our lawyers. This is the grandson of William Lloyd Garrison.** And on down. Some of the members of the Beecher family† and those—they were all in it. And the religious men—the Unitarian minister John Haynes Holmes was one of the number. Not too long ago somebody here got the John Haynes Holmes award for his liberalism. He's your father of Unitarianism. He's your highest Unitarian man. Miss Mary White Ovington, whose father was president of the New York–New Haven Railroad, and she cast her lot in that little cubbyhole down there at West Fifth Avenue in New York to help us bring it up. I knew those people. I sat down with them; Mary White Ovington was chairman of the board that said, "Yes, let her go ahead and sell the seals in the name of the association." That was Miss Ovington. James Weldon Johnson was a Negro poet and our first diplomat. He took over as executive secretary from [John] Shillady, this gorgeous Jewish fellow they beat to death on the steps of the courthouse in Austin, Texas.[1] Then when he died, came James Weldon Johnson. Mr. Shillady was one of the most handsome men you ever looked at. They beat him to death. He came down just to ask questions. He had no idea; he died from beatings; they broke him up. And his picture is on the list of founders. James Weldon Johnson came, a poet, a writer; he was the one who wrote *The Autobiography of an Ex-*

*Nickname for the 1925 trial of John Scopes, a Tennessee high school biology teacher, tried for teaching Darwinian evolution.

**New England abolitionist; founded the *Liberator,* antislavery newspaper.

†New England family that included abolitionist minister Henry Ward Beecher and Harriet Beecher Stowe, author of *Uncle Tom's Cabin.*

Colored Man, and he autographed all of his books and gave me a copy as they were written.

One of the big things of the state was the hundredth anniversary of the Emancipation Proclamation. It lasted a whole year and we held it in conjunction with the state celebration because the state was one hundred years old, June 20, 1963. We were part of the celebration. Out of seven or eight floats developed to commemorate the anniversary in the state, we had one of them set up and staffed by the Negro people. And in the cities of the state where they would have the celebrations, and the floats would go in, our float would go in. The people living in the city would staff it with persons living there because we had no money to transport people and the queen and all. We had a queen and they would pay her way there but the rest would be staffed with the local people. It was quite an advertising and it spelled to the people quite a thing—that we had progressed to this point where we could be so much a part of this celebration on the same level.

The same man who designed the Rose Bowl floats—the floats for Hollywood, designed the floats for this state with the exception of the part that I added to ours because I wanted to use children to stress the children's role—why we were having it and what it meant to West Virginia. So I suggested an extra part on each side with gold stems that the children could hold to for safety's sake. And there were six children who represented six things that we were stressing for the historical part of it; for instance, there was a little girl, Mrs. Smith's little girl was just five or six then; she was the little girl on our float who was dressed in her school clothes with her book under her arm that represented, as the story goes, three and a half million schoolchildren in the area of integration—their fight. The next was a little boy, little Stephen Johnson. Steve had on his doctor's uniform and he had his stethoscope around his neck; he was fit for a doctor and I said, "Get up there, Dr. Kildare." He said, "Oh, Mrs. Garrison, I'm Ben Casey."* So he had to represent the advance in medicine and the work of Dr. Daniel Hale Williams, who made the first operation on the human heart. And then we had a little girl with her music

*Characters in popular movies and radio and television series.

—her roll of music and her instrument and all, which represented the gift of the Negro in the music world. On the other side was a little boy that resembled Martin Luther King; he dressed like him, had on his clerical collar and his Bible under his arm, which signified the work of the church in the role of the Negro's search for freedom and equality. And the next little girl was Henderson's little girl who represented academic excellence in the field of learning. And we told in the story how many Negro Phi Beta Kappas there were and how many scientists and what they had done—that they were above average in the educational field. The last little boy was the little Allen boy, Mickey, we call him. Mickey had him a red football suit. It was beautiful; he had his helmet, his football— all of his trappings, and beside him lay a baseball and some other things. Mickey represented excellence in sports. It had come to a point that it was said by the news media and all that Negroes were excelling in the world of sports at that time. There was the football hero, Jim Brown, and the rest of them. And there was Jackie Robinson and his baseball and there was a basketball there on the float. The story that was being broadcast over the loudspeakers when those floats would be passing through educated many of the public. Of course, people who would have left otherwise would wait until this float came along to see it. And then, so many afterwards who heard of it wanted to know, "What was the significance of the children on there?" So we had a little pamphlet published by the state that you could get along with the rest of the literature. The people didn't know that we were looking forward, not to what we were already doing in the state, not to what we had done, but to the future, and that's what we were fighting for. This dramatized very, very vividly the Negroes' part and the "why" of this integration fight. And it may have eased some tensions here and there to know what the float was really about. I guess that was the biggest thing. We also went to the science camp. There was a Negro boy sent to that science camp, and he ranked high because he was the only one among that number who came from across the country to this camp. At every type of celebration that the state put on we, in some manner, were a part of it until we closed with the queen and ball at the big auditorium in

Charleston. Mrs. Barron* came in to crown the queen that was to reign over the whole thing—the whole picture at our closing time. Then we gave the awards and prizes on Sunday afternoon with Jennings Randolph** and some of the other politicians present. So, all in all, this was said, conceded to be, the best and most meaningful observation of the Emancipation Celebration among Negroes in this country. And it was sponsored by the state branch and the National Association for the Advancement of Colored People. Rev. C. Anderson Davis was our president at that time—a very fine worker, an ace-one organizer and he is now working in the area of urban development for the association in Houston, Texas. He has that.

I was vice president of the National Board of the NAACP from 1963 to 1966. I served three years. I attended the board meetings, which met every three months in New York City. The board meetings were a sounding board of what was happening through the country, the work that was being done, the things discovered that should have been done, the status of the movements in certain states—who was moving forward or backward or not moving at all, the problems encountered, the new persons who were taken in to act in certain fields of the association. For instance, I think we added a large number of lawyers to the staff that serves the NAACP; that section of the NAACP finally had a hundred lawyers. They were moving in that direction because it was going to be strictly a thing where they needed legal council. And you could get a lawyer for most anything. The fact of it was that we were the only civil rights organization that had a legal staff. CORE [Congress of Racial Equality] didn't have any, SNCC [Student Non-violent Coordinating Committee] —nothing. No group had a legal staff except the NAACP, and we fought all of their battles; we paid all their bills and then furnished the legal work while they went out and made trouble and got in jail and what have you. We'd go and defend CORE. They had no legal staff, none of them had. And not until now do they have a legal staff; they used the NAACP staff. So that's why the NAACP's spoken of as the leading civil

*Wife of W. W. Barron, governor of West Virginia at that time.
**Democratic senator from West Virginia (1959–85).

rights organization in the world; it really is and we have some of the finest lawyers in this country. We also had some of the finest labor men in this country on our staff. At a meeting in Mississippi, I went in to hear Herbert Hill, the head of the labor department who was white. I think Herbert was of Jewish origin; it seems that I heard that. Anyway, he was standing up there saying that something had happened in this labor field; he was being very emphatic about it and said, "They can't do that to us." So we got a big kick out of his using "us," you know; we'd had Herbert so long that he'd turned into us.

I was elected to the national board by the board of directors, which named the vice presidents. The whole board approved of a selection and then, of course, Mr. Wilkins had his say in it, too. He would notify you that you were selected to be vice president at such and such a meeting, and say that, "We hope you will be present and share in the problems of the association." We went in January; the first meeting was the friendship meeting and the presidents of branches across the country came and met with us at the friendship dinner in New York. Then there was a business meeting at which we elected new members for the years or continued the members whose terms were expiring; they were staggered, you know. There were sixty members on the executive board, and it always looked like they were present to me. At least, the majority of them were present, and any business, any problems that were to be solved, any grievances to be resolved, it was all done at those meetings. We met the first Monday in January; we had another meeting in April, and another meeting at the association, and one in the fall, in the late fall.

They did not pay all expenses for the meetings. They paid transportation. You got your round-trip fare; the expenses of the travel and your hotel, all the rest you did yourself. It was your contribution to the work; it was taken care of by you personally. And most of those who came are people who didn't mind, who were willing to do that, either one way or the other, you've contributed anyway. And the dinner, of course, I don't think we paid for the dinner. I think that must have been furnished.

There were sixteen vice presidents, sixty people on the board of directors, and, of course, the staff—Mr. Wilkins and the staff. I didn't count them, but there must have been twelve or fifteen of those, and there may have been others; for instance, those presidents who came from around the country. They may come into the meeting, but they did not vote or participate in the immediate business. But if they had a problem to solve, they may bring it there and attend the meetings, but they could not do any voting.

I didn't miss many of the meetings. I attended all of the January meetings. I liked the fellowship dinners and maybe I went at Easter time. I attended two out of three meetings. There were four meetings a year; maybe I attended two. At other times I attended three out of four. Sometimes the weather was such that I didn't like the flying and the exposure of traveling and the changing and waiting on schedules after the trains got so undependable; that was too much. That's why I missed those. It wasn't that I didn't want to go. I always wanted to go. It's the pull, the draw—you're so involved with it.

In attending the national meetings, I've usually served in some capacity and even at this last one they put me on for membership and fund raising; it was in a problem clinic. I had helped set up a problem clinic in Denver and helped staff it, but this time it was a meeting that everybody could come to and ask questions or give suggestions instead of bringing problems for the one person to make suggestions about. When I attended the meeting, I found out that it was an extension of what we had been doing in the problem clinic. I didn't contribute anything to that but the suggestions that were already there. We had a very fine organizer, Miss Simmons, who was a lawyer, Althea Simmons. She was on the west coast for a while, but I think she was a Texas girl. She did a fine job of organizing in all the areas where there was extra help needed.

The NAACP is quite unlike anything that Negroes've ever had before. In the years of organizing to meet the needs of this present time, they have covered just about everything and every part of the situation that has any bearing on civil rights causes. For instance, there was a lobbyist, Clarence Mitchell, who got the Spingarn Award.* He was a lobbyist extraordinary, so much so until the people in the Congress of the United States called him Senator 101. They just have a hundred, you know, but

*NAACP award named for an early board member, Arthur B. Spingarn, and given for high achievement.

that's the name they gave him, our Senator 101, Clarence Mitchell. He was an affable man, and he mixed; even though he didn't have a vote in that Senate, his influence made him a person to be sought after.

I also served as a national secretary on special assignment, kind of a troubleshooter. Maybe a branch had gone down, maybe a branch had been divided, maybe they had two factions and they both were tearing up. I was supposed to even things up and get that branch back together. Sometimes it'd be in my state; sometimes it'd be out of state. And I've worked with problems here. I've organized two or three times in West Virginia. I think I've organized the Logan Branch three times. I'd go to the meetings. I'd go and find out who they were, and that would save the national office a trip of sending an officer down. They'd pay my expenses.

I've been called to Ohio and I've been in Indiana. I went wherever something had to be done. Sometimes I would go to run a membership drive where a branch had just nearly gone to the wall or for some reason was split. I went to Richmond, Virginia, and to Charleston twice to set up their drive. They won't let you work at home, in your own county. I'd always have someone there to fight me. I still have them. Sometimes they talk just as good and then the next time they won't even look my way. Anyway, I went to Cincinnati. I stayed fourteen weeks there as a field secretary on special assignment. I brought that branch from 65 members to around 7,000, somewhere in that neighborhood. You've worked when you've done that, no hours—night and day.

To get that many members, I had special methods. It's laid down how to conduct a successful membership drive. Information's been taken from persons who have been doing it all over the country. When I went to Indianapolis, I think I was five or six weeks there, and I left with—I don't know how many members, but it was up in the thousands. Richmond had 6,000 when I left. Charleston came up to 885. Twice I was up there and they had fine membership drives each time. I went around anywhere they called. Sometimes there were places that I couldn't go to spend time, and when they were finishing their membership drive, they would send for me to come to the mass meeting to make the last appeal. Now, for going to branches, setting up those drives, the national office paid me a weekly salary. That's the only pay that I ever got when I was away from home working with the branches setting up their drives. Then I went to San Francisco to the national and conducted a week of workshops to tell how I had gotten this done. I had a manual, "How to Conduct a Successful Membership Drive," but the people who came to the workshop could ask questions and all. I had a full house.

I served as national field secretary for 7½ months, all told, not at the same time; the time that I served was over a four- or five-year period, but it would equal that. The work was reorganizing branches and that total equaled 7½ months for which I was paid. It's funny how people think that everything you do you get paid for. Some people don't think that you're dedicated to anything, that anything is a duty or moral duty that you can't just throw aside, that you do things because you should do them. It's hard for people to understand. They think, "She's getting money for it. She's getting hundreds of dollars for it." They think all of that, but it isn't true.

My one thought was of making the NAACP felt. Everything I did to benefit Negroes, I'd label it NAACP, like the Negro Artists' Series and all. Some of the Negroes didn't even know that the NAACP was being organized. But the thing of it was that it was doing something of great worth for people. It had to be the NAACP, that's why I did it. I knew about the NAACP so, really, I wasn't misrepresenting it at all. And the same thing is true here in Huntington. If I'm having something to raise funds to help out in the area of scholarships, or meeting the needs of youth, or soothing over questions that have brought about a lot of disagreement among groups, to me, it's the NAACP that moves in. And then in this poverty program—the NAACP has stood behind it. I guess they've stood behind everything that law and order stood for in order to protect the interest of people. They haven't had any trouble or anything to do about it but you knew they were there when any group called on them. If anything went awry that bordered on taking people's civil rights from them or taking their privileges from them, whether they were white or black, the NAACP was there for it. So, it's selling yourself completely on the program that motivates you; that's all that keeps me in it. I take all the kicks and bumps now, not because I like it so well to disagree or to be lambasted sometimes by the people who disagree with you because of what the NAACP represents. The cause you represent overlaps the unpleasantness that comes to you—I mean, it overshadows all of that. I feel like sometimes I would like to throw it all up, throw it at the people who make me so disgusted with it. But it doesn't come that easy. You can't quite do it; you still have a consciousness about the matter. I say I look over into the promised land; I'll never make it, but I know it's over there.

chapter 25

Problems of Integration in West Virginia

Governor Barron appointed me to the West Virginia Human Rights Commission from 1963 to 1966. The Human Rights Commission came in under Governor Barron because of the help that the president of the state NAACP, C. Anderson Davis, had given to Barron's campaign. Anderson was quite active in the church program and in the conference and all; he was one of the top Methodist men in his area of conference, and he was a Democrat. I don't know if he had always been a Democrat or not; anyway, he was one of the managers of Barron's campaign. Barron got elected governor and he said to Reverend Davis, "What is it you want?" You know it's a payoff, always. To the victor belong the spoils. Reverend Davis said, "I don't want anything, but I'd like for you to do something for my people," and he began to outline. He wouldn't take anything for himself; he wouldn't take any position in the statehouse or appointments in other commissions. That was out, he said. He mentioned the fact of a commission that would be presided over or sponsored by the state where you could bring your grievances and where there would be a director who knew how to conduct this sort of organization. So that was the beginning of the Human Rights Commission.

This was the first one and it was under Barron. You were named to the commission to serve three years, and the commission still remains under this governor. Many of the commissioners were Democrats and a smaller number of them were Republicans, being the minority political setup. The first commission was headed by a man by the name of Mr. McKinney, Howard McKinney. I think he came from Pennsylvania near here. I think he was with the Pennsylvania commission. We were staffed in Charleston at the state house. We had an assistant director after we got into the work and needed an assistant to go into the field. He was a Negro by the name of George Earl Chamberlain. Mr. McKinney was white—a Quaker minister by the way. We didn't know that until a long time after. Mr. Chamberlain came in about the second year when they needed someone in the field.

I was not the only Negro on the commission. There was one more, a minister from Bluefield. There was another woman, a white woman. The commissioners were from all over the state. One, a lawyer, was from Wheeling. They got all of these complaints from throughout the state before the commission. We were denied service in the eating places when we traveled. The commission came to Huntington when they were picketing the White Pantry [restaurant]. Things like that would bother the head of the commission. He would come here sometimes and go in with them to see what it was all about, or he would stand out and watch it. They were picketing Bailey's Cafeteria and the theater and the White Pantry. That's where they used the cattle prod, electric cattle prod on one of Marshall's students, Phil Carter. The White Pantry man, downtown —he's the one, and Phil Carter was the one that he used the cattle prod on. There were other sitters there, but I guess Phil was the biggest and looked like he could stand it. Phil is a tall, heavy-set black fellow. Phil said that he was wondering what the cattle prod felt like when "WHAM" it hit him. He said he fell on the floor. We could see why it was so objectionable. They had been using it in Birmingham and Montgomery and all. The cattle prod was much in evidence. Phil said it was a very bad experience. It didn't last long, but the very fact of using this on people, like the very fact of using the dogs on people, was bad.

Huntington didn't have the dogs, but we had the dogs in Birmingham and Montgomery, and we had the boy that the police held—the picture came out of the police on each side of this boy holding him while the dog nibbled at his vitals. We had that boy with his bandages on at the national NAACP meeting in Chicago. It was a terrific thing. It was something that made you kind of sick—a country that resorted to that kind of punishment for human beings. That boy was torn and bitten clear across his stomach.

Well, all that figured in this in Huntington. They put them in jail, and a fellow by the name of [Andrew] McDade, who is president of the NAACP now, went bail—put up his property and bailed all ten of them out. And he'll do that anytime they put them in jail. At Bluefield, I said, "Mac, pray that they don't leave the country." And he'd go down there to this judge—district judge. He'd say, "I ain't got no children, but I'm a Negro. I'll go those bails." He did the same for that Bluefield bunch. That isn't generally known how he has gone to the front like that for them. And I doubt if many people here know that he has done that—that he has been that loyal, but he has. He may be on somebody's bond now up there. If any of them are in jail, he is.

Then I was involved in the national committee on community relations, President Johnson's committee. A letter, a two-page telegram, came from the president of the United States expressing the why and what the program stood for and appointing me to the commission with the hope that I would accept the appointment and become a part of this. And of course, I felt very flattered. LeRoy Collins was appointed to head it. He was then the governor of Florida. We said that he was the converted governor of Florida because he was a rabid racist until his last years. It was under the Commerce Department that [former governor Luther H.] Hodges of North Carolina headed and meetings were held in Washington at the call of the president and the head of the department. They were held in the Department of the Foreign Commissions. All meet in there—the foreign representatives, the ambassadors. It was held in the department that they occupied for their meetings and we were served from the dining room in there. It was a chamber of mirrors. It's a beautiful place and the dining room was beautiful. Each table was numbered, and a special waiter was assigned to each table. West Virginia had seven representatives, and aside from being there to attend to business, it was an insight into how great and how fine this government is. It was a terrific thing. The ladies' room was the part that was mirrored. There were mirrors everywhere and over all the dressing tables and the carpet felt like you were walking on down. This government is a very affluent thing when it comes to putting into practice its governmental duties and the setup. There were four hundred of us on this committee, which made it very selective for a group of that size to cover the country to further better relationships in communities that had no particular interest in it even though they had the problem. Out of that four hundred they got together and selected one hundred persons as speakers for this committee and for the government, and you were scheduled to go here and there through the country wherever you were called by any part of this commission to help solve problems or to speak or to tell them what was going on. I was one of the hundred who was a national speaker for this bureau.

I didn't go anywhere outside of the state to speak. I attended some meetings that were outside, but I didn't speak anywhere. I was scheduled to go because then after that time the commission changed heads and it came under the head of the Justice Department with another head. And finally it came under the head of Roger Wilkins, a Negro under the Justice Department. He's a nephew of Roy Wilkins of the NAACP. You could see where we were moving. We were moving into the field of civil rights, and my three years were up by that time. I was no longer there; I didn't get reappointed. Roger said, "Oh, yes, you're there," but I didn't get any official notices and I wasn't called for the meetings anymore, so I knew that others had come on.

VI

community life

THIS amazing woman never retired. In the last years of Garrison's life she continued to take on major projects. Why are we not surprised that she organized Girl Scout troops for the young black girls in the Huntington area? And why does it seem so logical that Garrison would connect the need for textbooks in newly liberated African countries with the surplus of textbooks in her own community? Both of these examples simply reaffirm the content of her life. One gets the feeling that had she continued to live in good health, she would still be pounding away, finding appropriate causes and speaking to social needs. She herself identifies this in chapter 17, when she says: *All I have done in the world is to meet a need.*

And so what do we learn from this remarkable life—a life Garrison characterizes thusly: *Living has been great for me—the experience of living?* What does Memphis Tennessee Garrison continue to teach *us?* It is sometimes too easy to dismiss a historical account as irrelevant to the present, or not applicable to a current situation. Garrison had no email address and never used a cell phone. Yet today she is featured in a web site (http://www.marshall.edu/orahist/) and is the subject of a book that will be sold on Amazon.com.

It would be easy to describe her in platitudes—as "resilient of spirit," or "guided by strong principles." But that is not what she was about. Memphis Tennessee Garrison was about challenging the world she found—a world that lacked respect for hardworking people, failed to support its needy children, and proved unable to provide security for all its citizens.

That world continues to exist today. The southern counties of West Virginia are mired in poverty, and the terror of violence still stalks the streets of American cities. People of color the world over are being exploited in sweatshops owned by multinational corporations, and women continue to face domestic violence and degradation. Memphis Tennessee Garrison would be looking for the openings, those places where individual initiative and vision would make a real difference. And in doing so, she would make a difference. The message of her life is clear: making a difference provides meaning to life—gives it a richness unobtainable by any other means. This is her legacy. This is the lesson.

chapter 26

✳

Girl Scouts

I got involved with the Girl Scouts in my district when I was still living in McDowell County where the Houston Coal Company had mines. Mrs. Houston was a Cincinnati girl and she had been a Girl Scout. She married one of the Houstons and came down into the McDowell County coalfields. She began to interest people that worked in Girl Scouting, the white people, in our area; and she began telling the local people what scouting meant. She had the club women behind her, and the company gave a beautiful place up in the mountains and cleared it and set up a modern Girl Scout camp. It was named Camp Marian Houston. It was the first one in the county, perhaps the first one in West Virginia because those things were for the cities, you know, not for the mountains. Well, it worried me so because we didn't have a Girl Scout troop and we didn't have the know-how or the wherewithal to get one. And, we were told that Negro Scouts couldn't be recognized by the Council. Well, you couldn't be a Girl Scout unless you were a member of the Girl Scout Council. So I said, "Well, this, too, shall pass," and it did.

We finally came to the point where the schools began to take note of scouting, and the superintendent, Mr. Bryson, called a group together and asked us what did we think of a scouting program. "Well," somebody said, "Memphis has been trying to get a troop for twenty-five years." That was, of course, not true, but they always liked to go to extremes or something. He said, "Well, this is her chance," and he told us about the scouting. He would have the Girl Scout Council in our area send in persons to train for leadership; we'd need a committee to set it up. We did that.

I was one of those first ones to be trained. I think that was in '41 or '42, somewhere along there. And we had about fifteen who were trained as leaders, perhaps more; we liked it. We all became girls again and we had the camp and the cooking out—the whole program of Girl Scouts. And then, we had permission to go into the schools and recruit. Then after that here came a man with the Boy Scouts, and my husband took off to the Boy Scouts. The principal and teachers began to recruit for the Boy Scouts and the principal became a Boy Scout leader. It was a new thing for them. Everybody said, "Don't you wish there had been Boy Scouts or Girl Scouts when you were a girl." So, we had some very nice troops. I suppose we had through that county about twelve or fifteen troops. All were staffed by trained workers and many of them were teachers.

I helped organize the troop in my district. And then they'd have Girl Scout field day and, of course, the committee would be in on it. We would train the children, have them ready to be a part of that. We also had camping. We had the recreation place in Gary with the pool and pavilion, and we got that for the Girl Scouts. Buses would bring them; we couldn't have anything but day camping because we didn't have tents or anything. The schools loaned their buses for the scouting and the children would be brought in each morning. We'd have all the children in the county. We just had the one scouting session because the council didn't have much money. We'd have a camp director, an assistant director, and all of these helpers. I was one of the directors. It was very fine. We had a cookout. We brought nosebags [bag lunches], but the nosebags were never enough and we decided to cook.

I was amused at one little girl who came and brought a nosebag. Her momma didn't understand what a nosebag was. Her momma cooked up some nice pork chops and made some nice pork chop sandwiches and things like that and cake and all and gave it to her.

So she said, "Momma, this isn't a nosebag."

Her mother said, "You take that on; you've got to have something to eat. What is a nosebag?"

"Peanut butter sandwiches and all," the little girl said.

"Humph!" Her mother said, "I ain't going to have you starving. You take that bag and go on."

And she was the most popular thing in camp. All the kids wanted a bite of the porkchops. "Girl, give me a bite. Give me some of that." So after that she always brought that kind of lunch. "This is a real nosebag," they called it. "The real nosebag." They knew what she was going to have. Momma was going to cook and send it.

There were a lot of nice members with children, and there were a lot of nice things that girls should know. They made such fine friends early that they wouldn't have had a chance to make if they hadn't had scouting. Then we had a county meeting which brought all of the scouts together. The white and Negro Girl Scouts met at the Pocahontas Theater to practice for this big thing that they were going to have. And I remember the little white girls were timid about taking the hands of the Negro girls. They hadn't had too much contact because the places where they lived were small and they lived away from Negroes and they were separated in church and in school. There was one little girl who didn't know whether to take this little colored girl's hand. She started to take it and then she pulled her hand back. One mother, Mrs. Chapman, who was the wife of Dr. Chapman, the head of Grace Hospital, was on the committee; she was there with her little daughter who was just beginning scouting. She saw this little girl and said that she was becoming nervous because she thought somebody was going to make her take hold of the colored girl's hand. And Mrs. Chapman said to the leader, "Put my Alice there; she understands." So Alice Chapman said, "What is it you want me to do?" She walked on in there, snatched the little colored girl's hand, took it and went on.

You know, that did something for me when I saw that. I talked to a lot of the mothers after that, and I said, "The title to this little five-minute talk that I'm going to give you is 'A Little Girl Who Understands.'" And I told them what had happened. I told them I really think that those little experiences threw their influence farther than we knew.

In the years since I've been living in Huntington, I would go back to Welch for my physical examination. I'd go to the hospital to Dr. Chapman, and I told him, "I'm going to tell you something about your wife and you never knew it. I admire your wife. You'd never know how much." And I told him why. I said, "Now, I'm telling you that because I want to ask you something. Alice is grown; she's out of college; she has her own job. Does she still understand?"

He said, "Yes, she does. Alice is a trained social worker. She works in Pittsburgh; and she works in the Hill District with Negroes."

That was just ten years from the time of the incident with the little girl. So scouting has been a whole lot of things to me.

When I came to Huntington, they didn't have Girl Scouting among Negroes. They just had white troops; they began white troops in 1936. They have no record of Negro troops being held then. So, they went to a regional meeting where they were inquiring about the troops and Huntington. Mrs. Jean Carter reported that they had no troops among Negro girls and one woman spoke up and said, "But you're going to have one now." She gave Mrs. Carter my name and street number and said, "See her, and she'll set up her troops for you." So, Miss Crickmer, Mrs. Carter, and Mrs. Humphreys and the whole bunch descended on me here and said, "You have to help us." That was in the fall of '52. I was just moving to town, hadn't even straightened up. I said, "Give me until spring and I'll see what I can do."

So by February, after Christmas, I started and I got the churches, got the Catholic and all the churches, to send a leader to the office in town to get the training that it would take for the troops. The office held the training sessions. In the meantime, I got enough churches, and we organized troops, a total of a hundred and some girls. We had to have groups. They met on a different day, but that way we accommodated more girls. They met at the churches and they had the leaders and we carried through the program.

We had a field day. I was neighborhood chairman for a big event. We fixed the programs; we had a big demonstration at the fieldhouse. The Girl Scouts learned all kinds of folk dancing and made costumes. Parent committees helped make the costumes and the public was invited. They filled that fieldhouse for those Girl Scout days.

I handled Girl Scout cookies for our troops. One little girl who lived near me sold $1,000 worth. I didn't want to see a cookie after that. Cookies were from my front steps to the back porch. In addition to the Negro troops, there was a white troop here who got their cookies from me. Finally, the white troop moved on to another section, but one little girl named Mills was left. She'd come and said, "Auntie, can I come to your group?" I said, "Sure you can." She'd have to leave her school to get to the meeting. She rode her bicycle. If she didn't get there on time and we were going someplace, I'd put a note on the door. "We're at Ritter Park at such and such a place." It wouldn't be long before here would come this bicycle. We'd cook down at Appalachian Power Company and we'd take Mills. If she was a little late, I'd see a bicycle someplace and start looking for her because I knew she was there. She stayed with us until they moved to another part of the city and her mother set up a troop in the west end. I went down to help them set up that.

chapter 27

✻

Books for Africa

I was in Los Angeles and there were
quite a few African representatives from the different countries which
were seeking their freedom from the different countries who owned all
the interest in them. For instance, Belgium was being pushed out of
Africa as was England and all those. There were a lot of the top men
from those African countries that had been educated in the schools of
France, and there were Rhodes scholars from England. Those people
had come to the United States; I think their presence must have been
a sounding board on how the U.S. felt about them because they were
about everywhere. They were being entertained by all groups, not Negro
groups, but all groups that were there. All those people were paying
attention to those folks who were, I guess, goodwill ambassadors from
their countries.

I met Mr. Okunu from Nigeria and he was interested in the educational setup in that he said that textbooks were so scarce in his country
that ten children—ten youth—would have to use one book. They'd copy
it in longhand and learn from it—the desire was so great. If they were
willing to do that, you can imagine how desirous they were of getting
ready to become a part of the freedom that was to come to their country. So, he was wondering if he could get a club somewhere in the country to help, or a club there in Los Angeles. I didn't know about the other

parts of the country, but my friend, a music teacher who lives in Los Angeles, and I said we would join, so we added our names and addresses to the list.

After I came back home I was at the board of education office one day and I saw a lot of books lying around there, and I said to Mr. Brooks or one of them, "What are these books?" He said, "They're discontinued texts." Some of them were new; some of them—the boxes hadn't even been unpacked. They had decided not to use that publisher. And, oh, then I began to think to myself of some plan. What could be done about those books?

I went to Mr. Nutter [superintendent of Cabell County schools] and sat down with him and told him that I'd like to have those texts, and what I was going to do with them, and why. I told him about the conditions in Africa, and he said, "Well, I don't see any reason why you can't have them. We'd like to get them out of the way. Some places have been burning them up."

Well, that got it then. I said, "Well, burn no more, and I'll arrange for them."

"Where are you going to put them?" he wanted to know.

"I'll arrange some place, " I said.

"I'll tell you what I'll do," he said. "If you find a place, we'll load them up and bring them to you."

So I found the basement of the Sixteenth Street Baptist Church. Reverend [J. Carl] Mitchell said that the books could be put there until such a time as we could get the materials to pack them to send away. So the board of education sent its trucks and unloaded, oh, around 1,500 or 1,600 books there and said I could get more if I wanted them. Well, I thought that was quite enough. So then the lady who's the president of the Homemaker's Club was a former pupil of mine. I taught her when she was little. So she said, "Oh, my club will do it. We'll help you pack them. When do you want us to come?"

Well, then I went to the Armstrong people and asked what they could do to give us some strong cartons. They said, "We'll furnish you with cartons. How many do you want?" Another company furnished us that tape for sealing the boxes and the heavy twine for packing, and then those people in this Homemaker's Club were going to sort the books and mail them. So we took days there sorting the books into sizes that would fit in the boxes and noting the kinds of books they were and checking over what we had put in each box—so many texts of this and the other. It took quite a while; it took about six weeks to get all that done.

Finally, we got it done and in the meantime, while this was being done, I got in touch with the embassy. Nigeria had become an independent state and they had gotten an embassy in Washington and they had staffed it. They had a department of education and Mr. A. Y. Bida, a Rhodes scholar from Oxford, England, was heading it. He was quite a fellow, quite a man, quite an educator. He was a vocal sort of person and he said, "Send them to me." They had a steamship company which plied back and forth to new countries; that was their contribution and they would take these books. So we got them to the embassy in Washington. The embassy in Washington paid all the transportation to the Point Express Company here, and they came to the Sixteenth Street Baptist Church and took them out. The books were received in Washington and the thanks came from Washington and they said they would be very happy to have me visit. And later on I got a picture of them unpacking these books in Africa. I ran across an article in a magazine that said there were a thousand books that had arrived at that place for that school. I have the picture. They were unpacking these books. Then Mr. Okunu wrote that he had a part in the new state. He was head of T.V. and Radio Services for the new country, and he invited me to Nigeria. He thought it would be wonderful if we could get a group to come. There would be a special welcome for us because of what we had done. Ken Hechler, who was then our congressman, wrote to say that ours was the first gift from the United States to the new republic. Others sent gifts but ours arrived before any of the others did. That was the first gift from America, and he complimented us and said that he was glad to represent this district that had done that. It turned out to be a very successful. I could have gotten three thousand more books, but I was too feeble to pack any more.

chapter 28

✻

Awards

I received the Walker Medal in 1929.
This medal was given by the Walker Company. It was set up by Madam
C. J. Walker, the first Negro woman to have a hair business—hair straight-
ener; we used to have that. She had everything for beauty for the Negro
woman. She became—well, they said a millionaire; I say wealthy. Her
company gave me this gold medal with a hundred dollars in gold. The
medal is stamped with her picture and on the back it is engraved to
whom it is given and where and for what. They were giving it each year
at the annual NAACP meeting. There are eight of those medals, I think.
She died and in settling the estate, the practice dropped out. But there
are eight of those medals, and I have the fifth one. I got it for distinguished
service to Negroes in the United States through the NAACP. It was the
fact that I had raised money with the Christmas seals for the trial of the
two little Negro boys who had been jailed in Mississippi.

Our state NAACP conference awarded me the T. G. Nutter award for
my work up to that time in the field of Christian service and civil rights
—education and civil rights to the people of West Virginia. And that
included my community activities and church and religious activity. It
included a citation from the state for excellence in teaching and from the
county for the scholarships raised for Negro children and for the work
done at Bluefield State College. I was always available for everything. I

would speak at chapel at Bluefield State. I would speak at their celebrations. I was one of the speakers at their fiftieth anniversary celebration. My interest in general was in the educational setup. And then civil rights, of course, including my long-term service and activity with the NAACP. That was what the T. G. Nutter Award was for. That's issued by the state. T. G. Nutter was from Charleston and was a member of the national legal committee; and he met with the groups in Atlanta and New York, wherever the legal committee had to set up or to go for a briefing or to find out things, or to make guidelines for the integration picture. He was also the founder, the organizer of the state conference of the NAACP and he was president until he died in 1959.

The certificate from the state was issued by the state superintendent of schools and was given to me after I retired. It was for thirty-five years, and says "who for so many and so many years has done this." I guess, they had a general record that you had done work beyond the second mile in anything that had to do with the school and teaching and education. I had served as secretary of most everything they had. If I wasn't secretary, I was president of it. I had organized in our schools the Parent Teacher Association and had come to the meetings in Charleston to speak on the whys and wherefores of it. They had a very fine man there who was head of it; one of the first Negro assistant state superintendents, he organized the PTA among Negro schools. He's dead now—W. W. Sanders. I knew him and I had gone to meetings at his invitation and served on state programs and things like that. I'd been a part of the whole state setup so far as the schools were concerned. I had sponsored the first physical education demonstration that they ever had. Whatever it was, if I had time to do it, I would. They knew all that; they knew all that from the superintendent and the local place.

There were also some NAACP life membership dinners named for me and given in several communities in West Virginia. We were stressing life memberships because they afforded us surplus finance that we didn't get from the $2 memberships. You don't get much from the memberships when you divide them between the branch and the national. So the life membership is the same thing, but it provides you with more money inasmuch as life memberships are $500 each. When anybody pays a life membership, $200 of it may be used for local purposes and $300 is for the national work. Life memberships cost you just 15¢ a day. We figured it down to that to show people that anybody could be a life member, and that the life memberships meant so much more than the little $2 membership. You can't buy freedom anyway; $2 wouldn't buy anything, wouldn't buy the word "freedom" hardly. We would tell them that if they felt that they could become life members, they wouldn't have to do without anything—15¢ per day is not much. At the end of the year they'd have $55, and that $55 is what they'd pay each year on their own life membership. If they wanted to take it on that scale, it would take them ten years to pay. Well, anybody can become a member at that point, so we were pressing the importance of having this stable group that has paid, who was there and who was recognized by those bronze plaques with their name or their organization on it. Organizations could do the same thing; churches and all could combine. So the organization got the idea that rather than just asking the branches to get life memberships, they'd have a special kind of meeting, a special kind of dinner, and that it would be named for someone who had done a special kind of work over a period of time, which happened to be me. I don't think that any of the members wanted to be as old as I am and none of them want to be there as long as I have been, so they had no choice but take me. And the persons who come pay for the dinner which takes care of local expenses as well as helps get a prize for the branch which has brought in the largest number of life memberships. That is, has brought in the initial payments on life memberships. In Fayetteville, I think, $16,500 worth was subscribed to; they can pay it off at $50 a year. At Charleston, I think it was $10,000, and at Logan, I didn't get the exact amount from Mr. Henderson, but I think it was around $10,000. It wasn't far off. Now, they've made a pretty good amount—about $36,000 will be coming into the treasury for the next group over the next ten years.

[In recognition of her contributions to the civic life of the state of West Virginia, Mrs. Garrison was awarded a doctorate of humanities by Marshall University in 1970 and the M. L. King, Jr. "Living the Dream" Award in 1988.—Eds.]

VII

conclusion

chapter 29

Epilogue

Memphis Tennessee Garrison died in
Huntington in 1988. She was ninety-eight years old and had lived most
of her life in West Virginia—more than sixty years in McDowell County
and the last thirty in Huntington in Cabell County. She left friends in
both places and a legacy of achievement that remains inspirational.

"The only tangible reminder that I have of Mrs. Garrison," said long-
time friend Evelyn Payne Starling of Memphis, Tennessee, "is a letter I
saved, written October 1974. It begins, 'My dear, dear friend: Due to ill-
ness during the past year I have not been in touch with a number of
friends though I have not forgotten you and Maxine' [her daughter]. It
was signed 'Memphis T.' as usual. That excellent penmanship just flows
across the page—clear as always. I remember Memphis Tennessee Garrison as a woman who was intelligent, focused, well read, witty, a public
speaker than whom there was none better . . . and a friend."

Attorney Herbert Henderson, a McDowell County native who man-
aged Mrs. Garrison's affairs over the last years of her life, reminisced
about her:

> I knew of Mrs. Garrison ever since I was in high school, too many
> years ago for me to think of. Every black person in McDowell County
> knew about Memphis Tennessee Garrison. You couldn't grow up there if

you didn't know about her. We knew about Gary; we knew about the things that she brought to Gary. We knew how she had U.S. Steel to bring in the Count Basies, bring in the black entertainers, the black intellectuals, the Marian Andersons. She was just it.

I used to listen to Heywood Simpson [music teacher] and Dr. Gunn and some of the other people from McDowell County who were living in Huntington at the time talk about Mrs. Garrison. Probably more than anything else, she had the respect of all those people. She had learned how to be a survivor for her people. She was committed to the worth of the individual and always taught people to be proud of who they were.

My first real relationship with her was when I came to Huntington to practice law. I came here and didn't know anybody. It was in the summer of 1958 and it was about the time that Mrs. Garrison came. She had no close relatives here, but she had relationships. Reverend Smith and I and others would go there and sit and listen. We'd talk and listen. She was a very wise person. She was very neat, very thrifty about money matters, and very much a lady—a person with great character.

Immediately, we became bonded and from that time on until the very end, I spent a great deal of time with her—in her home, and on trips. One of our common bonds was our love of the NAACP. She's the one who taught me. She had a picture or a program of everything that had happened in the NAACP almost since its founding. We spent hours poring over the various conventions, leaders, people in the NAACP from all over the country. That's how I fell in love with the NAACP. So did a lot of other people, I think.

I remember my golden opportunity to meet Thurgood Marshall* in Minneapolis. She encouraged me to go. "Go and talk to Thurgood," she said. She knew the Whites, the Wilkins. She knew people. I would go here and there and she would say, "Henderson, get in touch with so and so and tell him I said, 'Hi.' He'll help you." She knew Afro-American people who were in the civil rights movement throughout this country. The "do-ers"—she knew them all. And she enjoyed the reputation among them as a person who was dedicated to the cause.

Concerning Garrison's political activities, Henderson noted,

*Black attorney who was a major figure in the *Brown v. Board of Education* case and became the first black Supreme Court justice.

She had been active on behalf of Republican causes and Republican individuals who sought office, but most of the time that I knew her she talked about her political work, but she didn't seem to have the same pride and enthusiasm for political work that she did for her NAACP relationships. It was as if she had put politics behind her and concentrated on the NAACP.

But "Mrs. Garrison's great legacy," Henderson believes,

is her influencing so many young black women in McDowell County to seek an education. I know that from the people who were in the NAACP with me as late as the 1950s. Many of the female students from McDowell County at Bluefield State College were there because Mrs. Garrison sent them. She'd say, "Take your two dresses and go on. You can make it." She has that legacy. She was a person with dignity, pride, and empathy for those who were less fortunate. She was proud of her race and tried to reach out to help, particularly to African American women, to teach them the scheme of life—about everything from cleanliness to the church. She was the embodiment of everything that I consider good. Most people that she touched grew intellectually and morally. Without her a lot of things wouldn't have happened. She was a bright star in the southern coalfields.

Similarly, Charles Holley, who had been one of Mrs. Garrison's first-grade students, recalled, "In the twenties we had no voice. Everybody was a miner. Mrs. Garrison was our spokesperson. She was a pioneer for our rights. She was very active and widely respected."

Holley also remembered Mrs. Garrison's kindness and humane concern for the children she taught. "She was my first teacher and was well respected in our area. We had no school buses in certain of our communities, especially in Number 6. Children walked to school from the Number 6 'holler'[1] in the wintertime and about froze," Holley said. "Mrs. Garrison would make cocoa for the kids to warm them on those days. She cared about us. She sponsored activities for us—the Ninth of April Celebration, May Day, public speaking competitions, and so on."

John Settle of Moorpark, California, knew Mrs. Garrison as his second-grade teacher, a next-door neighbor, and a community activist. "Mrs. Garrison was doing things that most other women didn't do. She was a woman who was far ahead of her time," Mr. Settle commented. He spoke of her involvement with the NAACP Christmas seal project, with Republican politics, with the Ninth of April programs, and with other community work. "She also made great improvements in our recreational opportunities," he recalled. "We couldn't use the white facilities, so she started some for us. We called our place Number 5 Country Club. It had a skating rink and a pool; the building was primitive, no screens on the windows or anything, but we could have dances and other activities there."

Marshall University professor of English Dolores Johnson rented an apartment from Garrison when she was first married. "She was a wonderful lady and she was always the teacher," Dr. Johnson said.

Although Gary native Carolyne Brown, now a social worker in Huntington, did not have personal experience of Garrison as a teacher, Brown's mother had been one of Garrison's students. "I had heard about Mrs. Garrison through my parents and through relatives and neighbors," Mrs. Brown said.

> She had taught my mother; I got to know her when I came to Marshall in 1961 and immediately fell in love with her. She was a dynamic, vibrant person and she liked having people from Gary with whom she could talk visit with her.
>
> I had also heard about Mrs. Garrison's civic activities. She was very active with the NAACP, and to a great extent, that got her in trouble with her employers. In particular, her civil rights activities made it extremely difficult for her in the school system in McDowell County at that time. McDowell County did not integrate schools until 1965, eleven years after the Brown Decision, so you can imagine what some of the racial attitudes were like in the county. It was said that the power structure felt that Mrs. Garrison didn't know her place. Her civil rights involvement showed a lot of courage. She was a dynamic woman and did things that other people did not do. But among us, she was well respected, well thought of—almost held in awe because of the things that she did and the way that she carried herself.

"At some point," Evelyn Starling said, "I began to request that Memphis do an autobiography and include the 'Free State of McDowell' account"—after a term coined by Tom Whittico, publisher of the black newspaper, the *McDowell Times;* "the whole bit—as faction, not fiction. I wanted all that good positive activity told as history. After Memphis's family had died she moved to 1703 Tenth Avenue in Huntington. On one of my trips back home I made it my business to stop over and spend at least one day with Memphis. I found her sprightly, but the years had taken their toll and she was frail to fragile. But that mind was acute, her memory seemed excellent, and she said she was gathering materials to put together that story I kept asking her to complete and publish."

Although Garrison did not actually put pen to paper to write her memoirs, and in spite of the fact that most of those artifacts she had so diligently saved were lost or damaged by a water leak where they were stored in her house, Bernard Cleveland of the Marshall University faculty did record the audio tape with her from which this document has been drawn. And along with her own story, Garrison did provide an account of some aspects of life in the "Free State of McDowell."

chapter 30

✴

Commentary

Ancella R. Bickley

Memphis Tennessee Garrison's story of her life in West Virginia brings a needed voice to material of and about Appalachia. Although there has been a black presence in the area almost since the beginning of non-native settlement, that it is seldom reflected in any organic way adds to the general "invisibility" of area black people. What has traditionally been presented as "Appalachian" is a pervasive image of agriculturally based rural people who create quilts, crafts, and country music, most growing out of European-derived customs and worldviews. The almost universal adoption of such a description offers little understanding or acknowledgement of the black presence. Further, both the emphasis on a Euro-Appalachian identity and the near indifference to other ways of life prevent many blacks from accepting their birthright. Many find it difficult to relate to the popular Appalachian images and retreat to an often state-specific, but more definitive and personally satisfying, generalized black identity.

Garrison's "story," however, her emotional and intellectual grounding in the history of black people and her commitment to an Appalachian black community, challenges many prevailing assumptions. For example, although the literature does report that there were black miners, Mrs. Garrison's unequivocal statement, "Negroes built this coalfield; that's it" lays claim to an Appalachia that few have acknowledged—a place where black people were not simply users, but creators; where their labor helped to open a new industry; where they built community and exercised their will to make a life for themselves in spite of great odds. To my knowledge, nowhere else in currently available Appalachian material is there such a sensitive firsthand account of black life in a mining community in an essentially southern state. For example, nowhere in another West Virginia document is the poignant account of black children finding a rope used to hang a neighbor, or learning to count using apples and acorns, or of a black teacher's fledgling attempt to help her slow-learning students in spite of administrative neglect.

Beginning her exposition of black life in a mining community with the time that the mines began to operate, Garrison also deals with West Virginia black people as shapers of their lives and environment. They built institutions such as churches and lodges and began to assert themselves on both local and national levels. Locally, they began to demand a more equitable educational system and developed astute leaders who learned to use both political and social systems to advance their people's causes. In this regard, Garrison was a prime practitioner. She adapted whatever was available to teach, to learn, and to improve the quality of life of those within her sphere, whether it was by developing her Negro Artists' Series or a skating rink, establishing a Girl Scout chapter or sending books to Africa.

Subsequent to their early hardscrabble community-based development, West Virginia blacks, including Garrison, connected to state and national black communities. An important feature in this effort was the NAACP, which brought organizational force to their activities. Other than in Garrison's account, the stories of these lives, of these developments, have not found their way into the literature of the state. Certainly, Memphis Tennessee Garrison's story does not parallel every black woman's life, but it is a black Appalachian story to which many of us can relate and whose telling is long overdue.

Memphis Tennessee Garrison and West Virginia's African American Experience

✳

HISTORICAL AFTERWORD

Joe W. Trotter

Memphis Tennessee Garrison's story is closely intertwined with the history of African Americans in the Mountain State. Bordered by parts of Ohio, Pennsylvania, and Maryland to the north, and by Kentucky and Virginia on the south and southeast, West Virginia was a product of the Civil War. When Virginia seceded from the Union, citizens in western Virginia seceded from it and formed a new state. Anti-secession sentiment was also strong in other upcountry areas—eastern Tennessee and western North Carolina—where the extent of slaveholding was far less significant than elsewhere in the South, but unlike West Virginia the struggle over secession did not lead to new states there. Unfortunately, the new state of West Virginia refused to couple statehood with the abolition of slavery. As one historian notes, "Several times during this formative period, the opposition of the pro-slavery group became so strong that it appeared that only a small minority in what is now West Virginia really desired separation from Virginia."[1] Even so, the legislation that admitted West Virginia to the Union provided for the gradual abolition of slavery. This ambiguous legacy of slavery and freedom, justice and inequality, would shape the experiences of African Americans through the nineteenth and twentieth centuries.

West Virginia's black history is inextricably connected to the history of slavery in Virginia. In 1619, when "a Dutch man of warre" sold twenty

Africans to the British settlers in Virginia, it established a beachhead for the growth of West Virginia's black population. African Americans entered western Virginia in the 1750s. They settled in Greenbrier and New River Valleys with the slaveholding family of William and Mary Ingles. While some African Americans soon joined Native Americans against European invaders, most sided with Europeans, partly because they were frequently the target of Indian attacks along with whites. In April 1782, for instance, Native Americans captured the wife, children, and slaves of Thomas Ingles. Under the impact of the French and Indian Wars, and, then, the American Revolution and the westward expansion of the new nation, slavery continued to spread into western Virginia. Although the Continental Congress rejected proposals to use black troops, the Virginia legislature approved the enlistment of slaves, promising masters $1,000 for each enlisted slave, and slaves $50 and freedom at war's end. African American enlistees defended the colony and helped to broaden the base of European settlement in western Virginia. Slaves cleared land and posted claims for white men such as George Washington in Kanawha, Randolph, Monongalia, Mason, Greenbrier, and other counties in the future state of West Virginia.

During the early national period, the number of slaves and free blacks in western Virginia increased significantly. The number of slaves increased from slightly more than 5,200 in 1790 to almost 20,000 in 1830, while free blacks rose from just over 600 to nearly 2,200. While some blacks worked on large plantations in Greenbrier, Hampshire, Pendleton, and Berkeley counties, most labored on small farms, in households, and as common laborers in the region's slowly developing iron, coal, and salt industries.

As elsewhere in the antebellum South, following Nat Turner's rebellion and the rise of the militant abolitionist movement, blacks in western Virginia suffered growing restrictions as slaves and free people. During the early 1830s, the Virginia assembly ordered free blacks to leave the state within a year of manumission; outlawed the teaching of slaves to read and write; prohibited the service of slave preachers; and denied free blacks trial by jury. The black population soon declined from 11 percent of the total in 1830 to 6 percent in 1860; the absolute number of blacks also declined from a peak of 23,500 in 1850 to about 21,110 on the eve of the Civil War.

Despite the difficulties they faced, slaves and free blacks developed a keen sense of justice and a fierce determination to fight inequality. Their struggle not only was depicted in major events like the American Revolution, but also surfaced on a day-to-day basis. As early as 1801, for example, a free black named Jack Neal was the first person to be tried in the Kanawha County Court, when he resisted slavery by killing one slave driver and injuring another. Although denied access to the legal system, slaves initiated procedures for their own manumission. In a letter to a white attorney, the slave Amos Timmons of Ohio County revealed the process: "Dear Mr. [Philip] Doddridge, I have wrote to you to know whether you can free me or not sire. . . . And if you pleas to undertake this Business sir I will give you good security for yore trouble in this matter. Your humble servant. Amos Timmons."

The advent of the Civil War transformed the lives of African Americans in western Virginia. In 1861 Virginia seceded from the Union and joined the Confederacy, but the western delegates voted against secession, and set in motion a movement for statehood. When West Virginia gained statehood in 1863, however, it did not become a haven for slaves and free blacks. During the war years, the state's black population actually dropped from more than 21,000 in 1860 to about 17,000, or 3 percent of the total, by war's end. This was partly a consequence of how emancipation came to blacks in West Virginia. Although the law provided for the gradual emancipation of slaves, the Mountain State entered the Union as a slave state. The law provided "That slave children, 10 years of age and under shall be free at 21 and that slaves over 10 and under 25 shall be free at 25." Although some whites advocated the complete and full abolition of slavery in the new state, most hoped to make West Virginia a white man's state. Before the constitutional convention approved legislation for gradual emancipation, the original provision stated that "No slave shall be brought or free person of color come into this state for permanent residence after this constitution goes into effect." Only in February 1865 did the state end chattel slavery in West Virginia.

As elsewhere, blacks in West Virginia played a crucial role in their own liberation. Some "voted for freedom with their feet." During the Civil War, Washington Ferguson, Booker T. Washington's stepfather, escaped from slavery and followed Union soldiers into the Kanawha Valley. He would later send for his wife Jane and his children, including the young Booker T. Other blacks migrated further north and joined the Union Army there. West Virginia blacks served in the Union forces of Ohio, Pennsylvania, and other northern states, making up four companies in all. Born in Charlestown, Jefferson County, Martin R. Delaney, the most renowned of the West Virginia blacks to serve, became a medical officer and attained the rank of major. When emancipation came in 1865, African Americans in West Virginia could claim a role in bringing it about.

The first generation of freedmen and -women faced the challenge of making real their citizenship in a democracy. In order to claim full-fledged citizenship, blacks had to gain not only emancipation, but the right to vote and hold public office, serve on juries, and testify and act as witnesses in courts of law. Unfortunately, until the suffrage amendment of 1920, these efforts would favor black men over black women, although black women would play an indispensable role in the social, economic, and political life of African Americans.

The status of blacks in the first years of freedom remained ambiguous. In February 1865, when the state ratified legislation outlawing slavery, it also approved the Fourteenth Amendment, extending to blacks full citizenship rights (ahead of the amended United States Constitution). Nonetheless, the acquisition of democratic freedoms was a slow and arduous process for blacks in the Mountain State. In 1866, the legislature introduced a measure permitting blacks to testify and serve as witnesses in courts of law. Opposition to the bill was fierce and bitter. Opponents believed that blacks were incompetent to act as witnesses, that such a bill would encourage black suffrage, that it would weaken the Union Party, and that it would create racial antagonisms. The governor of West Virginia eloquently defended the measure, and it finally passed.

Ratification of the Fifteenth Amendment, guaranteeing to blacks the right to vote, also produced sharp opposition. Because the Fifteenth Amendment barred rebels from the franchise, many whites refused to support a measure that enfranchised blacks and disfranchised whites, whatever the reasoning. Thus, before black men could secure the suffrage in West Virginia, the Flick Amendment, extending the suffrage to ex-Confederates, was also adopted. As elsewhere in the South, the Democratic party led the movement for white supremacy. In 1870, at its state convention in Charleston, the Democratic party pledged itself as the "white man's party." At the state's constitutional convention in 1872, the Democrats also led the fight to disfranchise black citizens. Although the new constitution enfranchised blacks by a vote of 36 to 30, it denied blacks the right to serve on juries, approved the segregationist clause that "white and colored shall not be taught in the same school," and sanctioned a racially stratified and unequal society that would persist into the twentieth century.

Blacks in the Mountain State resisted efforts to curtail their citizenship rights. In the constitutional convention of 1872, for example, sixty-two black citizens of Jefferson County presented a memorial to the convention. Under the leadership of Charley Arter, for whom there is little biographical data, they urged the adoption of a provision that would permit black men to serve on juries in the state's courts of law. Unlike several other southern states, however, West Virginia's blacks were a much smaller percentage of the total electorate. Thus, they carefully allied with key Republican leaders and pushed their claims upon the state with substantial success. Drawing their cues from the sentiments of blacks, some whites eloquently articulated the position of African Americans. In his address supporting the right of blacks to testify in court, governor Arthur Boreman stated that "Until this act of justice is done, all other guarantees are fruitless, and these unfortunate people are left to the mercy of anyone who chooses to inflict injury upon them." Another white Republican endorsed black suffrage, emphasizing how blacks bore the burdens of citizenship and should therefore enjoy its privileges and protections: "In war you send the Negro to the front . . . in peace you impose upon him all the duties of citizenship; why not let him vote? Republicanism makes no distinction before the law on account of race or color." Only during the 1890s and early 1900s, however, would blacks increase their proportion of the state's voting-age male population from negligible numbers following the Civil War to about 17 percent.

Under the impact of industrialization following Reconstruction, African Americans faced the complicated transition from southern agriculture to life in coal mining towns. The black population increased from 25,800 in 1880 to more than 64,000 in 1910, and to nearly 115,000 in 1930. The growth of the bituminous coal industry underlay this dynamic population growth. Coal production increased from less than 5 million tons in 1885 to nearly 40 million in the southern counties alone by 1910. Although the industry experienced sharp cyclical swings, southern West Virginia mines produced more than 120 million tons in 1925. Blacks made up more than 20 percent of West Virginia's total coal mining labor force from the 1890s through the early twentieth century.

African Americans played a key role in the growth of the state's coal industry. Blacks from rural areas of the upper South, mainly Virginia, helped to lay track for the three major railroads that helped to open up the bituminous fields: the Chesapeake and Ohio, the Norfolk and Western, and the Virginian. It was work on the Chesapeake and Ohio that produced the black folk hero John Henry. As each railroad completed lines through the region, contingents of black railroad men remained behind to work in the coal mines. They were later joined by growing numbers of blacks who went directly into the mines. While blacks from the nearby upper South and border states of Virginia, Kentucky, and Tennessee dominated the migration stream to West Virginia during the period, the advent of World War I brought growing numbers of migrants from the Deep South states of Alabama, Georgia, and Mississippi. From the turn of the century through the early 1930s, African Americans made up between 20 and 26 percent of the total coal mining labor force in southern West Virginia. They also gradually increased their percentage in the mines in northern West Virginia, but they would remain a much smaller percentage of the total there. Coal companies actively recruited black workers, but black men and women also established their own kin and friendship networks, and helped to facilitate their own movement into the coal mining towns. Moreover, since coal mining required the acquisition of new skills and work habits—especially safety procedures in the new volatile work environment—blacks also helped to transform themselves into a new industrial working class.

As the African American population increased, racial hostility escalated. In 1919, for example, a white mob lynched two black miners at Chapmanville, Logan County. During the early 1920s, chapters of the Ku Klux Klan emerged in Logan, Mercer, and Kanawha counties. Moreover, racial injustice before the law also prevailed, as in several cases of black men accused of crimes against whites, especially charges of rape. In 1921, for example, the governor denied a plea for clemency and permitted a black man to hang despite evidence that suggested his innocence.

As they made the transition to the new industrial era, African Americans developed a variety of institutional and political responses to inequality. Although black business and professional men would dominate leadership positions, black workers and women also shaped the growth of black community life. Predominantly Baptist and African Methodist Episcopal (AME), membership in black religious organizations climbed from less than 15,000 in the pre–World War I years to nearly 33,000 in 1926. Membership in black fraternal orders and mutual benefit societies reached similar proportions, about 32,000 before declining during the late 1920s. The emergence of West Virginia branches and affiliates of the National Association for the Advancement of Colored People (NAACP) and the Universal Negro Improvement Association (i.e., the Garvey Movement), the McDowell County Colored Republican Organization, and the black weekly *McDowell Times* rounded out the institutional life of blacks in West Virginia before the onslaught of the Great Depression. Under the editorship of Matthew Thomas Whittico, a graduate of Lincoln University in Pennsylvania, the *McDowell Times* voiced the civil rights struggles of blacks in West Virginia. Moreover, Whittico envisioned the black press as an alternative to the biased reporting of the white papers: "The white press champions the cause of all people except the negro, and upon the question of his rights . . . it is left to the negro papers to wage an unceasing warfare upon the enemies of the negro." Whittico also popularized the phrase, "The Free State of McDowell," the state's largest center of black population and political influence.

The expanding network of black institutions underlay the vigorous political mobilization of blacks in the state. Unlike their counterparts in most southern states during the era of Jim Crow, lynchings, and disfranchisement, African Americans in West Virginia retained the franchise. They strengthened their traditional political alliance with the Republican party, but, unlike the earlier period, as their membership increased they also elected their own representatives to state and local offices. In 1918, for example, blacks sent three black men to the legislature: the Charleston attorney T. G. Nutter, the Keystone attorney Harry J. Capehart, and, most significantly, the coal miner John V. Coleman of Fayette County.

After receiving the suffrage in 1920, black women also increased their influence in the political life of the state. In 1927, when the black legislator E. Howard Harper died in office, his wife, Mrs. Minnie Buckingham Harper, served the remainder of his term. Mrs. Harper became "the first woman of the negro race to become a member of a legislative body in the United States." At the local level, black women also gained election to significant posts, particularly to city council. Moreover, they often took leading roles in the West Virginia branches and affiliates of the NAACP, UNIA, and MCCRO. Memphis Tennessee Garrison, the schoolteacher and civil rights activist, was among the prominent black women in the institutional, social, and political life of the state. During the 1920s, she initiated the NAACP's national Christmas seal campaign, and later won the organization's coveted Madame C. J. Walker Gold Medal Award for her work.

Based on the activities of black men and women, elites and workers, African American political campaigns produced significant results in the Mountain State. Black legislators soon helped to pass a state antilynching law, a statute barring the showing of inflammatory films like *The Birth of a Nation,* and appropriations for the expansion of old and the creation of new social welfare and educational institutions. By 1930, African Americans claimed access to two state colleges (West Virginia State and Bluefield State); a tuberculosis sanitarium; homes for the deaf, blind, aged, and infirm; schools for delinquent youth; a Bureau of Negro Welfare and Statistics; and an expanding number of public elementary, junior high, and high schools.

Under the impact of the Great Depression of the 1930s, blacks shouldered a disproportionate share of the unemployment and hard times.

Their percentage in the state's coal mining labor force dropped from more than 22 percent in 1930 to about 17 percent in 1940. The Depression and World War II also unleashed new technological and social forces that transformed the coal industry, and stimulated massive out-migration in the postwar years. Although coal companies had installed undercutting machines in their mines during the 1890s, the handloading of coal remained intact until the advent of the mechanical loader during the late 1930s. Loading machines rapidly displaced miners during the 1940s and '50s. As one black miner recalled, "The day they put the loading machine on our section, the coal loaders went in to work but the boss was already there and he said that the men not on his list could pick up their tools and leave." A black miner recalled that the mine management "always put them [loading machines] where blacks were working first." Black men, he said, could not "kick" against the machines.

Mechanization decimated the black coal mining labor force. The percentage of black miners dropped steadily to about 12 percent in 1950, 6.6 percent in 1960, and 5.2 percent in 1970. By 1980, African Americans made up less than 3 percent of the state's coal miners. To be sure, the white labor force had also declined, dropping by nearly 36 percent, but the black proportion had declined by more than 90 percent. Under the leadership of John L. Lewis, the United Mine Workers of America adopted a policy on technological change that reinforced the unequal impact of mechanization on black workers. As Lewis put it, "Shut down 4,000 coal mines, force 200,000 miners into other industries, and the coal problem will settle itself."

As the state's black coal mining labor force declined, racial discrimination persisted in all facets of life in the Mountain State. In 1961, according to the West Virginia Human Rights Commission, most of the state's public accommodations—restaurants, motels, hotels, swimming pools, and medical facilities—discriminated against blacks. Moreover, applications for institutions of higher learning contained questions on race and religion designed to exclude so-called undesirable groups. Finally, and most importantly, as blacks lost coal mining jobs, they found few alternative employment opportunities. The state's Human Rights Commission reported that "Numerous factories, department stores, and smaller private firms had obvious, if unwritten, policies whereby blacks were not hired or promoted to jobs of importance or positions in which they would have day-to-day contact with white clientele."

Building upon the traditions bequeathed by preceding generations, African Americans responded to declining economic and social conditions in a variety of ways. Many moved to the large metropolitan areas of the Northeast and Midwest. Smaller networks of West Virginia blacks emerged in cities like Cleveland, Chicago, Detroit, and New York. Others moved to the nearby upper South and border cities of Washington, D.C., and Alexandria, Virginia. Still others moved as far west as California. Indicative of the rapid outmigration of West Virginia blacks, the state's total African American population dropped from a peak of 117,700 in 1940 to 65,000 in 1980, a decline from 6 to 3 percent of the total.

Still, other West Virginia blacks remained behind and struggled to make a living in the emerging new order. The dwindling number of African Americans did not sit quietly waiting for things to change under them. Charles Brooks, a black miner from Kanawha County, served as the first president of the Black Lung Association, which in 1969 marched on the state capital in Charleston to demand compensation for miners suffering from the disease. In 1972, the Black Lung Association also played a key role in the coalition of forces that made up Miners for Democracy, a rank-and-file movement that resisted the growing autarchy of the United Miner Workers of America's top leaders like Tony Boyle. As early as the mid-1930s, along with blacks elsewhere in America, West Virginia blacks had reevaluated their historic links to the Republican party and found it lacking. They joined the Democratic party and helped to buttress the volatile New Deal coalition of northern urban ethnic groups, organized labor, and devotees of the so-called "solid South." As suggested by their declining numbers in the coal industry, however, the black alliance with the Democratic party produced few lasting benefits in the Mountain State.

Under the impact of the 1954 *Brown v. Board of Education* decision, blacks in West Virginia pushed for full access to the state's public schools, colleges, and universities. As late as 1963, most African Americans continued to receive education within a segregated public school system.

The tradition of all-black public institutions nonetheless gradually came to an end. As early as 1956, the state had terminated the Bureau of Negro Welfare and Statistics. Bluefield State College and West Virginia State College became predominantly white by the mid-1970s. At the same time, local school boards closed one black high school after another, bringing to a close one of the major public institutions in black life during the era of Jim Crow. As R. Charles Byers, professor of education at West Virginia State College, states, the fall of black high schools was a "heartbreaking" development, "but what was more deplorable was the injustice that took place in West Virginia. The artifacts, trophies, books, yearbooks, and records now referred to as memorabilia were burned or placed away in boxes and forgotten."

Partly because of the often bitter fruits of integration, African Americans in the Mountain State retained their own institutions. They struggled to maintain black churches, fraternal orders, social clubs, civil rights and political organizations, and the black press. Formed in the 1950s, the *Beacon Journal* replaced the *McDowell Times* as the preeminent organ of black public opinion in the state. In 1988, the First Baptist Church of Charleston hosted the First Annual Conference on West Virginia's Black History. Spearheaded by the Alliance for the Collection, Preservation, and Dissemination of West Virginia's Black History, the annual conference has featured a variety of papers, speeches, and comments on the state's black heritage. It also has reflected an enduring commitment to African American institutions, values, and beliefs.

Although characterized by enduring patterns of class and racial inequality, the history of African Americans in West Virginia is not one but many stories. The first generation faced the challenge of transforming themselves from slaves into citizens in the larger body politic. While this goal was only partially realized and would persist over the next century, the next generation confronted its own unique challenge. During the late nineteenth and early twentieth centuries, African Americans in the Mountain State faced the difficult transition from life in southern agriculture to life in coal mining towns. Despite important class and gender differences, between black men and women and between black workers and black elites, African Americans built upon the traditions of their predecessors, bridged social cleavages, and protected their collective interests. Like preceding generations, the current generation is reckoning with the impact of mechanization, the decline of the coal industry, and the massive outmigration of blacks to cities throughout the nation.

How well black West Virginians succeed in building upon the lessons of the past is still to be seen. Yet, Memphis Tennessee Garrison's life provides an extraordinary source of inspiration for their efforts. When queried about her unique name, Memphis Garrison once replied: "My mother had never been to Biloxi, Mississippi." Born in Hollins, Virginia, on March 4, 1890, Garrison died in Huntington, West Virginia, on July 25, 1988. The youngest of two children of former slaves, Wesley Carter, a coal miner, and Cassie Thomas Carter, Garrison grew up in the coalfields of southern West Virginia. After receiving her elementary education in the segregated public schools there, she earned her B.A. with honors from Bluefield State College in West Virginia and pursued advanced study at Ohio University in Athens. Twenty-five years after the historic march on Washington, Garrison received the Governor's "Living the Dream" Award for distinguished service to West Virginia and the nation.

In 1908, Memphis Garrison launched her public school teaching career in McDowell County. She taught there until her retirement in the early 1950s. Garrison later recalled that she had wanted to be a lawyer, but her mother could not afford the required training. Garrison married Melvin Garrison, a coal miner. They had no children. If they had, it is likely that Garrison's teaching career would have been cut short, since as elsewhere, West Virginia openly discouraged the employment of married teachers with children.

Beyond completing a distinguished career as a public school teacher, Garrison also influenced the political life of the region. As secretary of the McDowell County branch of the National Association for the Advancement of Colored People (NAACP), her activities covered a broad range of local, regional, and national projects. In addition to local campaigns against racial inequality before the law, she spearheaded the national Christmas seal campaign during the late 1920s and early 1930s. Under the motto, "Merry Christmas and Justice for All," the Christmas seal campaign generated widespread support for the NAACP and netted substantial sums for the national office.

Until her death in 1988, Garrison continued to serve the state and nation. She served as the first woman president of the West Virginia State Teachers' Association, 1929–30; treasurer of the NAACP West Virginia State Conference, for twenty-two years; NAACP National Field Secretary, 1956–59; national vice president of the NAACP Board of Directors, 1964–66; member of the West Virginia Human Rights Commission, 1963–66; and member of President Lyndon B. Johnson's National Citizens Committee on Community Relations, 1964. For her distinguished public service, Garrison received numerous awards and honors: the NAACP's Madam C. J. Walker Gold Medal Award, 1929; the T. G. Nutter Award for outstanding achievement and service in the field of civil rights, 1959; the NAACP Distinguished Service Award, 1969; honorary degree of Doctor of Humanities, Marshall University in Huntington, 1970; and, as noted above, the governor's "Living the Dream" Award, 1988.

Although Garrison gained recognition for fighting racial injustice, her activities demonstrated a keen interest in equity across gender and class lines. Despite her professional training, Garrison retained close ties with the black coal-mining working class. In two illuminating essays on black Americans in southern West Virginia, she exhibited unusual sensitivity to the ideas, aspirations, and grievances of black workers. During the 1920s, Garrison challenged the gender distribution of power within the McDowell County Colored Republican Organization, which often held the balance of power in West Virginia politics. The career of Memphis Tennessee Garrison takes on added significance because the southern Appalachian mountains are often perceived as isolated from the main currents of American history. Her contributions deepen our understanding of life in the Mountain State, link black West Virginians to a national black community, and highlight the interplay of class, race, and gender in American society.

notes

✵

Introduction

1. In the early part of the twentieth century, there was tremendous backlash against immigrants, particularly those from southern Europe. Those who had been born in the United States considered themselve "natives." Organizations to protect the privileges (and jobs) of the native-born were formed—the largest of which was the Know Nothing Party. Adherents of the anti-immigrant movement were called "nativists."

2. Dorothy C. Salem, "Black Women and the NAACP, 1909–1922: An Encounter with Race, Class, and Gender," in *Black Women in America*, ed. Kim Marie Vaz (Thousand Oaks, Calif.: Sage Publications, 1995), 54–70.

3. Historically, slavery emerged with the development of large-scale societies and standing armies. The institutional form that slavery took varied greatly depending on cultural context. It was only with the development of capitalism, however, that the slave ceased to exist as a person and became "capital." This worldview held that these human beings were not "human" but could, instead, be "used up," just as a machine or animal could be used. Lerone Bennet Jr., in his classic work *Before the Mayflower*, describes capitalist slavery as "a social system as coercive as any yet known erected on the framework of the most implacable race consciousness yet observed in virtually any society" (New York: Penguin Books, 1982), 86. And he argues that slavery in Protestant North America was "the deepest pit," in comparison to the French and Spanish colonies (51). See Joe R. Feagin and Clairece Booher Feagin's discussion in *Racial and Ethnic Relations*, 5th ed. (Upper Saddle River, N.Y.: Prentice Hall, 1996), 30–56. For a historical discussion of oppositional culture in the American slave community see Howard Zinn, "Drawing the Color Line," in *A People's History of the United States* (New York: Harper/Colophone Books, 1980), 23–38.

4. George P. Rawick's study *From Sundown to Sunup* (New York: Greenwood Publishing Group, 1972) remains the classic study of how the slave community created its own culture.

5. Vaz, *Black Women in America*, xvii.

6. Fuller detail of the role of African Americans in the coalfields and the state of West Virginia is provided in the historical afterword by Joe W. Trotter.

7. This difference in perspective is analyzed by Linda Gordon, "Black and White Visions of Welfare: Women's Welfare Activism, 1890–1945," in *Unequal Sisters,* ed. Vicki L. Ruiz and Ellen C. DuBois, 2nd ed. (New York: Routledge, 1994), 157–85.

8. Carol Stack's careful study of the urban black community (*All Our Kin: Strategies for Survival in a Black Community* [New York: Harper Torchbook, 1975]) was the first to show the importance of such networks for survival. Jacqueline Jones's history of the movement of southern blacks into the industrial North (*America's Underclasses from the Civil War to the Present* [New York: Basic Books, 1992]) also describes the function and importance of such networks.

9. Henry Shapiro, in his insightful social history *Appalachia on Our Mind: The Southern Mountains and Mountaineers in the American Consciousness 1870–1920* (Chapel Hill: University of North Carolina Press, 1978), argued that the folklore about Appalachia served a functional purpose for American identity.

10. Wilma Dunaway, *The First American Frontier* (Chapel Hill: University of North Carolina Press, 1996).

11. Timbering in West Virginia is still one of the most dangerous occupations, but the industry remains unregulated by the state.

12. This quote is discussed by Janet Wells Greene, "Camera Wars: Images of Coal Miners and the Fragmentation of Working-Class Identity, 1933–1947" (Ph.D. diss., New York University, 2000), chapter 2.

13. Howard B. Lee, *Bloodletting in Appalachia* (Parsons, W.Va.: McClain Printing Co., 1969). Denise Giardina's *Storming Heaven* (New York: W. W. Norton, 1987) is a carefully researched novel that traces the rise of the union movement in southern West Virginia.

14. At one point early in the century, there were so many Italians in West Virginia that the Italian government opened a consulate in the state.

SECTION I: FAMILY HISTORY

Chapter 1: Remembrances of Slavery

1. Memphis Tennessee Garrison, née Carter, was the daughter of Cassie and Wesley Carter, both of whom had been enslaved. Her mulatto father and his red-headed sisters were the children of a white slave owner about whom Garrison knew little other than the name, Aldridge, probably his given name.

2. The Emancipation Proclamation freeing the enslaved in the states in rebellion against the Union was issued January 1, 1863; Garrison makes the point that it had no effect on the lives of plantation slaves such as her mother until the surrender of Confederate General Robert E. Lee to Union General Ulysses S. Grant at Appomatox Courthouse, Virginia, on April 9, 1865, which in effect ended the Civil War.

3. Blacks were used in the Confederate Army, generally as laborers or body servants. Some volunteered, some were impressed or conscripted, others were bor-

rowed or rented from owners, and a number accompanied owners to war. In 1924, Virginia granted state pensions to black state residents who had served during the Civil War. Marshall Thomas had died by that time. See Ervin L. Jordan, Jr., *Black Confederates and Afro-Yankees in Civil War Virginia* (Charlottesville: University Press of Virginia, 1995).

Chapter 2: Origins

1. John Henry was an ex-slave who helped build the Big Bend Tunnel at Talcott, West Virginia. He was memorialized in a ballad for winning a race against a drilling machine during the construction of the tunnel and dying from the effort.

SECTION II: FAMILY AND YOUTH
Chapter 3: My Mother

1. Memphis Tennessee Garrison's mother, Mrs. Cassie Carter, had been born a slave. Of Garrison's mother, Evelyn Payne Starling wrote:

> In 1936, the year that I was graduated from Bluefield State Teachers College, I married a man from Gary. His family and the Garrisons were friends and I was accepted, as were the Starling children, as young friends of the Garrisons.
>
> Over time I was welcomed into the Garrison home and met Mrs. Garrison's mother who began life enslaved. It was a joy to listen to her and to get answers to some of my questions about life way back then and about the "peculiar institution." I shared some very interesting learning moments in the presence of this short plump little lady who often boasted of her voracious appetite and who could be as funny as she could be serious. Mrs. Garrison encouraged her to answer my questions, so I had no qualms about what I asked.
>
> On one occasion, I stopped in at the Garrison home and the conversation turned to the physical and emotional treatment of the enslaved by those who claimed to own them. Before my visit was over, I'd been shown the permanently ravaged back of that little old lady, scarred by a slaver's lash. I was not aware of the depth of memory left by that sight until, sitting in a theater watching *Beloved*, I saw it again. I almost screamed. It was the same raised flesh. Only the pattern was different. (Email, March 31, 1999)

Chapter 5: The Family Land

1. The Bureau of Refugees, Freedmen, and Abandoned Lands, commonly known as the Freedmen's Bureau, was a federal agency established in March 1865 to aid people displaced by the Civil War.

Chapter 6: Schooldays

1. In accordance with the West Virginia Constitution of 1872, black children and white children were not educated together. This did not change until after the 1954 *Brown v. Board of Education* decision. In the years just after the Civil War when black education was beginning in the state, black children were taught wherever space could be found—in homes, churches, or other available places—and supplies were limited. Most of the black teachers who worked in these schools had received their training outside of the state. Later, some teachers were qualified by examination and others were trained at Storer College, a private institution in Harpers Ferry, West Virginia. As the black population of the state grew, school boards began to construct buildings specifically for black schools, and the state developed the West Virginia Colored Institute and the Bluefield Colored Institute (now West Virginia State College and Bluefield State College) with normal school divisions devoted to training black teachers.

2. African American folktales handed down by oral tradition, later recorded in southern dialect and published (beginning with *Uncle Remus: His Songs and His Sayings* in 1880) by Joel Chandler Harris. In these tales, the small, weak rabbit is able to triumph over larger, stronger animals through wit and trickery. Garrison's grandfather probably knew the stories through the oral tradition.

3. The uniform examination was established by West Virginia law in 1903 to bring statewide uniformity to teacher certification by examination.

SECTION III: WORKING LIFE
Chapter 7: Teaching

1. When West Virginia set up its public school system, the organizational unit was the district. In southern West Virginia, these school districts were often dominated by the coal companies. In 1932, the district system was replaced by the county unit system.

One of the struggles of black teachers in West Virginia was to achieve school terms for black children equal to those of white children, that is, to assure that the number of months of schooling was the same for black children as for white children.

Chapter 8: Participation in Teachers' Organizations

1. In keeping with segregated education, support organizations (such as the PTA) and teachers' organizations were also segregated. The black state teachers' organization was the West Virginia State Teachers' Association (WVSTA) and the black national teachers' organization was the American Teachers' Association (ATA). Their white counterparts were the West Virginia Education Association (WVEA) and the National Education Association (NEA).

Chapter 9: Beyond Teaching

1. The end of slavery was celebrated locally on April 9, because Confederate General Robert E. Lee surrendered to Union General Ulysses S. Grant at Appomattox Courthouse, Virginia, on that day in 1865.

2. According to former McDowell County resident Charles Holley, the movies, which both blacks and whites attended, were shown in the white high school.

3. After the school governance unit changed from the district to the county, Garrison "got in bad with the county" and lost her teaching position. During the time that she was not employed as a full-time teacher, she became a welfare worker for the U.S. Steel Company. In employing Garrison in this capacity, U.S. Steel, the owner of the Gary mines, was creating a position similar to ones in Pittsburgh steel mills. According to Peter Gottlieb, "The black welfare workers were key figures in the company schemes for migrant workers' free time. Some served in a general capacity as interpreters of the employers' policies to the migrants, but most of them directed the organizations for black workers, did social work in the communities adjacent to the mills and factories, or helped recruit black labor for their employers" (*Making Their Own Way: Southern Blacks' Migration to Pittsburgh, 1916–1930* [Urbana: University of Illinois Press, 1987], 30).

SECTION IV: LIFE IN THE COALFIELDS

1. See, for example, Herbert Aptheker, ed., *A Documentary History of the Negro People in the United States* (Secaucus, N.J.: Citadel, 1974); John Hope Franklin, *From Slavery to Freedom: A History of American Negroes* (New York: Knopf, 1974). Few people understand the enormous profitability of slavery in that period. Howard Zinn cites James Madison's statement shortly after the American Revolution that he could make $257 on every Negro in a year, and spend only $12 or $13 on his keep (*A People's History of the United States, 1492–Present* [New York: Harper Perennial, 1995], 33).

Chapter 11: Racial Separation in the Coalfields

1. Although only racial separation in schools and a prohibition against interracial marriage were a part of the legal code of West Virginia, segregation by race became a part of the social and economic fabric of the state. In accordance with Garrison's recollections, scholars such as Joe William Trotter in *Coal, Class, and Color in Southern West Virginia* and Ronald Lewis in *Black Coal Miners in America: Race, Class and Community Conflict, 1780–1980* (Lexington: University Press of Kentucky, 1987) note that the coal companies promoted segregated housing, churches, and entertainment, and held black miners to dangerous, low-paying jobs.

Chapter 14: Miners and Unions

1. The coal operators fiercely opposed the establishment of unions and used black strikebreakers to disarm the threat of work stoppages staged by miners demanding rights. Black workers were recruited in the Deep South and brought in by what was called "transportation"—transport provided by the coal company, travel costs to be paid back later. Both Garrison and Joe W. Trotter note the cooperative bond that formed between the growing numbers of educated blacks and black miners. This bond facilitated progress for black people in politics, education, and legal and social areas.

In addition to attempts to organize the United Mine Workers (UMW), miners were also developing independent unions. According to Garrison, the company saw the independent unions as less of a threat than the UMW. Referred to by Garrison as "the law," the Wagner Act (officially the National Labor Relations Act), passed in 1935, officially established the right of miners to organize.

Ronald Lewis in *Black Coal Miners in America* says that initially black miners gave their institutional loyalty to the operators but later transferred this loyalty to unions. Although in many instances Garrison followed her own agenda, she was largely loyal to the company.

2. In *West Virginia: A History* (Lexington: University Press of Kentucky, 1985), Otis K. Rice describes Mother Jones as "diminutive" (224).

3. According to Mike Hornick, author of an article in the *Welch Daily News*, June 30, 1983, entitled "Gary Celebrates 100 Years of Mining," there were twelve U.S. Steel Mines by 1909. The staff of the Eastern Regional Coal Archives at Bluefield, West Virginia, identified two U.S. Steel Mines established in the 1940s, bringing the total to fourteen. The mines were established in the following order: 1902—Number 1, Wilcoe; Number 2, Alpheus; and Number 3, Gary; 1903—Number 6, Ream; 1904—Number 4; Thorpe; Number 5, Leslie; and Number 7, Elbert; 1905—Number 8, a second Elbert; 1907—Number 10, Venus; and Number 11, a second Thorpe; 1908—Number 9, Filbert; 1909—Number 12, Anawalt; 1942—Number 13, Moses; and 1948—Number 14, Monson.

Wilcoe was named for William H. Coe, chief engineer on the Norfolk and Western Railway; Gary and Elbert were named for Judge Elbert H. Gary, of U.S. Steel; Ream and Filbert were named for Norman B. Ream and W. J. Filbert, corporation comptrollers, and Anawalt was named for James Anawalt, who worked for the Union Supply Company.

4. See note 3.

Chapter 16: Politics

1. Until the election of Franklin D. Roosevelt in 1932 (served 1933–45), it was through the Republican party in West Virginia that blacks felt their interests could best be advanced. Thomas Posey, who was a professor of economics at West Virginia State College, suggests that the election of 1888 was instrumental in abetting that party's discovery of black political usefulness. In that election, Republican Nathan Goff ran against Democrat A. B. Fleming for the governorship of West Virginia; Goff won the election by a minuscule number of votes. The Democrats challenged the election, saying that the Republicans had encouraged a number of newly arrived blacks to vote Republican before they had fulfilled the proper residency requirement. The election was finally settled in the West Virginia legislature; the Democrats won the governorship. However, in *The Negro Citizen of West Virginia* (Institute, W.Va.: Press of West Virginia State College, 1934), Posey indicates that the closeness of this election made blacks realize that the black vote could be the swing vote in the state if used intentionally. Blacks did choose to vote Republican, and in 1896, Republican George Atkinson was elected governor of West Virginia. Garrison points out that in 1896 blacks began to use their association with the Republican party to run for office themselves. Republican Christopher Payne, the first black legislator in West Virginia, was elected from Fayette County in 1896.

Chapter 20: Public Executions

1. Public executions in West Virginia took two forms: legal and illegal. Illegal executions by mobs were sometimes called "lynchings." In the early days of the state, legal executions were carried out in public places after the accused had been found guilty by a jury and sentenced. In McDowell County, Garrison had heard about one such execution—the public hanging of John Hardy. The law was later changed to require that all such executions had to be performed at the state penitentiary.

By 1919, nationwide lynching of blacks had escalated. Although the killings in West Virginia did not reach the proportions that they did in the Deep South, there were, nevertheless, some instances of lynchings in the state. This led to West Virginia's passage of the antilynching law introduced by McDowell County black legislator, Harry J. Capehart.

Although Garrison recalled hearing about only the Greenbrier lynchings and the one in her community from which she and her childhood companions found the rope, there were others.

Chapter 24: State and National NAACP Activities

1. John Shillady, a white social worker who served as the first professional secretary of the NAACP, was injured in Austin, Texas, in 1919 when struck in the face by a member of a group that included a judge and a constable. He did not die from the blow, however. He returned to New York and recovered from his injury in body but not in spirit. He resigned from the NAACP in 1920. See *Inheritors of the Spirit: Mary White Ovington and the Founding of the NAACP* by Carolyn Wedin (New York: John Wiley, 1998).

SECTION VI: CONCLUSION
Chapter 29: Epilogue

1. Community near Number 6 mine. According to Carolyne Brown, also from Gary, there was a "pecking order" to company home assignments in the "hollers" (interview February 15, 1999). Blacks were given the least desirable location. Native-born whites lived at the mouth of the holler. Italians, Hungarians, and other ethnic groups were next, and blacks were behind them, at the very back of the "holler."

Historical Afterword

1. Unless otherwise noted, direct quotes are from J. W. Trotter, "West Virginia," in Jack Salzman, ed., *Encyclopedia of African American Culture and History* (New York: Macmillan Publishing Company, 1996).

sources

�֎

Primary

The main primary source for Memphis Tennessee Garrison's account of her life is the audiotape and transcription of her oral history recorded by Bernard Cleveland in about 1968 and preserved by the Department of Social Studies, Marshall University, Huntington, West Virginia (Oral History of Appalachia Collection, #541).

Interviews

Brown, Carolyne. Huntington, W.Va. February 15, 1999.

Henderson, Herbert. Huntington, W.Va. February 15, 1999.

Johnson, Dolores. Huntington, W.Va. June 9, 1999.

Telephone Interviews

Carruthers, Ruth. Washington, D.C. June 13, 1999.

Carter, Alma. Columbus, Ohio. June 13, 1999.

Garrison, Allen. Greensboro, North Carolina. June 9, 1999.

Holley, Charles. Indianapolis, Indiana. April 8, 1999.

Rhea, Barbara. Columbus, Ohio. June 13, 1999.

Settle, John. Moorpark, California. August 14, 1999.

Correspondence

Starling, Evelyn Payne. Memphis, Tennessee. Email, March 31, 1999.

Secondary

Corbin, David A. *Life, Work, and Rebellion in the Coal Fields: The Southern West Virginia Miners, 1880–1922.* Urbana: University of Illinois Press, 1981.

Dix, Keith. *What's a Coal Miner to DO? The Mechanization of Coal Mining.* Pittsburgh: University of Pittsburgh Press, 1988.

Eller, Ronald D. *Miners, Millhands, and Mountaineers: Industrialization of the Appalachian South, 1880–1930.* Knoxville: University of Tennessee Press, 1982.

Franklin, John Hope, and Alfred A. Moss Jr. *From Slavery to Freedom: A History of Negro Americans.* New York: Alfred A. Knopf, 1988.

Gottlieb, Peter. *Making Their Own Way: Southern Blacks' Migration to Pittsburgh, 1910–1930.* Urbana: University of Illinois Press, 1987.

Haskins, James. *Black Music in America: A History through Its People.* New York: HarperCollins, HarperTrophy, 1987.

Henry, Florette. *Black Migration: Movement North, 1900–1920.* New York: Anchor Press/ Doubleday, 1975.

Jackameit, William P. "A Short History of Negro Public Higher Education in West Virginia, 1890–1965." *West Virginia History* 37 (July 1976).

Johnson, D. "Memphis Tennessee Garrison: The Real Gains of a Life, 1890–1988." *Beacon Digest* (August 30–September 7, 1988).

Jordan, Ervin L. *Black Confederates and Afro Yankees in Civil War Virginia.* Charlottesville: University Press of Virginia, 1995.

Laing, James T. "The Negro Miner in West Virginia." *Social Forces* 14 (March 1936).

Lawrence, Randy. "Black Migration to Southern West Virginia, 1870–1930." *Goldenseal* 5 (October–December 1979): 30–31.

Lewis, Ronald. *Black Coal Miners in America: Race, Class and Community Conflict, 1780–1980.* Lexington: University Press of Kentucky, 1987.

Mauer, B. B., ed. *Mountain Heritage.* Parsons, W. Va.: McClain Printing Company, 1980.

McGehee, Stuart. "Gary: A First-Class Operation." *Goldenseal* 12 (fall 1988): 218–32.

Posey, Thomas. *The Negro Citizen of West Virginia.* Institute: West Virginia State College Press, 1934.

Rice, Otis K. *West Virginia: A History.* Lexington: University Press of Kentucky, 1985.

Sheeler, John Reuben. "The Negro in West Virginia." Ph.D. diss., West Virginia University, 1954.

Simmons, Charles W., John R. Rankin, and U. G. Carter. "Negro Coal Miners in West Virginia, 1875–1925." *Midwest Journal* 6 (spring 1954).

Smith, Douglas C. "In Quest of Equality: The West Virginia Experience." *West Virginia History* 37 (April 1976).

Stealey, John E. "The Freedmen's Bureau in West Virginia." *West Virginia History* 39 (January/April 1978).

Trotter, Joe William, Jr. *Coal, Class, and Color: Blacks in Southern West Virginia, 1915–32.* Urbana: University of Illinois Press, 1990.

Trotter, Joe William, Jr., and Ancella Radford Bickley. *Honoring Our Past: Proceedings of the First Two Conferences on West Virginia's Black History.* Charleston: Alliance for the Collection, Preservation and Dissemination of West Virginia's Black History, 1991.

Turner, William H. "Special Issue: Blacks in Appalachia." *Appalachian Heritage: A Magazine of Southern Appalachian Life and Culture.* Berea: Berea College of Kentucky, 1991.

Turner, William H., and Edward J. Cabbell, eds. *Blacks in Appalachia.* Lexington: University Press of Kentucky, 1985.

Wedin, Carolyn. *Inheritors of the Spirit: Mary White Ovington and the Founding of the NAACP.* New York: John Wiley & Sons, 1998.

West Virginia Human Rights Commission. Annual Reports, 1985–86, 1986–89. Charleston, W.Va.

West Virginia Human Rights Commission. Public Hearing in Wheeling, February 1971. Charleston, W.Va.

index

✳

Photographs located in the unpaginated photo sections following pages 42 and 124 are indicated by the boldface designations 42f and 124f, respectively.